RISE

RISE

A SOLDIER, A DREAM, AND
A PROMISE KEPT

Daniel Rodriguez

with **Joe Layden**

HOUGHTON MIFFLIN HARCOURT
BOSTON · NEW YORK · 2014

For information about permission to reproduce selections from this book, write to Permissions, Houghton Mifflin Harcourt Publishing Company, 215 Park Avenue South, New York, New York 10003.

www.hmhco.com

Library of Congress Cataloging-in-Publication Data
Rodriguez, Daniel, date.
Rise : a soldier, a dream, and a promise kept / Daniel Rodriguez ;
contributions by Joe Layden.
pages cm
ISBN 978-0-544-36560-5 (hardback)
1. Rodriguez, Daniel, date. 2. Afghan War, 2001– –
Personal narratives, American. 3. Afghan War, 2001– – Campaigns.
4. Afghan War, 2001– – Veterans – United States – Biography.
5. Iraq War, 2003–2011 – Veterans – United States – Biography.
6. Iraq War, 2003–2011 – Personal narratives, American.
7. Soldiers – United States – Biography.
8. United States. Army – Biography. 9. Post-traumatic
stress disorder – Patients – United States – Biography.
10. Football players – United States – Biography.
11. Clemson Tigers (Football team) 12. Layden, Joseph, date.
I. Title. II. Title: A soldier, a dream, and a promise kept.
DS371.43.R63 2014
956.7044'342092 – dc23
[B]
2014016742

Book design by Brian Moore

Printed in the United States of America
DOC 10 9 8 7 6 5 4 3 2 1

I want to dedicate this book first to my friends who have fallen in the name of freedom, giving their last breath to this country. Second, I would like to dedicate these pages to my close friends and family who have been by my side over the years and will be in the years to come.

Author's Note

The Battle of Kamdesh remains one of the deadliest battles since the United States began military involvement in Afghanistan. While the author's experience in that battle plays a significant role in his life story, it is by no means the whole story. Nor does this book purport to be the definitive account of what happened at COP Keating on October 3, 2009. Entire books have been written about the Battle of Kamdesh. It is not the author's intent to explore or explain every detail of the battle here, but rather to present what he saw and experienced — from his heated but admittedly limited vantage point — as part of a larger story.

Acknowledgments

There are times I reflect and try to comprehend how exactly I am still alive. My life has been filled with many moments, but in all those moments were great people with whom I have had the privilege to share memories over the years.

Dad, you never let me quit anything and I thank you for that. You taught me what it means to work hard and provide for your family. There were times we didn't get along, but I always knew you loved me. I remember you telling me to go get your belt when it was time to get my ass spanked. I would cry before I even got hit, and you would tell me to stop crying and take it like a man because these were the consequences for my actions. I couldn't help crying after you spanked me, but you never hesitated to hold me in your arms and tell me "it hurts me more than it hurts you." I always thought you were full of shit, but I never doubted that you loved me. You were always there for me, and I can remember only one game you ever missed in my entire career in any sport. As a man now, I can't thank you enough for being the father you were. The shitty part is that you're not here for me to thank anymore and it sucks. I find myself back home about five days out of the year, and for forty-five minutes or so I sit bawling my eyes out in front of a tombstone with your name on it. I always ask you when I'm there if you're proud of me. And I always tell you I wish you could see me playing football now. I know you would love it.

Mom, I knew a long time ago I would never be anything even close to the kid you tried to raise. Even though I took a path that traveled far from the Bible book you hold in such high regard, I want you to know how much I love you and appreciate everything you have done for me. I have come to realize it isn't our points of view and the people we become that makes someone love us. It starts from the memories of that infant who slept by your feet while you finished the dishes, and the countless nights you scratched his back and prayed for him before he fell asleep. The compassion, love, and time someone dedicates solely to you is what unconditional love is, and I love you so much for being the best mother I could have asked for. Regardless of whether you agree with life choices I have made, you are a strong influence on the man I have become, and that is what being a mother is all about. Thank you.

Veronica, you are my sister, my blood, and my closest family member. Age was always a factor with us growing up, since you were hardly around to see me transform, but times have changed in recent years. The relationship I have with you is sacred, and even though I am sarcastic, an asshole, and always poking fun, I love you dearly. I know you hurt from the tragedies we have faced as a family and misfortunes in your personal life, and deep down they hurt me too. I am not the solid emotional stone that I appear to be. Yes, we have our means of venting as all do, but I hurt the most for you, and it's because I love you so much. You are the most dependable person in my life and I always know I can count on my sister—from the time you wired me money to get my car out of the tow shop so Mom and Dad wouldn't find out, to the time you wired me more money because I was stuck in a Third-World country. There is a reason that when a line on a form asks for an emergency contact I put your name down, and I put it without hesitation because you are my go-to in all my life ordeals. I once slipped you a piece of paper containing the names of all my friends, with you and Mom divvying up the life insurance money if I were to be killed at war. There are times when I wonder if my death would have benefited those around me who I love the most. Luckily, I didn't die and I'm still here to harass you. Love you, sis.

Stephan, you once told me "I tailor made your suit and I intend to ride the coattails all the way to the ground." You have not only helped stitch the outfit I currently wear, but you have been there for me for a very long time. I consider you a brother and my best friend. I have seen you marry the love of your life, and can't wait to see you as a father in the near future. There have been moments in past relationships when arguments erupted because I told you things first, and was accused of being in love with you because of how close we are, and was told to get my priorities straight. Needless to say, you and I are still close and those other relationships no longer exist. I have never had more of a bond with or trust in someone than I do with you. You never let me become someone I wasn't and would always call me out. Honestly, you made me a better person. You have called me stupid, crazy, and an idiot for things I have done, but the most important thing to me is that you call me a friend. Thank you for everything.

Joseph, our friendship goes very far back, and the picture hanging in my house showing us together playing parks-and-recreation soccer justifies it all. I want to say thank you for being there for me as friend, and, more importantly, for being there for my sister on multiple occasions. She wrote to me and told me how you and some of the guys helped her with the yard while I was away at war, and it always made me feel good inside knowing I had friends like you. It killed me not being home and hearing that the people I love were struggling, but the little things you did to help out mean the world to me and I will never forget them. Lastly, knowing this book will be in the hands of a lot of people, I want to clarify that I have dunked on you. Yes, you may have been the cause of a broken ankle on an attempt one time, but no matter what you tell yourself to sleep at night, you know, and everyone else who was there that day knows, I dunked on you.

Kyle, you never doubted for a second that I could play college ball, and whether you believed it or not, I sure as hell did. Thanks for being there for me and helping me achieve a dream. You and I are close friends to this day, and I am so thankful for you. I must note as well that I have never dunked on you, but there is still time.

Tim, I never told you this, but I hated seeing you deploy to Afghanistan. I had nightmares while you were overseas, and it killed me. You are one of my closest friends, and I want to thank you as well for being there for my family. You and Stephan driving cross-country to bring me a vehicle, and doing it again to help my mother move, are little moments in the past, but they are what make me appreciate you as a brother and as a best friend. Thank you for making me shoot from the Mexican three-point line.

Andrew and Sean, you guys are always there for me, and that's what friendship is all about. Love you both.

To all those who I served with . . . There are too many to name, but I want to thank you all for the friendships we made and the good times and tough times. A few I want to thank personally are:

John Breeding, for being one of the best men I ever served for and for teaching me so much. It was an honor fighting by your side.

Chris Cordova, you were one of the first people I met in the army and our friendship is still strong to this day. We have continued to share a relationship, and I enjoy being close to you and your beautiful family. The things you and I have gone through on and off the battlefield will forever keep us friends.

John Hammel, thank you for being able to talk so damn much and keeping me awake on guard shifts through two deployments. Long nights we talked dogs and guns and made a list of every food joint we could think of to go eat at upon our return.

Brad Larson, you are one of the finest men I have ever known and quite frankly, I think of you as a legend. You believed in me when I told you I wanted to play football, and that meant so much to me. In fact the night of my first game you were the only person I cared to call because, honestly, I was nervous and I knew you would be able to cool me out. It's always great talking to you and I can't wait to see you again.

Clint Romesha, you, my friend, are a badass, and more than that, you are cool as hell. We have a great relationship, and I always looked up to you when we served together because I knew that you would never back down from a fight and you didn't take any shit.

Zachery Koppes, you are a special person, and I am so glad that we are still in touch. We have had a rough road, but I assure you smoothness will someday come. Love you, brother.

Josh Emanuel, you may be the craziest SOB I have ever met, but I wouldn't trade a single second we served together for anything. You taught me more about a mortar system than I ever could have imagined, and I was a damn good soldier because of you squaring me away as soon as I got in-country. I'll never forget running up to your truck after it had just been hit, thinking I was going to see you in pieces, and finding you covered in black from the explosion. The only thing you said before you started spraying that 249SAW of yours was, "those fucks made me lose a perfectly good lip of Copenhagen." 2up 2down.

Jassey, Keith, and Cady, I think of us as a little team who bonded so well and won't forget all the good times we shared together. Cady, you and I are still close, and I love your family so much. As for Jassey and Keith, we have gone our separate ways and talk only every so often, but I would never hesitate to be there for you boys if you ever needed anything. Love you guys.

Joe Barela, I don't think you ever once called me by my name — it was always "shithead." Thanks for telling me to my face that I needed to tell you more about myself because if I died today you wouldn't know anything about me.

Also, thank you to guys I served with in Iraq: Johnny Robles, Mark Raines, Brian Hinkle, Gary S. O'Neil, Jeremy Snell, Christopher Walker, Frank Cohn, Billy Carter, Justin Flourny, Antonio

Keenan, and Doc "Crazy" Harris. And Afghanistan: John Hill, Doc Hobbs, Shane Courville, Ryan Schulz, and all others in Red, White, and Blue Platoon of Bravo Troop 3-61 CAV Black Knights.

Stephan Mace, I miss you so much, buddy. We had some great times and memories that will last me for the duration of my life. When I got word from Rasmussen that you didn't make it, I felt like they ripped out the last bit of life I had left in me that night. You were the toughest kid I knew, and I know you suffered the last hours of your young life, and that has always burdened me. I can't tell you enough how special your mother is to me, and how much she misses you. I see you in her eyes when I look at her, and to this day that is one of the hardest things I have to do. She is always there for me if I ever need to talk to someone, and I am always there for her. Although it is difficult to have our relationship based on these circumstances, I am so grateful that she is a part of my life, because I know if you were still alive you would be a part of it as well.

Kevin Thomson, there isn't a day that passes when I don't blame myself for not doing enough to get you home. You kept me sane out there in those mountains, and I cherish the relationship we had. I felt time stop when I saw you lying next to my feet, because I knew there was nothing I could do for you. Hours passed that day as the fighting continued, and I put my poncho over you when it started to rain a little, because I couldn't stand to see you lying out there getting wet. When the fighting stopped, I was the one who wrapped you up in a makeshift body bag and tightened down all the straps on the sled, and I watched as they carried your body down to the chopper. Tears streamed down my face in anger because those motherfuckers had killed my best friend that day, and I knew you weren't coming back. What I experienced that day triggered a nerve that will stay with me for as long as I live. I never think to myself that there is something I cannot achieve or something that can hold me back. I try to live my life in such a way that, if you were still here, you would be proud of me and enjoy watching me. To you and the other seven who lost their lives that day, October 3, 2009, I can't thank you enough for making me a better person, one who is appreciative and thankful just to be able to call himself an American, knowing he served with heroes.

Nick Wallace, you transformed my body and believed in me. I didn't have much money, but you kept training me. I hope my work ethic and commitment to you showed, because I don't think I would have been in half the shape I was if it weren't for your vision and expertise. I owe you a lot of credit for what you helped me achieve, and I will never forget our workouts.

Ryan Smith, your vision on that video was one I could never have imagined. I came to you with an idea, and you made it better than I ever could have dreamed. I gave you literally my last penny to make that recruitment video, and I must say the investment has been well worth it. Thank you and everyone at Wandering Hat.

Coach Swinney, you are the most passionate coach I have ever met. You are a little crazy at times with all your speeches and acronyms, but I never doubt for a second that you care as much about the lives of your players as you do about winning. At the end of the day, you would rather develop a man than a football player, and I can't thank you enough for having that type of program. You did so much and never gave up trying to get me to Clemson University, and I am forever thankful to you for that. I hope that when my time ends at Clemson you will be proud of yourself for giving me a shot on your team, and a little bit shocked that I turned out to be a better football player than you probably expected. Thank you, coach.

Also, a thank you to all the coaches and staff at Clemson; seeing what you do year in and year out is amazing, and understanding that you do it for us players is humbling. Every person on the staff is dedicated not only to winning, but also to bettering as people the players they coach. Specifically, I want to thank Coach Jeff Scott, my position coach, and Coach Chad Morris, our offensive coordinator. It's unfortunate for me that Sammy Watkins was so good, because I could have scored a lot more touchdowns.

To my teammates, I have been privileged to play with great

college athletes, but more importantly, I have been privileged to play with great friends. The hours we put into perfecting our craft are countless, but the memories we take away when we leave are priceless. I want to thank all my teammates for accepting me as a family member on our team, and for forever making me feel welcome.

Compliance – Andy, Stephanie Ellison, and my girl Amanda – you guys are the magic makers, and I know my file contains some thickness to it with all the waivers and paperwork. I want to say thank you so much for working with me and on my behalf. Your office is a safe haven, and I enjoy coming in and saying hello. One day, as I promised, I will donate a new door to your office in my remembrance.

Clemson University, I want to thank you for becoming a new home. I drove down to this little slice of heaven not knowing anything about it, and will leave here with roots connecting me back to it for as long as I live. I bleed Orange now, and couldn't be more proud to be a Clemson Tiger.

To the Clemson University faculty, fans, and community, you embraced me with open arms and countless ovations for minimal gains on the field. I could not feel more at home than I do there, and I attribute that to the culture and fan base that is Clemson University. Go Tigers.

Finally, thanks to everyone who helped make this book possible, most notably literary agents Scott Waxman and Frank Weimann, Susan Canavan and the team at Houghton Mifflin Harcourt, and my coauthor, Joe Layden. Without your support, I wouldn't have had the chance to tell my story. Thanks for believing in it.

Prologue

October 20, 2012
Clemson, South Carolina
The noise is almost deafening.

No question about it – when you put 80,000 people in one place and unite them in purpose, they can shake a building (and the surrounding countryside) to its core. As I stand here now, at the top of Memorial Stadium, preparing to lead the Clemson football team on the long downhill run to Frank Howard Field – there's a reason they call it Death Valley – I can feel the earth trembling beneath my feet.

I am at the front of the line, an unusual and somewhat disorienting position for a first-year walk-on. But then, this is no ordinary day, and I suppose I am no ordinary college football player. For starters, I'm twenty-four years old, which makes me the oldest guy on the team, despite the fact that I'm only a freshman. I've spent most of the past six years in the military, serving tours of duty in Iraq and Afghanistan. Along the way I had the misfortune of being involved in the infamous Battle of Kamdesh, one of the bloodiest encounters in the Afghanistan conflict. I lost friends that day, and no amount of hardware (I received the Purple Heart and Bronze Star with Valor in the aftermath) can ever change that fact or make the memory any less painful. But I guess this is one of the ways I deal with it: by fulfilling a promise I made to a friend who died that day, on October 3, 2009.

"Someday, when I get out of this shit hole, I'm going to play college football," I had said, although I didn't really know how I was going to make it happen.

And now here I am, dressed in orange, padded up, at five-foot-eight, 175 pounds, the smallest guy on the Clemson football team. But no matter — *ain't the size of the dog in the fight,* as they say. I'd be just as happy at the back of the pack, but today is unique. Not only are we playing Atlantic Coast Conference rival Virginia Tech, but it's also Military Appreciation Day. As I wave the American flag at the top of the stadium steps, generic cheering and shouting give way to something more organized, something more profound:

"U-S-A! U-S-A! U-S-A!"

I understand the reality of being a soldier in the modern army. I know that most people are deeply disconnected from the violent and exhausting work of the American military half a world away. I know that the patriotic chanting is a gesture soon forgotten. But you know what? That's okay. It feels good now, in this place and this time, and I'm honored to be a part of it. There's one other thing: it's my father's birthday. Ray Rodriguez, who was not just my dad but also my best friend, passed away shortly after I graduated from high school. I was still just a kid when he died, and not a particularly ambitious or focused one at that. I can't help but wonder how he'd feel if he were here now to share this day with me and to see the man that I've become. I like to think that he'd be proud.

Suddenly we're moving, careening downhill, nearly a hundred strong, rolling into the stadium, into Death Valley. It's a nickname, of course, and nothing more, signifying the supposed fate of Clemson opponents. I know the difference between Death Valley and the Valley of Death. I've seen both. Football is not war. Football is a game. But right now, for the moment, it's enough. I'm lucky to be here. I'm lucky to be alive. I was given a second chance, and I plan to make the most of it.

1

I T WASN'T UNTIL I enlisted in the Army and found myself
surrounded by kids who had dropped out of school or been
arrested or raised in poverty that I began to appreciate what a
comfortable life I'd led while growing up. Sure, there were some
challenging times, but for the most part I'd had it pretty good.

For a few years we lived in Prince William County, Virginia.
My father worked as an athletic director for the US Marine Corps
base at Quantico. He was a veteran himself, but by now a civilian.
Ray Rodriguez was a proud man. He wanted nothing more out
of life than to provide for his family. He'd grown up dirt-poor in
Lordsburg, New Mexico, a one-stoplight town off Interstate 10,
about three hours west of El Paso, Texas. Raised by a single mom,
he was one of nine children and never knew his father, so he was
committed to being a better model for his own kids. (I have a sister, Veronica, who's eight years older than me.)

There's nothing in that part of the country. It's beautiful, if
you like the desert, but opportunities are scarce. My father knew
that, so he got the hell out of Dodge when he graduated from high
school in 1974, then enlisted in the Army because he thought he

was going to get drafted. He did eight years, mostly stationed in Germany, then came home, went to night school, and earned his college diploma while working at Quantico. The importance of getting a college degree was always impressed upon me while I was growing up. My dad used to say, "Daniel, education is the only thing nobody can take away from you. You need education to succeed in this world."

I have vague memories of trailing after my dad when he went to work and running around the base. We lived in a high-rise apartment complex called Lyndon Park, not far from the projects. It wasn't the greatest area—there were four of us living in a tiny two-bedroom apartment where roaches were not uncommon and police sirens provided a steady sound track—so my parents scrimped and saved so that my sister and I could attend a private Christian school. After only a couple years my father got a new job as superintendent of parks and recreation in Fairfax County, one of the wealthiest counties in the state. We moved to a very nice neighborhood ("Aquia Harbour," it was called) fifteen miles down the road, in Stafford, Virginia. If people ask me where I'm from, I tell them Stafford. That's where I was raised, and that's where I went to school.

My parents would talk occasionally about hard work and ambition, but mainly they led by example. Dad was up every morning before the sun, then didn't get home until six o'clock at night. My mother, Cecilia Rodriguez, worked as an assistant in an ophthalmologist's office. They were high school sweethearts (middle school, actually!) who married young, started a family, and always worked long hours.

It was a busy, hardworking household, one that relied partially on the contributions of friends and neighbors and babysitters to keep it running smoothly. Reflecting back on it, I can see how much my parents sacrificed so that their kids could be raised with a degree of comfort and stability. But they never complained; whatever frustrations they might have felt were hidden from us. My father, in particular, was tireless. Despite the long hours, he always seemed to make room for a game of catch or pickup basketball; he'd take me fishing on the Potomac River or Aquia Creek. I have volumes of pictures from when I was a little kid, clearly showing the importance of sports in our lives. There I am playing T-ball in diapers, or dribbling a basketball when I can barely walk. I vaguely recall an exercise in which my dad would stick a fishing net into the ground and have me throw tennis balls into it because he wanted me to be a pitcher. But I never felt like he was drilling me. He always tried to make things fun, and I loved spending time with him. I can say with confidence that my father was not one of those psychotic sports dads. I know those guys—he wasn't one of them. And I can also say that I became an athlete because I loved to play, not because I was *forced* to play.

As I grew up and got more interested in sports Dad became my coach. Didn't matter the season or the game—my father was on the sideline. And I played everything: basketball, football, soccer, and baseball. I don't know how he found the time.

Genetics trumps everything. My father was about five-foot-eight, and my mother a shade over five feet; obviously I was never going to be a big kid. It didn't help that I was late to mature (in a lot of ways), but I tried hard not to let size be the defining factor in my life. Or fear. In the fall of my freshman year at Brooke Point High School, a crazy sniper terrorized Washington, DC. Midway through the season our school canceled football at all but the varsity level. I got called up to the varsity team, despite being only five-foot-one and 95 pounds. I didn't play much, but I had a uniform and a spot on the roster. Got my ass kicked every day in practice, as a receiver on the scout team.

The following year, as a sophomore, I started out on the JV. A couple weeks into the season the backup varsity quarterback got hurt and the coach needed someone to run plays for the scout team. I was maybe five-foot-three by then, but pretty quick, so they asked me to give it a try. Rain that day had turned the practice fields to mud, so we worked out in the gym, wearing sneakers and pads. As I looked over the playbook some of the older guys teased me, and a few of the coaches appeared concerned for my safety.

"Hey, kid. You sure you're fast enough for this?"

I nodded.

"You know how to run an option?"

I nodded again. Truth is, I had no clue how to run an option offense, didn't even know what it looked like. But after an explanation from the coach and a few minutes of practice, it seemed pretty easy. The option is all about speed, and I discovered that day that I was fast. I mean, I didn't exactly tear the defense apart, but I did manage to score a few times. These guys were all bigger and stronger than me, but they couldn't touch me. I was a foot shorter and a hundred pounds lighter than some of them, but I belonged.

After practice, as I was walking into the locker room, the coach, Jeff Berry, called to me.

"Hey, Rodriguez! Come here."

I jogged over.

"Yes, sir?"

"You don't practice on JV anymore. You're on varsity."

The very next game I suited up as the world's smallest varsity wide receiver. My primary job was to be a play runner — to act as a conduit between the coach and the quarterback. After a few possessions I got the impression that I was never going to see the ball, so here's what I did. When the coach called a play that was designed to result in a pass to one of our wide receivers, I decided to tell a specific receiver that I was subbing in for him. This was an act of deception. I was supposed to sub for someone else, but I figured it would be the best way to get a shot at catching a pass. I can still see the look on the kid's face — his name was Jamal, and he was the star athlete on the team and first option on probably 90 percent of our passing plays.

"Jamal . . . I'm in for you, man."

He stared at me. The whole huddle stared at me.

"What?" he finally said. "You sure about that?"

"Yeah, yeah. Let's go."

Jamal shook his head, yanked off his chin strap, and jogged off the field.

They all knew what I'd done, but I think they were too surprised to say anything. A few seconds later I ran a four-yard slant over the middle and made my first varsity reception. After that, I was on the team, more or less permanently. Sometimes, if you want people to see beyond the surface, you have to make your own opportunity.

For a while everything was great. Seemed that way to me anyway. In reality, things were far from perfect in our house. While I was in high school my parents began to drift apart. I barely noticed it happening, but I can see now that they were living almost separate lives—both of them working like crazy, Dad coaching my sports teams, and Mom making frequent trips to New Mexico to take care of my sick grandmother. On one of those trips, apparently, she resurrected a relationship with an old friend from high school. One thing led to another, the friendship became something more, and before too long my mom came to the conclusion that she wanted something else out of life.

After thirty-three years of marriage, my parents split up. To my father, it was like a slap in the face. To me it was both more and less than that. My mother is a woman of few words, so she never really came out and explained anything to me. I remember the phone ringing one night, and my father answering. I could hear him screaming at the person on the other end of the line (that person, as it turned out, was my mother's new boyfriend). Afterward there was an argument that went on for some time. My mom left, and my father came downstairs. I could tell he'd been crying.

"Your mom is going away," he said. "I'm sorry."

And that was pretty much it. Dad was a straight shooter. He didn't try to sugarcoat what had happened or give the false impression that this would be a temporary arrangement. Life was about to change, he seemed to be saying. Get used to it.

The transition was instantaneous. Suddenly it was just me and my dad. (My big sister had long since graduated from college and moved out of the house.) A part of me was bitter. I was furious toward my mom for her apparent abandonment and selfishness; at the same time, her departure was like a blanket of oppression being lifted. My mother had been very strict and religious, and I couldn't help but feel like her behavior was the height of hypocrisy. Really, though, I was just pissed off. And so I acted out. It didn't take long for me to figure out that my father was too busy to be an effective single parent — there was no way he could work sixty hours a week and also be the disciplinarian at home. I was sixteen years old, and he expected me to grow up and take responsibility for my actions. He needed that from me, and I let him down.

I'd never been the greatest student, but my grades had at least been acceptable. Boys will be boys, of course. I'd often been something of a class clown, and I rarely saw value in doing homework or studying in advance when you could put it off until the last minute. I did just enough to get by. But I'd never gotten in any serious trouble, never exhibited disrespectful behavior toward teachers or classmates. When my parents split up, though, I no longer had to worry about accountability. My grades tumbled. I became less reliable. In the summer after my sophomore year, I went to live with my sister Veronica in West Palm Beach, Florida. My father had reasoned that I was likely to get into some serious mischief if I was left home alone all summer, and he was right. Unfortunately, that arrangement caused me to miss a big chunk of preseason training for football. I had already been on the varsity for two years, but Coach Berry decided that I'd be demoted to JV as a junior as punishment for missing summer workouts. I stubbornly (and stupidly) declined that invitation and didn't play football that season.

The irony of that summer sabbatical is that it did not in any way prevent me from getting in trouble, as my father had intended; in fact, it had just the opposite effect. I played in a national AAU basketball tournament in Atlanta just a couple weeks after school got out. From there, my dad put me on a Greyhound bus for Florida. In my arrogance, I hadn't even bothered to talk with Coach Berry about my summer plans. I figured he'd cut me some slack since I was a good athlete with some problems at home. It was a self-ish, self-pitying approach to a complicated situation. I was young, but I still should have handled it differently. Instead, I took off for Florida and what I knew would be a fun-filled summer.

Veronica helped me get a job at the restaurant where she worked, but she was too young and busy to worry about keeping her little brother on a short leash. I worked mainly as a barback, running ice and replenishing supplies for the bartender. This was a fairly upscale restaurant, but with a serious party atmosphere. In other words, it was a great job for a sixteen-and-a-half-year-old kid with no parental supervision. I'd work hard all afternoon and night, make a pile of money in tips, and then hang out with all these beautiful women, many of them older than my mother, drinking and smoking pot and praying for a trip to Cougar Town.

And nobody really cared. I mean, the manager spoke with my sister, told her to keep an eye on me, but I think he realized the clientele liked having me around, so . . . no harm, right? A couple of my friends drove down late in the summer to join the party for a week, and they couldn't believe the way I was living. I was making a couple hundred bucks a week, all cash, under the table. I had access to drugs and alcohol. And women.

And no one to keep me in line.

I drove home with my buddies in late August, just before school was to start. My father must have known that I was a little out of control, because he immediately pulled me aside and gave me a lecture about school and grades. He also told me not to worry about money or getting a job.

"I'll take care of things," he said. "You don't need to work. Just concentrate on school and football."

Yeah, football. About that . . .

I made it back the day before preseason camp opened. The next morning I showed up at school, cleats in hand, acting as though nothing had changed. It honestly hadn't occurred to me that, by missing summer workouts, I might have not only pissed off Coach Berry but also shown disrespect for my teammates. They all sort of stared at me when I walked into the locker room, as if to say, *Where the hell have you been?*

This was late August 2004. Social media wasn't quite the beast that it is today; smartphones weren't all that smart. It was somewhat harder to keep track of your friends, especially if your friends weren't particularly interested in letting you know where they were or what they were doing. I didn't feel like I owed anyone an explanation. Not my teammates, not my coach. It wasn't long before I discovered that I had made a rather huge miscalculation.

I strutted into the locker room like I owned the place. But I did not own the place. This place belonged to Coach Berry and his football program. And I was about to find out that I was no longer a part of that program.

"What are you doing here?" Coach Berry said. He seemed legitimately surprised to see me. He was angry too. I don't blame him. Football meant the world to Coach Berry. His father had been the Brooke Point coach as well. The game was in their blood. They loved it, and they loved this school. And now I was sort of crapping on both at the same time.

"I'm here to play ball, Coach."

He shook his head in what can best be described as exasperation.

"Son, you haven't been here all summer. Nobody knows where you've been. You missed all the workouts. You can't just walk in here and think that you're entitled to something."

At that point I pulled the pity card, told him what was happening with my family and how we'd made a last-second decision that I'd live with my sister for the summer. Coach Berry generously agreed to give me a second chance.

"Come back tomorrow," he said. "We'll talk about it. But you're not practicing today."

That afternoon a friend who worked at a local hospital told me about a job opening. It sounded easy – taking food orders and delivering meals – and the pay was pretty good, about ten bucks an hour. So the next morning, before going to practice, I went down and filled out an application. They offered me a job on the spot, and I accepted. (There was, however, one little hurdle: a drug test that I could not possibly hope to pass. By this point I had developed a fairly healthy appetite for weed; with the help of a clean sample "borrowed" from a friend, though, I got the job.) I'm not sure what I was thinking, how I hoped to balance school, work, and football. But I accepted the offer and went off to practice. That's when Coach Berry called me into his office and laid out the parameters for my return to the team.

"We can work this out, Daniel," he said. "But you're going to have to start out on the JV. I think that's fair."

He was right. It was fair. Personal circumstances notwithstanding, I deserved some sort of reckoning for my behavior. So we shook hands, and I got dressed for practice. But the truth is, mentally, I'd already checked out. I went through the motions for a few days and then just kind of stopped showing up. Eventually Coach Berry confronted me, and I told him that my heart wasn't in it.

"I've got a job, and I have a lot of other stuff going on," I explained, not convincingly. "I don't think I want to play football anymore."

Coach Berry was shocked, hurt, upset – you name it. And I don't blame him. He had offered a reasonable compromise, and I'd accepted that compromise. Now I was quitting, and whatever I may have said, the real reason for my departure was embarrassment over being forced to play with the JV. That's one of the biggest regrets I have from my high school career. I let pride and ego get in the way of making a good decision. I should have just kept my mouth shut and done my time – it probably wouldn't have been more than a week or two. Then I would have moved up to varsity. I would have made so much more progress as a football player.

Instead, I found myself lying to people about why I wasn't playing and feeling pretty bad about who I was and the way I was behaving.

If there was a positive side to any of this, it was that I had plenty of time to play basketball, which was a sport I loved almost as much as football. I went to every session of open gym, worked to get in great shape, and wound up getting quite a bit of time as the backup point guard on the varsity basketball team – not bad, considering I was still only about five-foot-six.

In the springtime I began working out like crazy for football. I patched things up with Coach Berry and prepared for a terrific senior year. Sadly, that work ethic did not extend to the classroom, where I barely managed to maintain eligibility. I did a lot of reckless, selfish adolescent stuff my last two years in high school. I'm fortunate to have a completely clean record – never been arrested or anything – but it wasn't unusual for me and my buddies to skip classes and go swimming or fishing for the day, maybe knock back a few beers or smoke a few joints in the process. Sometimes I'd show up at my hospital job fully baked, eyes glassed over, and then sleepwalk through a four-hour shift. Some of these poor patients were so under the needle they couldn't eat their food, so I'd come back after an hour to retrieve their trays, and there would be a sandwich or a cheeseburger, untouched, sitting on the plate. I'd carry out the tray and scarf down their food in the elevator. It was an easy way to cure the munchies, although clearly against hospital policy.

I could get away with a lot of this behavior because there was no one around to stop me. That's on me, and I regret it. I'm just grateful things didn't turn out worse than they did.

There were friends and family members who knew what was going on and worried about me; I had a good support system, both in and out of the home. I had enough college-bound friends from solid middle-class families to know that not everyone chose to go down the path of self-destruction or just plain stupidity. Their influence cannot be overstated. Had I found myself in a different environment, I'm not sure where I'd be today. Dead or in jail, most likely.

Despite all of this, I had a great senior year in football. Historically, Brooke Point High School had been a mediocre football program. Nothing more, nothing less. We had some good players, even a few great players, but there was no real commitment. The fall of 2004, when I did not play, was a typical season: four wins, six losses. I was part of a potentially strong class, and I wanted to help turn things around. But I had fences to mend. So I went to Coach Berry and asked for a second chance. Well, a third chance, really.

"I'd like to come back, Coach. I think I can help the team."

To his credit, Coach Berry did not yell or lecture. He very simply and calmly stated his expectations.

"Well, you know our off-season schedule," he said. "Telling me you want to play doesn't mean anything. You have to show me, and you have to show everyone else. A lot of guys on the team make it to every workout. They need to know you're here."

He was absolutely right. And so I became a consistent performer in the weight room. I made just about every workout, but to do that I had to quit my job. I'm not proud of the way I handled that either. It's weird — until I left the Army, I'd never left a job properly. You know: walk in, head high, thank the boss for his time and support, and submit your resignation, no hard feelings. That's the mature, professional way to do things. But while I was athletic and very socially adept as a teenager, I was neither mature nor truly confident. Whenever I grew bored or weary in the workplace, I'd just stop showing up. When a manager would call me at home to find out what had happened, I wouldn't answer the phone. Eventually they'd give up. I'm not sure why I did this.

Maybe I was scared. I've always had an irrational fear of telling people no, or disappointing them. Same thing was true with football. Rather than quitting as a junior, I'd simply faded away.

Of course, people generally respect you more if you are honest and straightforward with them. It took me a while to figure that one out.

In terms of football at Brooke Point High School, things began to change in my senior year. We had a core group of seven or eight guys who had been playing varsity for three or four years and who really loved the game. Together, we decided to work our butts off in preparation for our final season. It paid off. We went 7-3, won our conference, and advanced through the district playoffs, eventually coming within two games of the state championship. That might not sound like much, but it was a unique accomplishment at Brooke Point. Frankly, it changed the complexion of the program. We've had a dozen players since then receive Division I football scholarships, and many more have played at the Division III level.

I'm proud to say that I am now one of those athletes, but I took the longest route imaginable. One of the most embarrassing moments of my life was when I got out of the military and began transitioning back into civilian life. To be accepted into a local community college I had to present a copy of my high school transcript, just to prove that I had graduated from high school. My grade point average was approximately 1.9. I felt sick just looking at it. I mean, I wasn't the smartest kid, but I sure as hell could have done a lot better than 1.9. At the time, though, I just didn't care, and because of that apathy, I had very few options when I got out of high school. Quite a few Division III schools had expressed interest in me. Though I was small, I was reasonably fast and strong; I could have been a solid player at that level, right away. But as soon as they saw my grades the interest waned. Academically, I was too big a risk.

It's actually amazing that I managed to stay academically eligible for sports throughout high school. But I did. I never quite fell below the threshold of eligibility. I'd cram for tests, make up work, and slip through the narrowest of cracks. My grades still sucked, but not enough to keep me off the football field or basketball court. And to keep my dad off my case I'd doctor my report card before he had a chance to look at it.

Today I can laugh at some of this stuff, even though it embarrasses me. If I wasn't here and hadn't gone through what I went through, I'd probably be working some dead-end job, and it wouldn't be funny, because it would be my actual life. It would be the ditch that I dug, essentially. But now, thank God, I have done something with my life and actually appreciate my education.

Somehow I managed to graduate from high school on time. But it was touch-and-go there for a while. Right up until the final day, in fact. Or so I thought.

First, a little background. Earlier in the year I'd gotten in a bit of trouble. See, we had a vending machine at school that sold these little crustless peanut butter and jelly sandwiches. I was addicted to these things—they got me through a lot of days. Well, they were a buck apiece, and one day on the way to class I stopped to grab one. Put in four quarters, prepared to grab my treat, and . . . the sandwich got stuck. It was wedged between the glass and that little corkscrew device that seems to work properly about half the time and must have been invented by someone with a really sick sense of humor. I gave the machine a gentle bump with my shoulder.

Nothing.

Gave it another bump, this time a bit firmer. Still nothing.

The bell rang, signaling the start of the next class. Now I was pissed. And really hungry. I walked over to the cafeteria, where I could buy a PB&J, but when I got there I realized that I didn't have my swipe card. Out of luck. I thought about trying to explain what had happened—that I'd gotten ripped off by the vending machine—but instead I waited until the lunch lady turned her head . . . and then grabbed a sandwich and ran off to class.

I know. Bad move. Knucklehead adolescent that I was, though,

I quickly rationalized the theft. Hey, I paid for the sandwich. I mean, there was a dollar of mine sitting in that machine, right? Ethically, it made sense, in a twisted sort of way. I had an accomplice too: my friend, Matt Cavalier, who was the class president and quarterback of the football team. I stole the sandwich, but we both ate it as we walked down the hall. A bite for me, a bite for Matt. By the time we got to class, the evidence had been devoured.

A week later I got called into the principal's office, where I was reminded in graphic detail that the entire school was heavily monitored by security cameras, one of which had recorded the theft and subsequent disposal of evidence. I got three days of ISS (in-school suspension) for that act of stupidity. Matt only got one day, because he had merely eaten the sandwich (an accomplice after the fact), whereas I had been the one who actually committed the crime. (To this day Matt is one of my best friends, and I still tease him about getting off easy because of his lofty standing at the school. Politics, man!) ISS was just about the worst punishment you could get as a high school student: seven hours of sitting in a cubicle, staring at the walls. Even the most boring class was preferable. Hell, a regular suspension would have been preferable.

Anyway, fast-forward a few months to graduation day. There I was, in cap and gown, milling about in a classroom with my friends, tossing a beach ball around, ten minutes before we were scheduled to walk into the Brooke Point auditorium and receive our diplomas. Suddenly the principal, Mr. McClellan, walked into the room, a dour look on his face. He scanned the crowd, finally saw me, and walked right over. McClellan was an impressive guy—big and athletic, a former college football player. He could be charming and funny, or tough as hell. Kids respected him, for the most part. Girls loved him.

"Daniel, we need to talk," he said.

"Okay, what's up?"

He shifted his weight from one foot to the other. I'd rarely seen

Mr. McClellan appear to be nervous or upset, but clearly something was bothering him.

"Listen, I don't know how to tell you this. We've never had this happen before . . ."

"What?" Now he had my attention.

"Daniel, I'm sorry, but your transcript did not go through. When we were calculating grade point averages, there must have been a mistake or something. You didn't meet the requirements. Your GPA is too low to graduate."

I could feel my heart rising into my throat. My grades sucked, no question about it. But I was reasonably sure that I had squeaked by.

"What happens now?" I said.

"You can't walk at graduation," he said. "We'll have to tell your parents, and then we'll try to get this all straightened out. You may have to make up some classwork over the summer."

I didn't know what to say. As I stood there, speechless, Mr. Mc-Clellan handed me a big envelope.

"I need you to open this and sign the document inside," he said. "Just to show that you understand."

I couldn't believe this was happening. I thought of my parents and my sister, sitting in the auditorium, waiting for me to walk across the stage and receive my diploma. They'd be furious. They'd be humiliated. I opened the envelope and slowly withdrew the contents. Inside was a letter, on official school stationery. But there was nothing written on the letter. Instead, a photograph took up most of the sheet of paper. I recognized it immediately. It was a still shot from the security camera footage of the great PB&J robbery. There I was, taking a big bite out of the sandwich as I walked down the hall. There was more: a big red circle had been drawn around the sandwich, with arrows pointing toward me and Matt.

I stared at the photo for what felt like an eternity. Finally, I looked up. McClellan was standing over me, hands stuffed in his pockets, trying to suppress his laughter.

"Are you kidding?" I said. "This is a joke?"

He smacked me on the back, said, "I'll see you inside," and walked away.

I think I was still sweating an hour later when I walked across the stage and became an official graduate of Brooke Point High School.

Given all that I have seen and experienced in the time since, I'm somewhat ashamed of the immaturity and selfishness that marked my high school years. I was too self-involved to even realize that my dad's health was in serious decline. Or maybe I was in denial. Regardless, I should have known that something was up when my mother came home late in my senior year. She and my dad had not divorced, but they were separated in every meaningful way. Looking back on it now, and putting the pieces together, I realize that her return was strictly a matter of practicality. Although she and my father both claimed otherwise, she was there to serve as my father's primary caregiver. There had been a "minor" heart attack (a misnomer if ever there was one), followed by extended time away from work. Over the course of a few months he grew progressively frail.

A couple days after graduation, I left with some friends for a weeklong trip to Myrtle Beach, South Carolina, a Brooke Point tradition that consisted primarily of lying around on the sand all day and drinking to the point of inebriation every night. We were only one day into the celebration when my cell phone rang. It was my mother.

"Your father is sick," she said. "You need to come home."

Her voice was flat, almost devoid of emotion. I'm sure she was trying to spare my feelings, but it had exactly the opposite effect.

"What happened?" I asked. "Is he okay?"

"Just come, Daniel. Now."

I didn't know at the time that my father was already dead. My mother wanted to tell me in person, which I respect and appreciate; unfortunately, the plan backfired. I got on a plane, turned off my phone, and tried to get some sleep. As soon as we landed my phone lit up with voice mail and text messages. The first one was from a neighbor of mine, a friend who was a couple years older.

"Hey, man. Sorry about your dad passing. Let me know if there's anything I can do."

There were others just like it, all offering condolences and emotional support. I walked off the Jetway and into the airport in stunned silence, hungover and shaken to the bone. My mother and sister were there waiting, along with a family friend. None of us were in any condition to drive.

My father died on June 19, 2006, and the void was instantaneous. No hug or handshake. No chance to tell him how much I loved him and respected him and appreciated everything he had done for me. No chance to say, "I love you, Dad," or, "I'm sorry for letting you down."

Nothing.

He was just . . . gone.

I insisted on seeing him at the hospital morgue, but that visit didn't offer any sense of closure or relief. The gray, lifeless form on the slab in front of me didn't even look like my father. It was just an empty vessel.

Unfortunately, I've encountered a lot of death in the years since, and the truth is, I've gotten kind of cold about the whole thing. You see enough of your friends die on the battlefield, you take enough lives with your own hands, your own guns and grenades, and you develop a defense mechanism. The skin thickens. I guess that's sad, but it's the truth. At the time, however, I'd never lost anyone close to me, and my father's death was absolutely devastating. Ray Rodriguez was not just my father, the man who had raised me – he was my closest ally and biggest supporter. And now he was gone? I felt utterly adrift.

Sadness quickly gave way to anxiety as I realized that I had to figure out something to do with my life. I imagined my father looking down on me, shaking his head in disappointment. My father was such a hard worker, and here I was, this carefree adolescent, taking things for granted and stuffing my face with a silver spoon. Shit, I never had to work in high school. I never needed a summer job to pay for clothes or sneakers. I just asked my dad, and he'd press a twenty into my palm. Any money I made from part-time jobs was strictly for discretionary spending; much of it went to pot, regrettably. My father took care of every necessity. All he asked in return was that I work hard in school and on the athletic field, and that I live up to the standard he had established.

On most counts, I felt like a failure. My friends were getting ready for college, attending summer orientation sessions, chatting with prospective roommates, figuring out class schedules. Me? I was just hanging out. A modest life insurance policy allowed my mom and my sister to keep the house and pay off some bills. But it was hardly a financial windfall; it was more like a safety net. After a couple weeks I started thinking about how my father had talked a lot about his military experience. It wasn't that he wanted me to follow in his footsteps – it was his dream to provide a better life for me, one that involved college and a good job – but he acknowledged with some regularity the benefits of his own experience in the Army. It was a good way to learn a trade and leadership skills, military experience always looked appealing on a résumé, and of course, it helped defray the costs of a college education down the road for anyone who chose to go that route, as my father had. He had come from nothing and made something of himself, and he believed the military had helped.

"But if you ever do decide to sign up," he urged, "don't be stupid. Don't go into the infantry."

Soon after graduation my good friend Tyler Pedersen and I both applied for jobs with Dominion Power, a utility company where his father worked. The jobs were dangerous and paid very well. If hired, we'd be on call 24/7 and get paid time and a half.

"Dude, we could make a hundred grand," he said one afternoon while we smoked a blunt in my basement.

"Sounds great," I told him. "But if this doesn't work out, I think I'm going to join the Army."

He laughed. "No way."

I don't know whether I was serious or not. Mainly I was stoned. But after filling out the application with Dominion and doing an interview, during which I realized that I was completely unqualified for the job, I started to think again about what I was going to do with the next chapter of my life. Before my father passed away, I had pretty much come to the conclusion that I would chop away at a degree while attending community college. There weren't a lot of other options, from an academic standpoint. I had talked to a few college football coaches, but as soon as they got a whiff of my grades they backed off. At first I tried to put a positive spin on things: "I'm smart enough to do college work; I just didn't try very hard in high school." That may have been true, but it was also the kind of thing that college coaches heard all the time, and it rarely swayed their opinion. A smart kid who won't do the work is almost worse than a less intelligent kid with a hefty amount of ambition. Most of my high school coaches and teachers liked me, but they were reluctant to vouch for my work ethic, and understandably so. I had earned neither their trust nor their respect. If I was serious about going to college and maybe playing football at a higher level, I'd have to prove myself in the classroom first. I figured I'd have some fun over the summer, then enroll at either Northern Virginia Community College or Germanna Community College. Then I'd transfer to a university.

Until the day my father died, I never seriously considered enlisting in the armed services. This is hard to explain, but I'll try, and I'll use a story from my own military career to illustrate the point. When I was in the Army, I had a sergeant named Joe Barella. He was a Mexican American from California, with a heavy Hispanic accent. He used to give me shit all the time about not being a "real Mexican."

"Dude, you're from Virginia," he'd say. "You don't even sound Mexican."

That was true. The fact is, you have to dig back four generations to trace my roots to Mexico. I don't even speak Spanish. Not a word. Doesn't mean I'm not proud of my heritage. Just means that I've always sort of considered myself a plain old American. Yes, my name is Rodriguez, and you can certainly take a reasonable guess as to my ethnicity simply by looking at me. But Hispanic culture was not a huge part of my life growing up. This became a source of endless ball-busting among my friends, who were predominantly white, middle-class, suburban Americans.

"Yo, D-Rod . . . you're pretty well-spoken for a Mexican."

"Fuck you, man."

Sergeant Barella would banter like this as well, especially when we were deployed together in Iraq. We'd be smoking cigarettes on guard duty, taking shit . . . and occasionally sharing some honest feelings. That's the way it works when you're on guard, filling the hours, waiting for something horrible to happen. You open up to each other.

"You know, the only reason I joined the military is because I didn't have anything going on back home," Barella said. "It was a way out."

Sergeant Barella knew a little about my history, how my father had basically been in the same situation. My dad didn't have anything growing up. He wore nothing but hand-me-downs. I remember him telling me a story about how he found a nickel hidden in a cabinet when he was like six or seven years old, back in the early 1960s. And he stole it to buy some candy, or maybe a soda. When he came home, he found his mother bawling, because she had hidden the money so that she could use it to buy lard for dinner that night. My dad went out and collected empty soda cans and then sold them back for the deposit so that he could repay my grandmother for the money he'd stolen.

"I knew we were poor," he'd say. "I always knew it."

He used to tell me stories like that all the time, but for some reason that one really stuck with me. My father had high expectations for me, but until that night when I stood guard with Sergeant Barella, I didn't really understand what that meant. I didn't realize that he had a lot in common with my dad. Joe had five or six kids; like my father, he wanted a better life for them.

"I will feel that I have failed as a parent if they think it's a necessity to join the military out of high school," he said. "If they want to join, fine. But it shouldn't be the only option."

That really got my attention, hearing it from a parental standpoint and knowing that my father had felt essentially the same way about his kids (even though he never said it in such explicit terms). And it made me feel pretty lousy, considering that I was given so much that my father never had: a better education; a roof over my head and a nice home growing up; new clothes; even private school tuition when I was younger. I had parents who loved me, who provided for me to the best of their ability. Did I know that we were actually in debt up to our necks? No, and I wouldn't know that until much later, when I realized that my parents not only worked themselves to the bone but also borrowed heavily to allow us to live the way we lived. Then again, a kid isn't supposed to know that stuff.

All that my father really wanted out of life was to ensure that his kids had more choices than he did, more options. For a long time everything went the way he planned. My sister had graduated from college. I was doing reasonably well. But then my parents' marriage began to unravel and my father's health declined, and suddenly there wasn't a push for me to hold up my end of the bargain. We all went downhill together.

In the middle of July 2006, roughly three weeks after my father died, I enlisted in the Army. It happened the same day I found out that I would not be hired by Dominion Power.

"You can apply again in six months," they told me.

I said thanks, hung up the phone, and drove straight to the recruiting center, which was located in a typical suburban strip mall. In a single trip you could pick up an Xbox at Best Buy, have lunch at Applebee's, and enlist in the Army – or the Air Force. Representatives from all branches of the military worked together in one building, and my plan was to enlist in the Air Force. Better benefits, I'd heard. Slightly better pay too. But when I poked my head into the room, the Air Force recruiter was not at his desk. I guess he was on break or something.

From across the hall, an Army recruiter could see me wandering around.

"Hey," he yelled. "Come talk to us, man!"

He seemed pretty friendly for an Army guy, and I was tired of waiting, so I walked into his office. I can remember vividly thinking to myself, *All right, fuck it. I've got to get out of here, I'm doing this.*

Like a lot of young men at that time (and this is probably true today as well), I had only a cursory awareness of the US military campaign overseas. I knew we were at war. I knew people were dying in Iraq and Afghanistan. I knew that the "war on terror," which had begun on September 11, 2001, had stretched out over years and across continents and showed no sign of ending anytime soon. But I saw it all from a distance. It had no impact on my life. And to be perfectly candid, there was no great swelling of patriotic pride that provoked my enlistment. Unlike some guys my age, I did not join the Army because I wanted a taste of battle. The honest truth? I just wanted to get the hell out of town.

I actually scored very high on my Army test. I could have had almost any job had I not been so damn transparent when I came to the part of the questionnaire that asked about drug use.

"Don't lie," the sergeant had said. "We will ask people, and we will find out the truth."

Most people lied anyway. I was truthful. Well, almost. I said I had experimented with marijuana on graduation night. Total bullshit, as I'd actually smoked weed on countless occasions. I wanted to look like an honest person, but not a total stoner. So this was my compromise. I shouldn't have bothered. Even this fudged admission was enough to flag my application and preclude any security clearance for at least a year. So, despite testing well enough to qualify for some of the best jobs in the Army, I was now relegated to the lowest tier — hell, I wasn't even qualified to be a truck driver. One option was to wait a year, reapply, and pass a drug test. But I wasn't that patient.

"If I join right now, what jobs do you have?" I asked. "Is the infantry available?"

The woman handling my application gave me a hard look. She seemed surprised.

"You do realize we're at war, right?"

"Yes, ma'am. I understand."

I didn't understand a thing.

2

NO TURNING BACK NOW . . .
That's what I kept telling myself on the bus ride from
Atlanta to Fort Benning, two hours of weirdness rolling
through the Georgia darkness. Everything had happened so fast.
Usually there's a month to six months of lag time between enlistment and basic training, but in 2006 the Army was pumping
out infantrymen to be wounded or killed, so the slots were immediately available – for anyone crazy enough to want one. There
wasn't much time to process or belabor the decision. I took my
mother and sister out to lunch, told them what I was doing, and
let them know I'd be leaving in less than seventy-two hours. My
mother, predictably, started crying. They both were completely
shocked. So were my friends, most of whom were heading off to
the comfortable world of college.

"D-Rod, you're crazy," more than one of them said at the time.
"You know what it's like over there?"

No, I did not. And neither did they. You couldn't possibly know
until you saw it for yourself.

As the bus lumbered along I stared out the window, didn't really talk to anyone. I didn't know another person on board, didn't have any idea what to expect when we arrived. I did get the feeling right away that the Army was going to be one hell of a melting pot. Kids flew into Atlanta from all over the country and then bused collectively to Benning. On my bus alone there were guys from Hawaii, Montana, and Puerto Rico. I could tell some of them were nervous; like me, though, they tried not to show it. A fair number of guys were exactly the opposite — all full of piss and vinegar, acting like they couldn't wait to put on a uniform and start fighting.

A lot of these guys had been in ROTC programs in high school or college and were on their way to becoming officers. They already had been indoctrinated to some degree. They understood Army lingo and tradition, and so they acted like cheerleaders on the bus, chanting out marching cadences, trying to get everyone else to join in, like we were at a bar on St. Patrick's Day or something.

"We are the soldiers of 11-B . . . !"

With each new verse, more of the guys on the bus joined in, but I just sat there, watching the moonlit countryside roll by, thinking, *What the hell is an 11-B?* It was during that ride that I realized just how little I knew about the military. My dad was a veteran, and he worked at Quantico, but I hadn't really paid attention. I can't say I was worried about being inexperienced or naive, but I did wonder what these guys were going to be like when we got to Fort Benning. I figured they'd be super-high-speed, trying to blow everyone away, that they'd know how to use their weapons and generally be better suited to not screwing up. In short, I figured I'd spend most of basic training playing catch-up. What I learned, however, is that first impressions are not always reliable, especially in such an intense environment. Basic training brings out the best and the worst in almost everyone. You never know how people are going to respond.

We arrived at Fort Benning around eleven o'clock, on a typically hot and humid summer night. What I knew about basic training in the Army I'd absorbed from movies and books and a handful of conversations with my dad. As I got off the bus I thought about how he must have gone through virtually the same thing thirty-something years earlier. At this very spot. He had been an infantryman. He went through airborne training at Benning. My father had made it, right? And if all those amped-up douchebags at the front of the bus were so excited, how bad could it be? Everything had happened so fast – there hadn't been time to process what I'd done by enlisting, or to consider the ramifications. Three days earlier I'd been sitting in a recruiter's office; now I was getting off a bus at Fort Benning.

The assault was immediate and profound and completely overwhelming.

"I want all you motherfuckers over here!" someone in a uniform bellowed. "And all you motherfuckers over there!"

I started to say something, to ask a question, and immediately one of the drill sergeants was in my face, spitting and snorting. He looked like he wanted to rip my head off.

"Don't fucking talk! You understand, asshole? Not a fucking word!"

I understood. We were all assholes and motherfuckers, no matter where we stood or what we did. That was the whole point. We were the lowest of the low, kids who had enlisted in the Army and hadn't yet learned a thing. We weren't soldiers. We were first-day grunts.

I tried to stand perfectly still, to do nothing that would betray my ignorance or anxiety. The truth, though, was that I knew absolutely nothing about proper etiquette – how to speak to a superior, how to stand at parade rest, how to salute. I didn't even know how to read rank. After several minutes of scrambling around and being screamed at, I went up to someone who looked like a sergeant and tried to explain that I was a bit out of my element and wasn't sure where I was supposed to go. This was truly a bad idea.

"The fuck you think you're doing?!"

"Uhhhh, just wondering where –"

He cut me off in midsentence. Then he pushed up against me, our chests touching, our noses an inch apart.

"On the ground!" he screamed.

For the next ten minutes this guy smoked me. I must have done a couple hundred push-ups and a couple hundred sit-ups, until every muscle in my body ached and I thought I was going to heave. The entire time the sergeant did not stop screaming. He called me every name in the book and some that aren't even in the book.

"Back in line!" he finally said.

By this time everyone was standing perfectly still. One of the guys next to me – one of the high-speed types who had been singing on the bus – whispered, "That's an NCO. If you're going to talk to him, you have to be at parade rest. But you're not supposed to talk to him anyway."

"Why didn't you tell me that earlier?"

He shrugged.

Lesson learned. After that, I kept my mouth shut. The best advice I can give to anyone going to basic training is this: blend in.

That initial dose of immersion therapy, which included having my head shaved, was a bit misleading, as "true" basic training did not begin for another week to ten days. Classes graduate every week at Fort Benning, and I had to wait for a slot to open. So for the next several days I just hung out in the barracks, eating, working out, trying to convince myself that I hadn't made the biggest mistake of my life. Every so often one of the high-speed dudes would drop to the floor and start cranking out push-ups.

"We're gonna be doing a lot of these, man. You'd better be ready."

Okay . . .

Finally, one morning we were told to grab our rucksacks, boots, and helmets. We were going downrange to begin basic training. We didn't know exactly what was meant by "downrange," and for some reason the Army didn't want us to know. We were rounded up, stuffed into a windowless cattle car –"nut to butt," as they say – and driven in circles for forty-five minutes before finally arriving at the barracks we'd call home for the next fourteen weeks. The idea of this little exercise is to provoke a sense of disorientation and isolation. After we graduated basic training, they took us back to the holding barracks where we had spent the first week. It was literally two miles away. Maybe a five-minute drive.

But it felt like we had plunged twenty miles deeper into the woods. And that was precisely the way we were supposed to feel.

"Yeah, we just drove you around to fuck you up," my drill instructor admitted afterward. Then he laughed. "We like messing with you."

His name was Drill Sergeant Baskerville, and like most of the drill instructors of that era, he was the real deal. I hated this guy ... for about six or seven weeks. See, that's the way it works. Your drill instructor is the biggest asshole in the world for roughly the first half of basic training. Then, once they start breaking you and you're competing against other platoons, they stick up for you – they'll go to bat for you. By the time you graduate basic, you have a pretty good relationship with your drill sergeant.

Drill Sergeant Baskerville was an impressive man, both physically and vocally. He was about six-foot-six, maybe 220 pounds, a black guy with a booming voice and an air of menace about him. You did not want to piss him off. Sergeant Baskerville was in his early thirties, so he'd been in the Army for probably fifteen years. The first time I met him I remember feeling legitimately intimidated. Not in an abstract way, but in a very concrete and visceral way. Like, this guy might actually kill me if I screw up badly enough. A lot has changed in the eight years since I went through basic training. Back then, the vast majority of drill instructors had been directly involved in the initial push into Iraq and Afghanistan. They had crazy, real-war experience, which is not like the half-assed, hands-tied-behind-your-back political bullshit of the last five years. I have tremendous respect for anyone who has served in the military, and especially for anyone who has been in combat. But the truth is, things were different ten, fifteen years ago.

Guys like Sergeant Baskerville fought under a different set of expectations and regulations. They would show us pictures and tell us stories that were hard to believe. They had a different mentality. And they had been taught by old-school drill instructors who were Vietnam vets. Nowadays it's not unusual to see drill instructors who have never seen a minute of combat. They have no practical battlefield experience, but once they reach a certain grade, they have to become either a recruiter or a drill sergeant. So today you have a lot of kids being trained by drill instructors who don't really know what it's like to be in a firefight. And the political atmosphere is totally different. Drill sergeants are still tough, don't get me wrong. But they aren't as abusive and terrifying as they once were. The threat of lawsuits and a philosophical shift toward "sensitivity" has seen to that.

Some people would say that's a good thing, but I'm not so sure. There were fifty-five guys in my platoon when I arrived at Fort Benning. Only thirty-seven made it through the nine weeks of basic training and the subsequent five weeks of infantry training (fourteen weeks total). And that was considered a healthy outcome. The point of basic training is twofold: to prepare each soldier for military life, in particular life on the battlefield, and to weed out those who are not up to the task. That might sound harsh, but it makes sense. If the training is not severe enough, you'll end up with unqualified soldiers on the field of battle. So it wasn't unusual to hear a drill instructor say something like this:

"If you guys want to go AWOL, the train station is right over there. Just hop on. There's a pay phone at the second stop. You don't want to be here, we don't want you here."

It was a constant, endless testing process in which the weak were identified and systematically culled from the herd. If you were viewed as a likely quitter, the drill sergeants would push you to the door and hold it open. The most obvious tactic was physical exertion: endless push-ups and sit-ups and pull-ups, or miles of hiking with a full pack. Equally effective, though, was the verbal abuse heaped upon new grunts. We all experienced the humiliation of having a drill instructor in your face, screaming at you, insulting you, daring you to respond in some way. We all felt the rage rising up, and the desire to push back.

But you couldn't do anything about it. I mean, you could, but that was a guaranteed ticket home. There was one kid in my outfit who totally lost it. One day he took a swing at Sergeant Baskerville. Before the sergeant could even respond, three other guys, myself included, jumped in and subdued the guy, bruising him up in the process. He was gone by the end of the day.

The absurd becomes almost normal in boot camp. We'd run to chow hall and have maybe three to five minutes to eat each meal. You couldn't ask for food; you'd just sit down, wait for it to be served, scarf it down on the way to the trash can, and then move along. You couldn't speak or look at anyone during mealtime. I lost eleven pounds during basic training. Felt dirty most of the time too. We'd shower an entire platoon in less than six minutes. There were twelve showerheads lined up in a row, some spitting hot water, some spitting cold. You never knew what you were going to get. The rationale for that one? I have no idea. Just to screw with us, to make us uncomfortable and edgy. To make us realize that we could get by with less than we had thought was necessary.

A lot less.

Every morning Sergeant Baskerville would do a white-glove inspection of the barracks, and if everything wasn't perfect — I mean, exactly in order and spotless — he would go ape shit. He'd start screaming, calling us names, throwing rifles and boots and helmets all over the place, emptying lockers, dumping shampoo on the floor. Then we'd have to clean all over again. This guy was a terrifying, relentless presence.

And I actually kind of liked him. He knew the Army, and he knew about life. In a very practical way, he had wisdom.

For example, one time I got into it with another recruit, a much older guy who was probably in his thirties. You see that sometimes in the Army – guys who flunk out of college or lose their jobs and suddenly decide that the military is a reasonable option. This guy was also a beast, at least as tall and wide as Sergeant Baskerville, and in some ways even more frightening, since Baskerville's behavior was calculated and purposeful. This guy was just big and stupid and mean.

One day we were out in the field training. He was in charge of one group, while I was working with another group. I forget the exact details, but I did something he didn't like. Or perhaps he was just looking for a reason to get in my face. My bunkmate at the time was a Puerto Rican kid from New Jersey named Johnny Robles. You bunk alphabetically, so . . . Robles and Rodriguez end up next to each other. Anyway, Johnny was my friend, a feisty little guy like me, and he was standing next to me when the big guy (who was white) got in my face.

"Chill out, dude," I said.

"Fuck you, spic!"

That didn't go over well with me or Johnny. We looked at each other. Next thing I knew, me and the big guy were toe to toe, yelling at each other. I'll be honest here – this guy could have broken me in half. It's all well and good to stand up for yourself and to demonstrate that toughness can come in a small package, but there are times when the laws of physics prove irrefutable.

This was probably one of those times.

Fortunately, it ended before I had a chance to find out. Another drill sergeant got between us, wanted to know what happened, and pretty soon there were four or five people all huddled together, cursing and yelling and calling each other names. No punches were thrown. The next day I got called into Sergeant Baskerville's office. I told him what happened, that I'd been provoked by the use of a racial epithet. I figured Baskerville, an African American, would understand. And he did . . . to a point.

"Okay, son, here's the way it works," he said. "You're going to be dealing with these racist motherfuckers your entire life, so you'd better figure out right now how you're going to handle it."

"Yes, Sergeant."

He paused.

"I'm going to be completely honest with you. You can file a complaint; that's your prerogative. I don't know what's going to happen if you get that ball rolling. Maybe this guy will get demoted. Maybe he'll get tossed. Is that going to make you happy?"

I thought about it for a moment. I knew the guy was married, had kids, and that things must have been pretty rough for him to have enlisted at that age. No doubt he was racist to the core, but Baskerville was right—those people were everywhere. No point in letting them get the best of you.

"No, sir," I said. "If that's how he's going to live his life, that's fine by me. I'm not one to ruin the guy just because he used a racial slur."

"You sure?" This was exactly the response Baskerville wanted.

"Yeah, I'm cool with it," I said. "Just let him know he can't be doing that shit. There's a few other Hispanic guys in the platoon, and he's going to have a problem if he isn't careful."

Baskerville smiled.

"Okay."

Just like that, the problem went away.

The thing about the Army—and I suppose this is true of any branch of the military—is that it is simultaneously the most diverse and racially insensitive organization you'll ever come across. It's true that men and women of various religious and ethnic backgrounds are tossed into one big cauldron the day they arrive at boot camp and by necessity must not only get along but also depend on each other and learn to work together to survive. This becomes even truer in a combat scenario. I can say with absolute certainty that you do not give a shit about a man's skin color when he's standing next to you in the middle of a firefight. But it's also true that soldiers tend to hang with their own kind. As in prison, the cliques in a military setting can be ferocious and isolating.

So even though I was like the least Hispanic person in the history of all people named Rodriguez, there was an expectation that I would be part of the Hispanic and Latin clique. And yet, when we'd hang around together, these guys would give me endless shit:

"Why do you talk like a white dude?"

"Why don't you know any Spanish?"

"And why the hell are you good at basketball?"

It was the last of these things that solidified my relationship with Sergeant Baskerville. When it came time for the company games—an athletic competition between companies (each company comprised four platoons)—drill instructors tended to favor the recruits who were best at PT (physical training) because these recruits were most likely to give their company the best chance to win. I was small, but I could run. (I had the best mile time in my platoon.) I maxed out my rifle score. And I could play ball, a fact that absolutely shocked a number of people in my unit.

The company games pitted the soldiers of Alpha Company, Bravo Company, Charlie Company, and Delta Company against each other in a daylong series of events. The competition was mostly traditional track and field events with a few others thrown in, like tug-of-war and boxing. But the company basketball game was easily the highlight of the competition. With more than 200 men across four platoons competing for spots on the company team, I figured the tryout would be fierce. (Each company had one day to practice and select competitors for specific events.) It wasn't. The games were voluntary, and roughly half the men in each company opted to be nothing more than spectators. That left about 100 men to represent each company (in my case at that time, Charlie Company).

"What do you want to do, Rodriguez?" Baskerville asked me.

"I'm pretty good at basketball, Sergeant."

He frowned. "Bullshit."

I'd heard that before, although not in quite a while. My high school years were spent in an affluent, suburban, mostly white school district. Demographically speaking, Brooke Point High School, class of 2006, had very little in common with my class at Fort Benning just a few months later. I was one of the few guys who wanted to play on the Charlie Company basketball team who was not African American. If self-promotion is to be believed (and it's not, of course), I was also the one person who hadn't been offered a Division I college basketball scholarship, only to see it slip through the cracks for one reason or another.

"Couldn't get my grades up."

"Coach got fired just before I was ready to sign."

"Offer got pulled at the last second."

I tossed a little bullshit myself — told everyone I was "recruited" by some D-III schools without saying which sport — just to improve my chances of making the team.

Physically speaking, it was an impressive group of thirty to forty men who tried out that day. Lots of big, athletic guys, tall and ripped. But here's the thing: as soon as we tossed out the balls and began running layup lines, many of these guys were instantly revealed to be posers. That's the thing I've always loved about basketball: you can't fake it. If you're big and strong and fast, you can play football. I know people who didn't even play until they were in high school, and yet they wound up getting D-I scholarships. Soccer requires more expertise, but if you're fast and reasonably skilled, you can blend in. Not so with hoops. Either you can ball or you can't, and the truth of that equation is made abundantly clear the moment you take your first dribble.

I've seen this phenomenon many times over the years. Basketball is a sport that can make even the best of athletes look ridiculously lacking in athleticism. One of my buddies at Clemson was a freak of an athlete, one of the best football players I've ever been around. If you saw him walking around in the locker room in his Under Armour, you'd swear he could play in the NBA. But I've seen this guy in a gym. He can't dribble, can't shoot ... can't do anything with a basketball. It's almost like a running joke on the football team (since everybody plays basketball too; in fact half the guys on the Clemson team were really good high school ballers). I tease this guy all the time. He's probably going to make millions playing in the NFL, but he literally cannot shoot a basketball to save his life.

And neither could most of the men trying out for Charlie Company. Within the first two minutes of warm-ups, I knew I was a more experienced player than just about anyone else in the company. They divided us into roughly four teams of ten and let us play round-robin pickup ball for an hour or two. Midway through the first game, after feeding Baskerville a couple times (each company team had at least one drill instructor on the roster), he said, "Okay, Rodriguez, you're on."

The championship was determined on the basis of total points, and even though we lost in the final of the basketball tournament, we ended up winning the company games. It's strange – I've played in a lot of athletic events over the years, but that game stands out as much as any of them. We lost on a last-second shot in front of a wild, profane crowd. I played well enough to earn serious street cred with the brothers, especially Sergeant Baskerville.

"Look at your little Mexican ass," he said afterward. "Where'd you learn to play like that?"

I just laughed. "Told ya'll I could ball."

I've always gotten a kick out of breaking down stereotypes and proving people wrong. When you're as small as I am, people don't expect you to be much of an athlete; they sure as hell don't think you can play basketball. Or Division I football, for that matter. So you either wilt under the weight of low expectations or you rise above them. Even today, when I show up in the gym or on a playground, I usually wear Army shorts and a regular T-shirt, maybe even New Balance running shoes. It's not enough that I'm small. I want to look like I have no idea what I'm doing, just so I can see the look on the faces of other people – guys wearing $200 Jordans or LeBrons – when it turns out the little Hispanic kid can actually play ball. I know that might sound cocky. But it's really not. I'm as insecure as anyone else. But I've learned that sometimes it's best to use perceived weakness as a weapon. It's a tactic that catches people off guard.

After the company games, I had no issues with Sergeant Baskerville. We got along great. In fact, I had no problems with anyone. It's funny how something as simple as a basketball game can change the way people perceive you.

I was fortunate to make a couple good friends during basic training. Johnny Robles was one. The other was Mark Raines. We called him Marcus, although I forget exactly why. Raines was a character. He'd grown up in Champaign, Illinois, and was working at a Pizza Hut when he decided that his life needed some focus and direction. Raines was twenty-seven years old when he enlisted and looked even older. He was incredibly skinny, maybe six-foot-one and 125 pounds, with thick glasses and hair graying at the temples. Chain-smoker too. When it came to the Army, Raines was all in. He'd given the whole thing a lot more thought than I had, although both of us had enlisted basically because we were looking for a way out of our current circumstances. (I suspect that is true of most enlistees.) Raines wanted an assignment to airborne school, but didn't make weight. I remember him chugging a gallon of water before getting on the scale. He couldn't hold it in and wound up running to the bathroom right before he was weighed. Poor guy ended up less than a pound short of the minimum, and the Army wouldn't give him a waiver.

"Damn, all I had to do was hold my piss two more minutes," Raines would say. "I'd have been jumping out of airplanes."

Raines was one of the scrawniest guys in boot camp, but he was a fighter. We were in Iraq and Afghanistan together. Like I said, appearances can be misleading. You just never know what's inside someone until he's tested.

• • •

By the time we neared the conclusion of basic training I had been sufficiently transformed. No longer was I simply an ambivalent kid running away from a bad situation at home. I'd become a soldier. Granted, I remained clueless about what that word truly meant, but I'd begun drinking the Kool-Aid, that's for sure. I wouldn't say that I was as gung-ho as the ROTC kids who chanted on the bus ride to Benning, but I liked the idea that I had acquired a whole new set of skills: mixed martial arts, weaponry, night-vision combat. I was lean and strong and confident. I liked knowing that I could handle myself in almost any scenario. Basically, it came down to this: three and a half months earlier I'd been a kid with a serious weed habit and no idea what he was going to do with his life, but by the time I got out of basic I felt like I was bulletproof. There's no such thing, of course, but that sort of mentality is precisely what the Army hopes to instill in its new recruits. All I knew was that I was stronger and fitter than I'd ever been in my life. And if someone wanted to bump up against me because I was a little guy, they'd find themselves in a fight.

Back in the day, in the peacetime Army, new soldiers approaching the end of basic training were allowed to put together a wish list of destinations where they hoped to be stationed in their first stint in the military. I had been led to believe by my recruiter that this practice still existed, so as our class approached the final weeks of boot camp I asked Sergeant Baskerville about it.

"Hey, Sergeant, where is this wish list I keep hearing about? I think I'd like to go to Germany."

Baskerville laughed, like I was the most naive kid who had ever joined the Army.

"Son, you enlisted in the infantry in a time of war. Uncle Sam is going to put your ass wherever the hell it's needed."

"Oh . . ."

Three days before the end of basic training, the final roster sheet magically appeared. We were all called into formation and informed of our duty assignments. I won't lie: this was a pretty intense moment – finding out where I'd be spending the next year of my life and whether I'd be kicking back in Germany or Italy or some stateside base. Either way, the likelihood was great that soon enough I'd be dodging IEDs (improvised explosive devices) in Iraq or avoiding sniper fire in Afghanistan. The announcements were made in alphabetical order, with each name followed by the name of a military base. Some of these bases, like Fort Bragg, were in the States; others were overseas. Most of the guys had committed the various possibilities to memory, and so they knew exactly what their assignment meant. As usual, I was a little behind in the homework department, so when my name was called, I reacted with silence and befuddlement.

"Rodriguez: Schofield!"

Now, I really didn't care where I was going, although Germany would have been nice. That's where my dad had been stationed, after all. In fact, when one of the kids ahead of me got Germany and expressed disappointment over the assignment, I quickly offered to trade places, without even knowing where I was going. When I heard the word "Schofield," I didn't know what to think, mainly because I had never heard of the place.

"What the hell is Schofield?" I said.

A couple of the guys near me shook their heads in amazement.

"Damn, dude. That's Hawaii."

Hawaii? No shit . . .

Now, one way or another, I was probably going to end up in Iraq, and I knew it. But for the next few months I'd be . . . well, I'd be in paradise. Not only that, but I'd be hanging out with some of my buddies from back home. You see, my best friend, Stephan Batt, who graduated a year ahead of me from Brooke Point, was already in Hawaii. Stephan is almost like a brother to me, and has been for years. He's a super-smart guy, but decided to forgo a traditional college experience and join four of our close friends who had chosen to attend community college in Hawaii. Then, if all went well, the plan was to finish up at a four-year school closer to home. And that's how it worked out for Stephan. He graduated from the University of Virginia and now works for the Department of Homeland Security.

Anyway, they packed their bags and flew to Hawaii, found an apartment on Oahu, and enrolled in community college. Schofield Barracks, as it turned out, was on the same island. I couldn't believe my luck! I'd be stationed in one of the most beautiful places on earth, and I'd get to reconnect with some of my best friends, who were still on the island. I called home to tell everyone that I'd received my orders, and they were all excited. Considering how recklessly I had approached this entire adventure, things were going pretty damn smoothly.

But the Army is nothing if not unpredictable, especially in a time of war. Long before I ever fired a rifle in combat, death changed my role and assignment. Less than twenty-four hours after being told I would be stationed in Hawaii, I was reassigned to Fort Carson, Colorado, as part of the 3rd Squadron, 61st Cavalry Regiment, 2nd Brigade Combat Team, 2nd Infantry Division. This was Bravo Troop 3-61, and it was where I spent my entire military career.

Apparently the Army had been taking casualties in Iraq and needed replacements in a hurry. This was a fairly common theme in the infantry at this time, during the height of what was colloquially known as "the Bush surge." American troops were getting killed on a daily basis, and fresh bodies were not in great supply. If you were an infantryman in the mid-2000s, you were going to wind up in Iraq or Afghanistan. It was just a matter of time. In my case, that time came very quickly.

I left Fort Benning right around Christmastime and spent a few days at home with friends and family. My mother was living in New Mexico at the time, but she came back to Virginia to see me. She and my sister met me at the airport, which was kind of emotional, although I tried not to make a big deal out of it. They recognized instantly that some things had changed. I was leaner and more muscular, and I had picked up a few military quirks, like addressing everyone as "sir" or "ma'am" and subconsciously marching in cadence when we did something as simple as walking through a shopping mall.

Mom was kind of quiet on that visit. I'm sure she was worried to death about her only son flying halfway around the world to serve as cannon fodder. I didn't look at it that way. To be honest, I still didn't have much of a worldview. I knew Iraq was a dangerous place, but I figured I'd be all right, that I could handle myself in any situation. Besides, it didn't seem real yet. For all I knew, I might be in Colorado for six months or more before deploying.

Then again, maybe not.

I arrived at Fort Carson on January 2, 2007. I didn't even know there was an airport in nearby Colorado Springs, so I had flown into Denver and taken a long bus ride to the Army base. What struck me most was just how cold it was at Fort Carson. I had grown up in Virginia and spent the previous four months in Georgia. I was not accustomed to the frigidity of a Rocky Mountain winter. Not that it mattered. There wouldn't be time to get acclimated. Much of Army life is about standing in lines and filling out paperwork. It happens every time you're reassigned. Well, I was such a rookie that I didn't understand the significance of what was happening to me – I kept getting shoved to the front of lines, and every piece of my paperwork was stamped with the word "expedited." It was kind of cool, like being a platinum member in an airline frequent flier program. Something should have told me that there was a reason for all this special treatment, and that it might not have been because I was such an accomplished soldier or such a good-looking guy.

The reason for the rush was very simple: I was being deployed. Not in a matter of months, but more likely days or weeks. It's the strangest thing to sit around waiting like that, knowing that as soon as another soldier is seriously injured or killed you will be shipped out. I took the place of a young man I never had the opportunity to meet. His name was Allen B. Jaynes. He was from Texas and went by the nickname "Fuzzy." He was twenty years old when an IED detonated near his vehicle while he was on patrol in Baghdad on January 20, 2007.

Four days later, on January 24, I was on a plane bound for Iraq, to take the place of PFC Jaynes. Robles and Raines went out on the same trip, along with another friend of mine, a kid from Maryland named Brian Hinkle. I remember calling my mother and my sister and telling them I was being deployed. My sister tried not to betray any emotion. My mom fell apart. "Please don't die," she sobbed. In fact, a surprising number of people offered exactly that same advice. I was offended. I didn't realize at the time just how practical and sensible it really was.

3

I SPENT FIFTEEN MONTHS IN Iraq without a single day of leave time. I arrived in late January of 2007, with absolutely no clue about what it meant to be a combat soldier, and I left a hardened killer. I don't say that with pride or satisfaction; it's just the way it was.

In neither of my deployments to Iraq and Afghanistan did I spend any time whatsoever on Team Hearts and Minds. In Iraq our job was to coordinate with satellite forces to pinpoint the location of "high-value targets" (these were people, not places) and then hunt them down. It was claustrophobic and urban and crazy. The streets of Baghdad were so hostile and dangerous that we'd routinely spend several days at a time living with the Iraqi police force in the city rather than driving back and forth to our forward operating base. It was a nasty, violent deployment, and we took a lot of casualties — eleven in my unit alone. I was lucky. I had a few close calls with bullets, even got hit in the helmet once, but managed to avoid being wounded. Combat, I discovered, is about luck as much as skill and training. There's only so much you can control. You learn to keep your head down and your guard up.

And you soon come to the realization that life can be snuffed out in an instant.

More than once I've been asked how quickly a soldier becomes acclimated to a theater of combat. The answer is twofold: immediately . . . and never. Like every other American soldier, I entered Iraq after spending a few days in Kuwait. I was actually jacked up when I loaded my bag onto a massive C-130 for the slow, lumbering ride to Balad Air Base in Iraq. From there we boarded a Black Hawk for the final leg of the journey, a roughly fifty-mile sweep under the cover of darkness into the flaming shit hole of Sadr City, located in the northeastern part of Baghdad.

Raines and I were on the same bird, and I remember looking over at him as we climbed aboard. He wore a blank expression, so I'm not sure what was on his mind. Everyone was nervous, but I can honestly say that I was also excited. For the first time since I'd enlisted in the Army, I felt like I had a purpose, and I knew exactly what that purpose was. As the chopper climbed into the night sky I could sense my heart racing. I pulled my night-vision goggles down to better see the landscape below. I ran my hand along the spine of my gleaming new M4 rifle.

I was badass. I was ready for action.

Until the tracer rounds started ringing off the side of the bird: *Ping! Ping! Ping!*

Not heavy fire (sometime later I'd learn the difference between deadly fire and scattershot small-arms fire), but enough to get my attention in a big way. Until that very moment, I'd been approaching this whole thing like I was playing *Call of Duty* on Xbox: with an air of detachment and fantasy. I looked at Raines. He looked at me. I could see him mouth the word *Shit*.

It was completely disorienting and frightening. I tried not to show the fear because, well, you don't want to look like a coward before you even arrive in-country. Honestly, though, I instantly fell victim to the phenomenon known as "puckering"— fear causing your sphincter to tighten so hard that you can barely breathe. I don't think my asshole relaxed until the next morning after that ride. And this wasn't even legitimate contact. This was just a routine flight into Baghdad. It happened all the time. It was like a rite of initiation for every soldier beginning his combat deployment.

Most of the guys on our bird were new and clearly scared. One exception was a sergeant, returning from leave, who just laughed as the bullets rang off the side of the Black Hawk.

"Fucking pussies!" he shouted over the roar of the chopper. "Always shooting. Like it's gonna make a difference."

He took a big dip of chewing tobacco, spit on the floor, and laughed again. As I watched him our eyes met. He nodded. Not in a friendly way, really. But there was something oddly reassuring about his demeanor.

This guy is crazy. I'm sticking close to him.

We landed at Camp Rustamiyah, a forward operating base manned by a couple hundred soldiers on the eastern side of Baghdad, about six miles southeast of Sadr City. I did not exactly make the most heroic of entrances. If you watch a lot of movies, you'd be fooled into thinking that disembarking from a helicopter as it idles in the landing zone is no big deal. Let me tell you something: it's trickier than it looks. The first part went well. I jumped out of the chopper, grabbed my two duffel bags, and began jogging away.

"Stay low!" someone yelled. Which made sense. You don't want to be the sorry bastard who gets decapitated two minutes after landing in Iraq. No one wants to lead the nightly kill count, and you sure as hell don't want to do it in a way that leaves a legacy of embarrassment. So I crouched low and kept moving, bags hoisted on my shoulders, weapon neatly slung. I looked and felt like a soldier.

God, I wish somebody would take a picture!

Thankfully, my wish was not granted, because about two seconds later the Black Hawk revved its engine and began to rise from the LZ, kicking up a storm of rubble and wind in its wake. Instantly I was caught in the vortex. I could feel my feet rising off the ground. For a moment I thought I might actually be able to fly. No such luck. The LZ was about three feet above the surrounding area, and the force of the chopper's departure caused me to lose my balance as I was transitioning to level ground. I landed awkwardly, lost my bags, and felt a knifelike pain rip through my calf.

Shit . . . I think I broke my leg.

I could just imagine the abuse I'd take if I were to be sent home in a cast after one day in Iraq. I don't think anyone would give me a medal for something so stupid.

But I was lucky. One of the duffel bags cushioned my fall, and the pain had been merely a cramp. It hurt for a couple days, but very quickly I realized that there were far greater concerns at Camp Rustamiyah.

Nicknamed "Mortaritaville" because it was shelled so often, Rustamiyah was a fairly compact little base in the middle of an urban center. Some of the bases in Iraq were massive, with multiple airstrips and giant recreation and dining facilities, as well as a range of medical services. Rustamiyah was far more modest. There was a little gym, a chow hall, and walls that had been erected to provide shelter from the constant onslaught of mortars and rockets. It was somewhat secure within the perimeter of safety that had been established, but we still got fired upon every morning.

The person who showed me the ropes was a country boy from Georgia, Sergeant Josh Emanuel. A good friend with whom I still keep in touch, Josh was exactly the kind of sergeant you want to meet early in a deployment, because he was both insanely funny and competent as hell. I woke up that first morning, my calf aching, my back sore from sleeping on a two-inch mattress, and within a few minutes there was Josh, standing in the doorway addressing Raines and me and a couple other new guys.

"All right, fuckers, get your stuff, you're coming with us," he said. "You're going to be in our platoon."

That was it. Those were the first words I ever heard from Sergeant Emanuel: *All right, fuckers, get your stuff.*

Then we started talking.

"Your name really Rodriguez?"

"Yes, sir."

"First off, don't call me sir, I work for a living. Bullshit! What's your full name?"

"Daniel Rodriguez, Sergeant."

"Where you live, Rodriguez?"

"I'm from Virginia, Sergeant."

He frowned. "The fuck you are!"

"Yes, Sergeant."

There was a pause as he looked me over.

"You hunt, Rodriguez?"

"Roger, Sergeant."

"Fish?"

"Roger that."

He nodded. "That's good. You smoke? Dip?"

"No, Sergeant."

"Well, you're going to start soon enough. I like Copenhagen, so when you start dipping, keep that in mind, so we can share."

My initial response was one of disbelief. I figured the sergeant was just messing with me; I sure as hell didn't plan on taking up either smoking or dipping. I'd been a bit of a pothead in high school, but I'd always considered tobacco to be poison and wasn't even tempted to start.

And of course, like just about every other Army grunt who ends up seeing combat duty, I became both a smoker and a dipper. More of the former than the latter, really. I dipped occasionally because it was so readily available and sometimes it was the easiest way to get a nicotine rush. (It was also an incredibly effective laxative, which came in handy when you'd been constipated for days on end.) But I never did get the hang of it. I hated the taste and was terrible at spitting. I'd stuff a wad into my cheek, let the juices accumulate, and then invariably some of it would trickle down the back of my throat. If you've ever been a novice dipper, you know what happens next. Instantaneous nausea. I must have vomited the first three or four times I tried to dip. It became almost a running joke in our platoon.

"Stand back! D-Rod's gonna dip."

Smoking is just as nasty as dipping, maybe even worse for your health, but your priorities change when you're on deployment. For example, the last thing you want is to fall asleep when you're pulling guard duty; you don't want to lose your edge when you're on a mission. Other lives are at stake. You can't afford to screw up. So you smoke or dip; you do whatever it takes to sustain that buzz in your brain, day or night.

I was a foot soldier who was attached to a mortar platoon. For the first two months in Iraq my job was pretty straightforward. We'd drive around in a convoy, set up checkpoints, bang on doors, and generally just look for bad guys. Oh, and try not to get blown up in the process. In the early spring of 2007, though, the surge kicked into high gear, and after about two months in-country my unit was relocated to something known as a joint security site (JSS), which in this case was a police compound right in the middle of Sadr City.

It was as hot as any location in the region, and I don't mean from the standpoint of temperature. I basically lived at this police compound for the duration of my deployment, working and patrolling alongside the Iraqi police force. In the beginning, we'd commute to the JSS in the morning and then return in the evening. Very quickly, though, as casualties mounted, this was deemed much too dangerous. In Iraq the more time you spent in a vehicle, traversing streets and highways, the more likely you were to get blown up. That was the primary difference between combat in Iraq and combat in Afghanistan. Both places were potentially deadly, but for very different reasons. Snipers and IEDs caused the greatest carnage in Iraq; in Afghanistan mortars and small-arms fire presented the greatest risk. Neither situation was ideal for a soldier who often felt he was fighting with one hand tied behind his back, but you learned to make the best of it.

So, after a month or so, to minimize the likelihood of casualties in and around Sadr City, we decided to cut back dramatically on the amount of commuting we did. For five or six days we would live at the JSS, with the Iraqi police force, patrolling our district. Then our sister platoon would come and take over, and we would return to Rustamiyah for a day or two of recovery. When we first arrived, the JSS was a total shit hole. It had nothing, just bare walls and thirty cots packed into one little room. We built bunk beds and trucked in some Port-a-Johns, along with enough food to last a week at a time.

Each stint at the JSS was preceded by something known as a "route clearance." Basically, this involved traveling behind mine-sweepers, at three miles an hour, as they painstakingly scoured the road and surrounding area for possible IEDs and roadside bombs. It was incredibly tedious and annoying. At the same time, it was safe. Better to be hot and bored and frustrated than to risk having another American soldier blown to bits because of impatience or recklessness.

For the first month or so I spent a lot of time manning a machine gun in the turret of a Humvee. I hated that. Too static and reactive. I preferred to be part of the dismount team – the guys who actually banged on doors and extracted the high-value targets. Boots on the ground – that's where the action was. We would clear houses for blocks on end, sweeping entire neighborhoods in search of one or two high-value targets. At times it was like trying to find the proverbial needle in a haystack. But at least we were doing something; we were trying to make progress.

The goal was not execution. The goal was extraction: to capture insurgents who might have useful information and to bring them in for interrogation. Obviously, this work brought up a lot of moral ambivalence. The US Army has the best intelligence and surveillance equipment and personnel in the world, but it was still hard to know whether we were breaking down doors that belonged to civilians or insurgents. Sometimes, frankly, they belonged to both.

As a soldier in Iraq (and this was true in Afghanistan as well), you learned very quickly to develop a thick skin and to not let yourself be affected by tears and shouting. This was the job; sadness and empathy only got in the way and increased the odds of American casualties.

Traditional shoot-outs and firefights were rare during my Iraq deployment. When we did fire our weapons, it was usually in response to mortar attacks or sniper fire. On those occasions we would be like unleashed animals, trigger-happy to an almost insane extent. I had two friends killed by snipers. You take that shit very personally. Imagine that you're walking through a concrete valley, with buildings rising up on both sides. All of these buildings have windows and flat roofs – a thousand vantage points from which a lone gunman would have easy access. You're walking along, quietly, carefully, looking for IEDs, waiting for intel to provide the coordinates of a high-value target, when all of a sudden you hear the crack of a rifle. Maybe someone to your left falls. Maybe not. Depends on the sniper's ability. Regardless, you respond with catastrophic violence.

"Light that shit up!" one of the sergeants would yell. And we did.

We called it the "mad minute," a brief but intense period in which we would unleash holy hell on the neighborhood, firing so ferociously that our gun barrels would almost melt. It was basically a free pass to spray everything in sight and to release all the pent-up anger and frustration that came with the job. Does this sound brutal? Primitive? Well, it was. And I don't expect anyone who hasn't felt the chill of a sniper attack to understand it.

On June 18, 2007, while out on patrol, we lost Sergeant Eric Snell. Snell was thirty-five years old, a big (about six-foot-four and 200 pounds), good-looking, athletic man from New Jersey who had been drafted by the Cleveland Indians out of high school and later played baseball at Old Dominion and Trenton State College. He'd also done some modeling. Snell was a good soldier, a nice guy, and, most important of all, the father of two boys. He had enlisted for them just a couple years earlier, to try to provide some financial stability in their lives.

There was nothing particularly unusual about the day Snell was killed. One minute he was on patrol, talking and laughing to ease the tension, and the next minute a sniper's bullet pierced his helmet. He fell in the middle of the street. I was on a relief mission with another unit when it happened; we arrived maybe two minutes after the initial ambush. I couldn't believe what had happened. That's the way it usually worked when someone got tagged by a sniper. There was a surreal, almost dreamlike quality to it. A few seconds in which all you could do was stop and stare.

Oh, no . . .

And then we returned fire, a massive assault that went on for at least the allotted "mad minute." One of our guys quickly got on the radio and reported that we were taking small-arms fire. Technically speaking, this was an accurate assessment of the situation. You never knew whether a sniper was acting alone or in concert with a half-dozen others. It wasn't unusual for the ping of a sniper's bullet to be followed by the crack of a dozen rifles, or the eruption of an RPG or mortar. In this case, we didn't wait to find out. If the insurgents got off another shot, it was completely drowned out by our hailstorm of bullets. I don't know if we killed anyone that day; I presume we did. But we certainly laid waste to an entire city block. The truth is, fighting often went down that way in Iraq. We traveled with a dozen AKs and cases of ammo, and we did not hesitate to use them at the slightest provocation. Unfortunately, that provocation often included the death of an American soldier.

That summer things really heated up. For a while it seemed like we were taking casualties every day. One morning we were hanging out at the JSS, waiting to go out on patrol, when a massive explosion ripped through the city. We could actually feel the walls of the police station shake, even though we were a couple miles away from the blast. Immediate chatter followed over the radio.

Some men from one of our sister units had been hit by a roadside IED. It had happened on Route Pluto, one of the most dangerous roads around Sadr City. So dangerous, in fact, that it went black by the end of my deployment—travel by US troops was completely banned.

As we rushed to provide support I felt a surge of adrenaline—I wanted to fight. But when we arrived on the scene, I was nearly overcome with fear and shock at what I saw. A Humvee had been practically incinerated, and three of the four soldiers inside had been slaughtered. There was a sickening stench in the air, the unmistakable smell of burning flesh. I was barely nineteen years old at the time, and here I was, climbing up onto this truck, a body bag in hand. When I looked inside, I could barely comprehend what I saw. Not only could you not identify the soldiers, you couldn't tell where one body ended and another began. It was utter carnage—a human stew.

What the fuck . . . ?!

Maybe "fear" is the wrong word. It's something much deeper and more profound than that. It's almost an inability to process. It's like your brain shuts down for a moment to protect you from the insanity of it. Look, I wasn't completely naive. I knew my job and was beginning to understand what war meant. But up until that moment I did not have a clear grasp of how horrific it could be. I knew one of the guys in that truck too, which made it much more personal. If it could happen to him, it could happen to any of us. It could happen to me.

Even worse than dying in this way was the prospect of living through such an attack. The one kid who had survived was sprawled across the floor of the Humvee, wailing in agony. His jaw was missing, and his midsection had been ripped apart; with one hand he was trying feebly and unsuccessfully to hold his entrails in place. Several seconds passed before I realized that both of his legs had been blown off as well. Miraculously, the medics got him stabilized, but he bled out on the way to the hospital. I remember thinking that it was just as well. It's true that soldiers injured on the battlefield in Iraq and Afghanistan often survived despite incurring devastating wounds that in another era surely would have resulted in death. I can't help but wonder sometimes, though, about the quality of their lives.

The cleanup took several hours. There is no way to sugarcoat it. It was foul work, emotionally and physically exhausting. While the remaining members of the caravan protected the perimeter, we erected a tarp around the Humvee and scooped whatever we could into body bags. The truth of a combat cleanup is this: Sometimes bodies are not sent home. Sometimes the caskets that travel halfway around the world are filled, not with bodies, but with "remains." Sometimes they are filled only with dog tags and uniforms and bags of sand to approximate the weight of a human body. I can't even imagine a military mortician's work. It must be devastatingly grim and sad.

After several hours of the grisly work, we were nearly finished. A truck was called in to haul out the wreckage of the Humvee, and helicopters hovered overhead to provide security. I was lying in the grass, keeping lookout, when suddenly my vision blurred and my head started spinning. I had trouble breathing. At first I thought I might be having some sort of panic attack. These were not uncommon in the military, and I had just witnessed some bad shit, so it was certainly a possibility. Nothing to be ashamed of. Except it didn't really feel like that. After a few minutes, my chest began to hurt. Not like a constriction or a coronary event, but something more palpable. It felt like I was burning. Like the skin on my chest was on fire.

I stuck a hand inside my shirt and fumbled for my dog tags. They were practically on fire.

What the hell is going on?

I turned to Sergeant Emanuel.

"Sergeant," I said, gasping for breath, "something's wrong."

Josh knew I wasn't a complainer, nor was I prone to exaggeration. I could tell by the look on his face that he was concerned.

"You all right, Rodriguez?"

I shook my head. "No! I'm freaking out here."

Josh rushed over, hooked his hand under my armpit, and pulled me to my feet. Together we walked briskly into a shady spot maybe thirty yards away. And as soon as we did that the symptoms subsided; there was instant relief.

"Probably just dehydrated," he said. "It's a bad day. Don't worry about it."

It was a bad day – the worst I saw in Iraq. But there was more to my breakdown than heat exhaustion or anxiety. You see, many of the armored vehicles in Iraq were equipped with "dragons": radioactive devices designed to detect and deactivate IEDs well in advance of an approaching convoy. Well, the dragon on this particular Humvee was still working throughout the cleanup, and apparently I'd absorbed a hefty dose of radiation. That's why my dog tags were practically melting while I was lying in the grass: I was getting baked by the dragon's radiation beam! As soon as I got out of range I felt fine. As fine as could be expected under the circumstances anyway.

Disgust was quickly replaced by rage. Anger is the predominant emotion in combat. When one of your buddies gets killed, you want more than anything else to exact retribution on the person or persons responsible. It's more of a desire to justify the insanity of the entire exercise than a desire for revenge, although there is some of that.

There were times when we detained insurgents who were strongly suspected of killing American troops. We didn't have proof. But we had solid military intelligence. And sometimes, even though it tested the rules of engagement, we would aggressively and forcefully interrogate the detainees, no doubt frightening and angering them in the process. And then we would set them free to spread the word. I don't doubt that this probably only made things worse, that it heightened hostility among the Iraqis. Frankly, I did not give a shit. The usual rules of civility and decency no longer seemed to apply. Additionally, after you've been on a combat deployment for a while, you start to wonder whether you'll ever get home alive; this thought is both liberating and dehumanizing. Essentially, your entire existence becomes guided by a single principle:

Fuck it.

We had a saying in the Army: it's better to be judged by twelve than carried by six. With a jury, you have a chance; with pallbearers, well, the discussion is over. I always knew that if anything ever came back on me – if there were repercussions about supposedly killing the wrong person or killing someone wrongfully (it's important to note that these two acts are not interchangeable) – I would take my punishment and sleep with a clear head. It turned out to be a lot more complicated than that. There's no shortage of things that happen in battle that can mess with your mind for years to come. You lose sleep for a lot of reasons, some of which you never anticipate until you get home.

I was fortunate. I can honestly say that I never knowingly shot the wrong person. But it could have happened to me, and obviously it did happen to others. Every day you're literally a finger away from killing somebody. It's such a scary thing. Here I was, less than a year out of high school, kicking down doors and breaking into houses. I would stand there holding a gun to the head of someone while his children screamed in the background, pleading with us to let him go, insisting that he had done nothing wrong. And maybe he hadn't. On the other hand, maybe he was an insurgent, aiding Al-Qaeda. Maybe he was Al-Qaeda. Maybe he had personally detonated an IED like the one I'd cleaned up after that day.

You never knew. You just fucking never knew.

All it would take was one wrong move by a desperate wife or child, or the sudden emergence from a back room of someone who might simply have been sleeping, and I could have lit up the whole house. And I'd have been justified in doing it. Thankfully, I never did any crazy shit like that. But I certainly didn't come away without any scars.

I took up smoking that day, and I stopped sleeping.

Coincidentally (or maybe not), I logged my first official kill that very same day; in some ways that was even worse. Certainly it was a psychological rite of passage. I was manning a roadside checkpoint with another guy, not far from the perimeter we had established in the wake of the IED explosion. Two or three hours later, it was still a very tense and hostile situation. Because car bombs were common in Iraq, this was stressful, important work. And given the all too recent incinerated Humvee episode, the job took on added significance and risk.

The rules of engagement in Iraq (and Afghanistan) were often murky; however, when it came to roadside checkpoints, there was no confusion. If a vehicle failed to stop at a checkpoint, it was fair game. In this particular instance, the driver panicked and tried to blow past us – usually an indication that a car was carrying illicit material of one type or another or that the driver was, to put it colloquially, a bad guy.

As the car approached, without slowing down, we began waving and screaming.

"Stop! Stop!"

We even fired a warning shot, but still he kept coming.

I don't know what the driver was thinking – there was some speculation afterward that he might even have had a seizure behind the wheel – but the inevitable result was a barrage of bullets from our M4 rifles. Between us, we must have put thirty rounds into the vehicle.

The car crawled to a stop. There were two of us who had lit up the car, and now we had to investigate the results of our work. The car was riddled with bullets, the windows shattered. I don't know which one of us fired the kill shot – it really didn't matter. We both had hit him. When we pulled the driver from the car and began to drag him away, the lower half of his jaw fell off and a large chunk of his brains slipped out and landed with a splat on my boots.

For a moment I froze, totally repulsed. My head began to hurt, and a cold sweat bubbled to the surface of my skin. I thought for sure I was going to pass out or puke. Or both.

"Gimme a minute here!"

And then I could hear the laughter, a dozen guys shouting insults and cracking up at the rookie's sensitivity. I bent over, put my head between my knees, and choked back the nausea.

That was the first and only time I ever felt sick about pulling the trigger. It sounds barbaric, but in a combat zone you quickly get over the natural human tendency to preserve life — unless it's your own life or the lives of your fellow soldiers. Killing becomes second nature. It's part of a chain reaction: something happens, you respond accordingly, and then you move on. Regardless of the outcome, there is no time to dwell on what happened.

You adapt. For better or worse . . . you change. That kid from Brooke Point High? The one who liked to play football and smoke weed with his friends? The kid with a laid-back live-and-let-live attitude?

He was gone. And I wasn't sure he'd ever come back.

Later that night I was hanging out with Sergeant Emanuel, the two of us sitting on the hood of a Humvee, smoking and dipping, trying to make sense of the day's craziness. Josh was by then already a veteran in every sense of the word. He'd been through crazy shit during the initial push into Afghanistan a few years earlier, when hardly anyone even realized that American forces were there, because the focus was all on Iraq. Josh used to tell stories about that deployment, about how they wrote the rules of engagement as they went along. This, he seemed to be saying, was the way it should be.

Josh knew I was upset and wanted to make sure I was okay. He was as tough as anyone I met in the Army, but he had a good heart too, and he knew that both the IED cleanup and the checkpoint kill had taken their toll on me.

"You good?" he asked, offering me a cigarette.

"Yeah, I'm all right," I said, which was a lie.

Josh nodded, looked right through me.

"Listen, you need to understand something. People in this world live to be a hundred years old and they will never ever see what you saw today."

"I know."

"Naw, man . . . no bullshit," he said, his Georgia drawl getting thicker as he spoke. This happened with Josh: the more emotional he got the more he betrayed his redneck roots. "Folks live for-fuckin'-ever, and they will never witness anything like what you just saw. Remember that. Nobody ever will understand what you've been through over here except for us. So don't ever be afraid to talk to me about it."

"Thanks, Sergeant. I appreciate that."

That was the extent of the pep talk, but it's funny – that one brief conversation stayed with me as clearly as any that I had on either of my two deployments. Josh was not an educated man. He was a country-ass Southern boy who joined the Army because there weren't a lot of other options. He was one of my best friends in the military, and I trusted him with my life. But let's be honest: he wasn't a psychiatrist. Nevertheless, that advice sticks with me as one of the smartest things I've ever heard. He was right. I was going to go home and see friends and loved ones, relatives who had been walking the earth for decades longer than I had. Presumably they possessed wisdom I did not have. But if they hadn't been in Iraq, or if they hadn't seen combat, there were some things they couldn't possibly comprehend. I was still in my teens, but already I'd been exposed to a part of human nature we'd all like to pretend doesn't exist. I had seen the worst that people are capable of doing to one another. I had done it myself. And there was no undoing it.

Later that night we lost power at the JSS. This sounds more catastrophic than it actually was. In fact, it happened all the time, for periods both long and short. Sometimes it was simply a matter of a local generator running out of gas. Other times it was a citywide mechanical malfunction. When these larger outages happened at night, they were a sight to behold. I often rushed to a rooftop just to look out over the desert sky, which stretched endlessly to the horizon. It was absolutely breathtaking – a million or more stars lighting up the exquisite, ancient architecture below. That was the thing that struck me the most about Iraq: it was undeniably gorgeous. As much as I hated being there and hated the people who were trying to kill us, as much as I failed to comprehend our reason for even being there, when it seemed no one wanted us there . . . despite all of that, I couldn't help but marvel at the sheer spectacle of its natural beauty. This country was broken and battered, but still, under the right circumstances, in the right light, it left me awestruck.

On this particular night I was alone on the rooftop when the power went out. I don't know what happened, or why it hit me the way it did, but as I looked out at the stars and thought about the horrible shit I had seen that day and how incongruous it all seemed – how such a beautiful place could hold so much death and destruction – suddenly I began to cry. I broke down and sobbed until my chest ached. And for some reason I began thinking of my dad, and how great it would have been to be able to talk with him, to ask for his advice, and to share with him some of the pain I felt. But I didn't have that. And I'd never have it again. Josh was right. All I had were the guys in this unit. No one else would ever understand.

4

IN THE SUMMER OF 2007, maybe six or seven months into my deployment, I got sick. That sounds like a little thing, and in fact it was quite common for US troops in both Iraq and Afghanistan to contract all manner of nasty bugs, usually of the gastrointestinal variety. At any given time it seemed like half a dozen men in our platoon were walking around with what can generously be called "flu-like symptoms."

But you learned to deal with it. Except in the most extreme cases, life and business went on as usual. If you were fortunate enough to be stationed far from the action, you could get a few days of rest and recovery when you got sick. Not where we were, though, not in Baghdad. Still, I found out the best cure for any illness is adrenaline. There were times in both Iraq and Afghanistan when I was sick as shit, feeling like I couldn't get out of bed – and as soon as the bullets started flying, or a mortar shell exploded, I felt instantly better. One minute I'd be in the fetal position, sweating my balls off, sick to my stomach, and the next minute I'd be up and armed, fighting like a madman. There was instant relief from the sickness. And not short-term relief either. Even after the fighting subsided, the symptoms would not return. It was like the massive surge of adrenaline flushed the infection right out of my body. This happened to me on more than one occasion, and I saw it happen to other people as well. So here's my advice: If you're ever sick and you want to recover in a hurry? Get someone to start shooting at you. Convince yourself that your life is coming to an end and almost no pathogen stands a chance.

I say "almost" because there are exceptions to every rule, and one of the exceptions to this one is cholera. That's right — cholera, a wretched and aggressive intestinal illness that killed tens of millions of people in the nineteenth century. In the United States and most of the developed Western world, we don't even think about cholera. It's one of those ancient maladies that's been largely eradicated through public health measures we take for granted, like chlorinated water, efficient septic systems, and the widespread enforcement of health standards in the food and agriculture industries. But in Third World countries, where sewage runs raw into streams and rivers and every other household slaughters its own food for dinner, cholera is alive and well.

I know this from personal experience.

Not that there was any benefit to knowing the source of the infection (because in all likelihood I'd go right back to old habits), but I'm pretty sure it was the eggs or chicken that made me sick. We were very careful about our drinking water — bottled only, shipped from the US. If you drank the local water in Baghdad, you were just asking for trouble. When it came to food, however, boredom sometimes led to imprudence. You'd get tired of the MREs and eat with the locals (we had an Iraqi cook at the JSS), forgetting that your immune system might not be up to Third World standards.

Like most mornings, that day started with a breakfast of scrambled eggs with some vegetables and chicken. Maybe some pita bread. The chickens, as I said, were not exactly of the free-range variety. These were filthy little birds that often ran wild in the streets, like pigeons. If you wanted eggs or meat, you'd just corral a few of them and do the butchering yourself. Well, the Iraqis would do it for us, actually. We'd just eat . . . and hope for the best.

I started to realize something was wrong when I began to sweat like crazy while out on patrol that afternoon. In itself, sweating was hardly unusual in Iraq, especially in the summertime, when the temperature would climb to 130 degrees. Inside a Humvee or armored tank, it could easily hit 140. The human body has a remarkable ability to adjust to such oppressive conditions, although the acclimatization process has some weird side effects. On a clear desert night in the summertime, the temperature would fall to 90 or 95 degrees. Still hot, of course, by any reasonable standard. But when you have grown accustomed to 130 degrees, it's funny how 95 can feel almost frigid. There were times when I would be standing outside, shivering, teeth chattering, and I'd look at the thermometer.

How the hell can it be 100 degrees?! I'm freezing!

Then I'd add another layer of clothing.

So at first I thought there was nothing out of the ordinary when I started shivering while on guard duty in a Humvee that night. It was a clear evening, probably in the low 90s, and the sweat that accumulated on my uniform had dried and cooled. This happened all the time and rarely was cause for concern. As the night went on, though, I began to feel worse. Not just cold or clammy, but really light-headed and nauseous. I left my post briefly (we always stood guard in pairs) to go to the bathroom. Right away I knew I was in trouble. If you've ever had food poisoning or any other digestive bug, you know how it works. The first bowel movement is loose. The second one is looser. Pretty soon you have raging diarrhea. I shit at least ten to fifteen times in the next hour. And then I began vomiting. Each time I'd come staggering back to the Humvee and try to resume guard duty. I'd stand at the rear of the Humvee, practically hugging the tailpipe to keep warm.

"Keep revving the engine," I begged the driver. "I'm freezing."

The usual response to someone getting sick was to bust his balls and tell him to get back to work. I'd done it myself. But this was different. I'd never experienced anything like it. Eventually the driver called for a medic, who quickly assessed the situation.

"How many times have you gone to the bathroom?" he asked.

"I don't know. I lost track."

"Are you going in the same spot every time?"

"Pretty much . . . I think."

"Okay, take me there."

I staggered into a patch of brush maybe twenty feet from the Humvee, with the medic holding me up as we walked. He pulled out a little flashlight and scanned the ground. Obviously it had never occurred to me to examine my own feces, but when I saw it now – when I saw that my excrement was laced with ribbons of white matter, like bird shit – I knew something was amiss.

"Yeah, this is bad," the doc said. "That's a symptom of cholera."

Cholera?

I couldn't even remember the last time I'd heard that word – probably during a high school history class.

"What's cholera?" I asked.

"It's like the worst case of dysentery you can imagine," he explained. "Basically, you shit yourself to death."

Oh, fuck . . .

"We have to get you out of here," he added. "Right now."

The urgency stemmed from the fact that cholera is extremely aggressive and swift – excessive fluid loss in the first few hours can lead quickly to dehydration and electrolyte imbalances and subsequent cardiac issues. Simply put, you don't mess around with it. The medic tried to start intravenous fluids right there in the JSS, but I was so dehydrated that my veins had already begun to collapse. It wasn't until I was taken to a hospital in the Green Zone, some twenty minutes away by chopper, that they were finally able to get an IV line running. One of the docs also gave me an injection of penicillin in the butt, which was surprisingly painful.

"This is going to feel like a railroad spike going into your ass," the doc warned. "And then it's going to feel like I'm injecting syrup."

"Okay, just give it to me." If it was going to help alleviate the symptoms, I wanted it right away.

There was a little poke, nothing too bad . . . and then . . . well, I don't remember too much else. There was a massive burning sensation – soldiers call it the "peanut butter and jelly shot"– that felt like sludge working its way into my skin . . . and then I passed out, a victim of pain and fever and dehydration. I woke a few minutes later, appalled to discover that I had literally shit the bed. I was completely exhausted and humiliated.

Oh, man . . . I came all the way to Iraq for this? My buddies are getting shot by snipers and blown up in Humvees, and I'm going to shit myself to death? You've got to be kidding.

I spent approximately forty-eight hours in the hospital, and then two days on bed rest at Rustamiyah. Then I went back to work. I was lucky. Had I not received treatment so quickly, things could have turned out much worse.

There are various ways to deal with the stress and boredom of a combat deployment. Not many of those coping mechanisms would be considered healthy. Not only did I start smoking and dipping in Iraq, but I also became a heavy drinker and a purveyor of black market goods.

I'm not proud of either of those things, but if I'm going to tell the story, I might as well be honest about it. It's part of who I am and the road I've traveled.

In high school I hadn't been much of a drinker. I preferred marijuana – it suited my laid-back temperament at the time. But weed was hard to come by in Iraq, if not downright impossible. Alcohol was a different matter. Despite being banned in Iraq, booze was available, if you knew where to look. It just took me a little while to figure out how things worked. For the first few months I did what everyone else did: I asked friends from back home to send liquor in cleverly disguised ways. We all received packages containing bottles of apple juice laced with whiskey, or orange juice cut with gin. Plastic water bottles were emptied and filled with vodka. I don't know how widespread this practice was throughout the Army, or even in Iraq, but I do know that it was embraced by practically everyone in my platoon.

The problem with this system was the fact that it took forever. A package would take weeks to arrive. So if you were fortunate enough to have saved up a little extra liquor, you could make a killing by selling it to your friends. And the markup was extraordinary! A twenty-ounce water bottle, the contents replaced with vodka, could fetch as much as $50. You had a captive market of young men who had almost nothing on which to spend their money. Guys who worked five or six straight days, sometimes seeing their friends get blown up, and then wanted nothing more than to smoke cigarettes, play video games, and get fucked up on their day off. In that environment an industrious person could do pretty well.

For me, personally, alcohol was primarily a sleep aid, a way to forget the awful stuff I'd see every day, all the myriad ways in which a person could die and a human body could be shredded. I'd go days on end with hardly any sleep when we were out at the JSS. But on the weekend I'd drink. And I'd forget. Along the way I stumbled upon a gold mine.

I've always been pretty good at figuring out my surroundings and adapting to new environments, establishing relationships and networking. It's interesting how these skills come in handy, regardless of circumstances. Doesn't matter whether you're in the boardroom or on a football team or deployed to Iraq or Afghanistan. Life is all about relationships. I like making new friends, hearing about what other people do with their lives, and figuring out ways we can help each other. In Baghdad I befriended a young man whose father was one of the highest-ranking Iraqi officials at the JSS.

He was a few years older than I was, probably in his early twenties, and there were huge language barriers — he spoke only a little English, and I spoke even less Arabic — but somehow we got along pretty well. It wasn't so much a friendship as a business arrangement. We started out with some rudimentary bartering. For example, I'd give him a *Playboy* magazine in exchange for a carton of cigarettes, which I could then either smoke myself or use as currency – just like in prison – with some of the other guys in my platoon.

For a while the transactions remained small, until one day I decided to up the ante.

"Hey, can you get alcohol?"

He shook his head and made a face, which didn't necessarily mean no. More likely it meant, "I don't understand you."

"Vodka," I said. "Liquor."

Again, nothing.

"How about whiskey? Can you get whiskey?"

He smiled, nodded. "Whiskey, yes! I get you whiskey!"

Now we were rolling.

"How much?" I asked, rubbing my thumb and forefinger together – the universal sign for cash. "You want money? Cigarettes?"

He shook his head. Then he smiled again.

"Condoms," he said. "You get condoms. And baby wipes."

I laughed. It made sense. The guy was pretty young, but he had several wives or girlfriends, and multiple children. He needed baby wipes. And condoms. Lots of them.

"American condoms good," he said. "You get."

"Okay . . . deal."

We shook on it. That weekend I hit the PX at Rustamiyah, where there was never a shortage of condoms, despite the fact that there were very few women on the base. Don't ask, don't tell, I guess. Baby wipes were always available, as soldiers used these in lieu of showers. So I bought a bunch of condoms and baby wipes and gave them to my new friend.

"Very good," he said as we stood outside the JSS, near his car. He looked around, to be sure no one was watching, and popped the trunk. Inside were several big bottles of whiskey smuggled in from Iran, Russia, and Turkey. He gestured toward the stash.

"You take."

I could almost feel the heat of the lightbulb that went on in my head. I knew how much I had been paying for a couple ounces of Jim Beam mixed into apple juice. I knew how much other people were willing to pay for it. And here, right in front of me, was a mother lode of pure, high-quality whiskey.

"How much do I take?" I asked, not wanting to seem greedy.

He struggled for the words, then reached into his car and withdrew an empty garbage bag. He snapped it open and held it out, as if to say, "As much as you can fit in here."

That's how the venture began. I'd fill up fifty-caliber ammo cans with whiskey bottles, then break it down into smaller servings, and sell it at a ridiculous markup. I never gave the police general's son a dime. All it cost me was . . . stuff. Baby wipes, condoms, diapers, soft-core porn (*Maxim, Playboy, FHM*). At first I told only a few people, but pretty soon word got out, and I became the liquor distributor for the entire company. I had to share some of the booze with one of my sergeants because I needed help smuggling the whiskey back to Rustamiyah in our Humvees. Like any other illicit venture, palms needed to be greased in order to keep everything running smoothly. Frankly, though, I didn't encounter much resistance. War sucks. Iraq sucked. Getting drunk on a day off made the experience slightly more tolerable.

It was kind of weird, though. Here I was, a private first-class. Low man in the chain of command — bottom of the barrel. I didn't even make specialist until the end of my deployment. Despite that humble status, I would have sergeants and first lieutenants approach me surreptitiously and say, "Uh, Rodriguez?"

"Yes, sir?"

"We need to talk."

Invariably the conversation would quickly evolve into a haggling session.

"I heard you can get me some whiskey?"

"Well . . . maybe, sir. But it's not easy, you know? Risky. Very risky."

"Right, right. Cut the bullshit, Private. How much?"
Shuffle feet, scratch head.

I'd throw out a number, we'd bat it back and forth a few times, and then we'd close the deal. It felt kind of strange at first, negotiating with my superiors, but rank routinely broke down in a combat scenario anyway. We were all in this cesspool together, so why not help each other out?

At its peak, my little enterprise consisted of approximately seventy regular customers. I'd procure six to eight bottles of whiskey every week. Each bottle contained roughly one gallon of whiskey. I'd sell it for close to $200. Then I realized I was being something of an idiot, business-wise, so I started breaking down the stash into smaller portions – selling twenty-ounce water bottles filled with whiskey for $40 to $50 apiece. That effectively increased my profit by nearly 50 percent: the $200 bottle of whiskey was now worth $300.

And then I got greedy.

If you've ever owned a bar or pub, or worked at a bar or pub, you know what happened next. I started cutting the whiskey with water, which again practically doubled the profit. No one noticed. No one complained. After a while, though, I started to feel like I was getting in too deep. The client list grew, so I needed more "product," which meant coming up with more stuff to barter. I started taking preorders, and then some people got pissed because I wasn't able to accommodate their needs.

It went on like this for at least three or four months. We'd finish a week at the JSS, then return to base and get hammered for two days straight on whiskey. It wasn't like a frat party or anything. You'd just play *Halo* or *Call of Duty* for hours on end, sipping whiskey and soda the entire time, until pretty soon you'd look at the screen and couldn't tell the good guys from the bad guys. Do that for ten or twelve straight hours and you end up on the bathroom floor, hugging the toilet bowl. After one particularly brutal night of drinking, we had a surprise inspection and inventory. Several of us had trouble getting through that one; guys were running into the bathroom to vomit, hungover nearly to the point of incapacitation. After that incident, some of the sergeants and officers understandably became less willing to turn a blind eye to what was happening. And I got the message:

Tone it down.

So I did.

In time, the business dried up entirely. I settled for exchanging just a handful of stuff for a small amount of whiskey, which I kept for my personal use, in comparative moderation, primarily to make sure I could sleep on the weekends. By the time I was through, I had accumulated almost $3,000 in cash, which I mailed home in small batches. I'd put a couple hundred dollars in an envelope and address it to myself, back in Virginia. I didn't want my sister to know what I was doing, so I'd ask her to collect my unopened mail and leave it in a safe place. All of my Army checks went straight into a savings account, so by the time I got home I had roughly $12,000 in the bank—one-quarter of which came from running whiskey in Iraq.

There is an arc to every deployment during a time of war. You show up clueless and scared, eventually settle into a routine marked by acceptance and stoic professionalism, eventually progress to ambivalence, and finally hit apathy . . . with a touch of nihilism.

I just don't give a damn.

You continue to do the job to the best of your ability—that much I should stress—but there comes a time when the job seems hopeless and the odds against making it out alive seem long. You just figure that things are totally beyond your control, and that if something awful is going to happen, well . . . there's not much you can do about it. So it's best not to care too much.

As you near the end of a deployment, however, and the prospect of going home becomes tangible, a different mind-set starts to take hold. This final, brief phase is filled with anxiety, paranoia, and, most of all, superstition. Any deviation from the normal routine—the one that has kept you alive for ten or twelve months—is like playing poker with the gods of war. You find yourself walking around mumbling under your breath: "You've only got a few weeks left. Please don't do anything stupid."

Meanwhile, as the departure date draws near, new soldiers are arriving every day. One unit leaves, another comes in. Early in a deployment you feel a sense of generosity toward newcomers. You want to help them and train them, as your own health and success depend on their ability to adapt and assimilate. As the deployment ends, though, you just want to keep your distance from the rookies. They're the ones most likely to screw up, and you don't want to be near them when that happens. Don't get me wrong: you still help them get oriented; you still do your job. But maybe with a little less enthusiasm . . . and a lot more caution.

Meanwhile, the military is constantly upgrading, so while you've been deployed for a year, the Army has been developing new technology. With each new unit comes another wave of technological innovation. New gear, new weapons, new surveillance equipment. All well and good, I suppose, except that someone has to figure out a way to incorporate all this new equipment as seamlessly as possible. That person is usually a lieutenant. However tolerable a deployment turns out to be depends largely on the outlook and ability of your lieutenant. I was an enlisted man, never rose above the rank of sergeant, so I don't want to sound like one of those grunts who thinks all officers are idiots. I don't feel that way. I had some great commanding officers in the Army; I also had some bad ones. The best were those who understood the value of listening to their men. The worst were those who thought they knew everything, despite having never fired a gun in the heat of battle.

Lieutenants have a hard job. I'll be the first to admit that. They're usually fresh out of West Point or some college ROTC program, and suddenly they're sent to Iraq or Afghanistan and asked to provide the sort of intelligence and leadership that will allow everyone to get home safely. Some of them overcompensate for their inexperience by acting like they know everything. Let me tell you: most of them don't know shit. Combat theory and battle-field simulators only approximate what a real deployment will be like. Until you've been there, you can't possibly understand. That's why the best newly minted lieutenants will lean on their sergeants, some of whom have been on multiple deployments.

"Listen, I know I took a different route from some of you guys, but we're all in this together, okay? We're a family here. Tell me what I need to know, and I'll stick up for you guys."

This is how you want a lieutenant to talk when he's new to the job.

For most of my deployment, our lieutenant was a man named Luke Pereira. He was one of the good guys. Knew how to listen to his men. Fought right beside us. Unfortunately, he was transferred to a different unit, and I spent my final two months with a guy who reminded me of the high-speed douchebags I'd seen on the bus to Fort Benning. A real rah-rah type who sought counsel from no one and believed there was only one way to do things: his way. He was an NCO, which meant he was an enlisted man who had come up through the ranks; at first that gave us hope that he might be a regular guy with some serious boots-on-the-ground perspective. Uh-uh. In the military, every position is identified by a Military Occupation Specialty code, more commonly referred to as an MOS. Well, when we asked the lieutenant about his MOS (just so we'd know a little bit about his background), he said that he'd most recently been an 02B.

I remember scratching my head at that one.

Most of the soldiers I'd come across were infantrymen, and virtually all of us had an MOS that included the number 11, the MOS code for infantry.

"What's an 02B?" I remember someone asking the lieutenant. He smiled.

"I was in the Army band."

This response did not provoke laughter. It provoked complete silence. Utter stupefaction.

"Really?" someone finally said. "The band?"

The lieutenant nodded. "Yeah, I played trumpet."

This was no joke. The Army had plucked a trumpet player out of the band and assigned him to an infantry platoon. He was as green as any PFC on his first day in-country, and yet somehow he was now responsible for the lives of more than forty men. And he wasn't leading from the relative comfort and safety of the Green Zone. He was in Sadr City, where kids were getting killed or maimed on a regular basis.

"Why the hell would they do this?" I asked one of my buddies. It was a rhetorical question, but he answered anyway.

"Guess they want us to die."

There are all kinds of bad leaders in the Army. Some are dictatorial; some are just dicks. By far the worst, though, are those who are just plain stupid. A jerk can get on your nerves, even drive you crazy when you're in garrison. But if he knows what he's doing and manages to keep everyone alive and in one piece, then you don't mind serving under him in combat. A clueless lieutenant, one who has no idea what he's doing, is benign in garrison; put that same guy in Iraq, though, where the stakes are much higher, and he becomes a potentially lethal liability. I honestly had no faith whatsoever in this man's ability to get us home. Hell, he was so reckless and unaware that I didn't think he'd last more than a few weeks. My only hope was that he wouldn't get the rest of us killed in the process.

We'd be out on a mission, tiptoeing through the streets of Baghdad on heightened alert, waiting for some sniper to take a shot at us or an IED to rip through one of our Humvees, and this guy would just stroll into open view, rifle dangling at his side, a cup of coffee in his hand. I never saw him fire his weapon; I'm not even sure he knew how to use it. In a time and place that cried out for aggressive patrolling, our new lieutenant was captain of Team Hearts and Minds. He'd walk up to people in the street, with no idea whether they were civilians or insurgents, and start making small talk. He'd distribute books and pamphlets like he was running for mayor or something, or recruiting for the Jehovah's Witnesses.

Now, I understand that some people consider this a logical, thoughtful approach for an occupying force. But after nearly a year of sniper fire and IEDs, I just didn't see it that way. And our company certainly had not operated in that manner. I saw it as a recipe for disaster. Maybe the lieutenant's heart was in the right place. Maybe he was a decent human being. I never really got the chance to know him that well. But his methods were naive and dangerous. Not to mention annoying as hell. Sometimes we'd get home from a mission at ten or eleven at night and just as we were dozing off, exhausted from a twelve-hour patrol, we'd hear the bleat of this guy's trumpet cutting through the night – not only preventing us from sleeping but making it easy to identify our position. I am not kidding! It sort of became a running joke in the platoon:

If the Iraqis don't shoot this idiot, we might have to do it ourselves.

Fortunately, by the time this lieutenant arrived we had already begun the transitional phase of our deployment and were spending less time on combat than on the logistical practicalities of changing personnel. Still, the last few weeks were fraught with anxiety. The closer you get to your departure date, the more likely it seems that you'll never live to see it. This is more a matter of perception than reality. It's just a colossal mind fuck, and every soldier on a combat deployment goes through it.

I left Rustamiyah in late December 2007. It took more than a week to get home – with stops at the Green Zone, Balad, Kuwait, and then finally Fort Carson, Colorado, where the families of 500 soldiers were waiting. We arrived on New Year's Eve, a caravan of buses greeted by fireworks and blaring music, by cheers and tears, and lots of hugs and kisses. Words can't possibly do justice to the emotion. My mother and sister were there waiting, both of them crying. I tried to be chill about the whole thing —"What's up, guys?"— but the truth is, I'd never imagined that just walking on American soil could feel that good.

I'd been on deployment for fifteen months without a minute of leave time. Now I was home. It was New Year's Eve in the USA. And all I wanted to do was sleep.

5

W HEN A DEPLOYMENT ENDS, it doesn't really end. You get to relive it and examine it in great detail through something known as "out-processing." It's basically the Army's attempt to ensure that every returning soldier is of sound mind and body and not irrevocably scarred by what he encountered on deployment. Some people bare their souls during out-processing; some reveal every bump and bruise, especially those who are about to leave the military and hope to claim benefits. But most just want to get the hell out of there as quickly as possible, and so they lie or say practically nothing and generally minimize their entire experience. I know that's what I did.

"Rodriguez, how's your hearing?"

"Fine, sir."

"Were you ever exposed to any loud gunfire or IEDs?"

"No, sir. I was lucky."

"Okay, you're good. Next!"

The truth? I came home from Iraq with severe hearing loss and tinnitus; it got even worse in Afghanistan. And it's still bad to this day. I presume it's permanent. Most of the men with whom I served suffered hearing loss. It was part of the deal, and you learned to accept it. But I wasn't about to acknowledge any problems in that setting, at Fort Carson. I knew that the quickest route to the exit door was to deny, deny, deny. Just tell them everything was fine. The moment you acknowledged a problem of any kind you were taken off the fast track and referred to a "specialist."

Your hearing is bad? Okay, go over there and see Dr. Smith.

Hypertension? Okay, come over here and see Dr. Jones.

Can't sleep? Nightmares? Off to the shrink . . .

If you weren't careful – in other words, if you spoke openly and candidly – out-processing could take days, and if you planned to remain in the Army, the results might not be to your advantage. I'd been counseled on all of this before I came home, so I simply took the path of least resistance. Virtually every question and psychiatric probe was met with a shrug and a smile.

"Private Rodriguez, how many people have you killed?"

"None, sir. Only fired my weapon a few times."

"Did you witness any of your fellow soldiers being killed?"

"No, sir. We were very careful."

"Good for you, Private . . . Next!"

And off I'd go. Before long I was out the door and ready to start thirty days of R&R.

It was ridiculously easy to slip past the initial line of interrogation, occupied as it was by young and inexperienced counselors who had never been deployed to a theater of combat. Their job was to push people through the line as efficiently as possible; if you didn't want help or didn't ask for help, no one was going to force it on you. I suppose some soldiers were so obviously damaged, psychologically or physically, that their issues would jump out at even the least qualified counselor.

You'd like to think so anyway.

But I'm not so sure.

• • •

There was a soldier in our platoon named Robert Marko. He was a specialist who had grown up in Michigan. Now, as anyone who has served can attest, there is no shortage of unique characters in the Army, especially in the infantry. People who are "normal" or "ordinary" simply do not sign up for the job. And I don't blame them. It's hard and thankless. It's dangerous. So it's fair to say that you have to be somewhat unusual to seek out this line of work. But Marko? This dude was just flat-out nuts.

Marko was my bunkmate throughout my deployment to Iraq. Obviously we spent a lot of time together and often were in close proximity, but I can't say that I really knew him well. He was a respectable soldier. Aside from the fact that he wasn't crazy about firing his weapon (some guys were just like that), he was competent and reliable. He would do whatever you told him to do. If you wanted Marko to stand guard, he would stand there for hours, refusing to leave for any reason whatsoever. On more than one occasion he peed in his pants rather than take a two-minute bathroom break. We had some terrific soldiers in our platoon; they all understood that it was okay to use the bathroom, even on guard duty. Marko was just . . . different. You couldn't get close to the guy; he was too strange.

How so? Well, first of all, he used to claim that he had descended from an alien tribe known as the Black Raptors. And when I say "alien," I am not referring to a country other than the United States. I'm talking about extraterrestrials. He had a Facebook page devoted to his alien culture and history, and he was supposedly writing a book about life on his home planet (wherever the hell that might have been), how the raptors reproduced, what they ate, the weapons they used. Marko would talk about this stuff endlessly, and without a trace of irony or humor.

The guy was totally serious. We figured he was kidding, that he had perfected this role and was playing it for the sake of his own amusement. But we'd grill him for hours, like curious college students peppering a history professor with questions, and

Marko would answer every question with a straight face and with unbelievable detail.

"On my twenty-first birthday, I'm going be reincarnated," he'd proclaim. "And I'm coming back as a black raptor."

Okay, Marko . . . whatever you say, dude.

I spent endless hours on patrol and standing guard with Marko, listening to him talk about the Black Raptor Tribe and how much better and different his life would be when he turned twenty-one and ascended to their ranks. That's the word he used: "ascended." It was like a religion to him. And I mean that literally. When you join the Army, on the section of the enlistment form devoted to "religion," you can write down anything: Christian, Jewish, Muslim . . . anything. Including religions that don't actually exist. The Army will take you at your word, going so far as to inscribe the name of the religion on your dog tags. One guy in our platoon was an atheist, so he put down "Jedi Knight" as his religion. (I guess he was a *Star Wars* fan as well.) I had "Christian Non-Denominational" on my dog tags.

Marco? According to his dog tags, his religion was "Black Raptor Tribe."

Strange as he was, I never considered the possibility that Marko was legitimately detached from reality — like, clinically insane — or that he was capable of violence in a civilian setting. Shit, the guy was barely capable of violence in a combat setting. Yeah, he was weird, but a lot of people are weird, and the inherent lunacy of war tends to overshadow the quirks and eccentricities of any particular individual. What might seem like a red flag in the normal world provokes nothing more than a laugh when you're on deployment. I was way too concerned about getting nailed by a sniper or vaporized by an IED to worry about whether Robert Marko was going to come back home to the United States and turn into some sort of deadly sociopath.

In retrospect, maybe we should have seen the warning signs. But in all honesty, Marko was merely a source of amusement to us, his stories nothing more than a benign diversion.

I have no way of knowing what happened to Marko during out-processing. It's hard to imagine that he didn't tell any of the various counselors or psychiatrists about his plans to ascend to the ranks of the Black Raptor Tribe. Maybe he did. I know only what I heard through the rumor mill and what I read in the newspapers a few months later, when the official Army reports were released. According to the *New York Times,* Army documents revealed that Marko had a "history of behavioral health issues that predated his enlistment" in 2006. The issues supposedly included alcohol abuse (that applied to almost everyone in our platoon) as well as Tourette's syndrome and a speech impediment. (Marko did have a lisp, which only added to the perception that he couldn't possibly have been dangerous.) He also displayed an "extremely active imagination."

Yeah, that's for sure.

According to Army documents, Marko underwent psychiatric evaluations on several occasions after enlisting and was even identified as having "symptoms of mental illness" while at Fort Carson in late 2006. But he was allowed to deploy to Iraq anyway, which demonstrates more than anything just how badly the Army needed bodies during the surge. In light of what happened after he returned, it would be easy to point a finger at the psychiatrists who deemed Marko fit for duty "without limitations." But I served with the guy, and while he may have been unusual, he was in fact a pretty good soldier. Whether Marko's experiences in Iraq contributed in some way to the crimes he committed is for others to decide. I do know that combat changes a person in ways both profound and fundamental; you can't scoop up the body parts of your friends and not be affected by it. In two deployments I saw more death and destruction than you can imagine. I killed people and thought that it didn't even bother me – until I came home and realized that it did bother me.

Even a soldier who is psychologically strong can suffer from post-traumatic stress disorder. It's not much of a stretch to think that someone with a tenuous grip on reality, like Marko, would be driven completely off the deep end by his battlefield experiences.

Or maybe he was just wired badly. Who knows?

All we have is a record of events and a lot of speculation. This much is certain: On October 10, 2008, while stationed at Fort Carson, Robert Marko raped and murdered a developmentally disabled woman he had met online. Three days later, on his twenty-first birthday, he led police to a mountainous spot outside Colorado Springs where he had left the woman's body. Law enforcement officials had tracked Marko through his Myspace account (on which he was identified as Rex290, an allusion to his fascination with aliens and dinosaurs, or maybe just alien dinosaurs). Among the most recent entries was this: "I'm becoming a cold hearted killer and can kill without mercy or reason."

Marko was later accused of sexually assaulting two other women, one of whom was only fourteen years old. In February 2011, he was convicted of first-degree murder. He's serving a life sentence, with no chance for parole.

When I heard the news about Marko's arrest, my first reaction was: *Not again!* You see, Marko was the sixth person from our brigade at Fort Collins to be charged with murder in a span of less than one year's time. The overall crime rate was through the roof: domestic violence, armed robbery, assault. We had three suicides as well. For a while my whole division was on lockdown while the Army tried to deal with a public relations nightmare.

PTSD neither fully explains nor excuses the violent and self-destructive behavior of some returning vets. But it would be irresponsible to dismiss it or to deny that it's a contributing factor. Every vet struggles in some way with the transition from the front lines to the home front. It's just a question of when and how.

There are advantages to going almost directly from basic training to overseas deployment. For one thing, I avoided the six months to one year of drudgery and demoralizing shit that is typically heaped upon a new grunt. In garrison, the new guys get all the lousy jobs and are generally treated like the incompetent rookies that they are. On deployment, though, most of that stuff goes out the window. It's less formal, more egalitarian. In Iraq a new private might address a sergeant by his first name. In garrison . . . not so much.

By the time I got to Fort Carson for my first long stint of stateside service, I was already an accomplished, experienced soldier. So, despite the fact that I was barely twenty years old, I found myself in charge of training groups of new soldiers, many of whom were older than I was. Included in this first group of trainees were five guys with whom I would eventually serve in Afghanistan. They would become my closest friends.

There was Keith Stickney, who had grown up in New Hampshire and had actually come within a few credits of getting his degree at Johnson and Wales, a culinary school in Rhode Island. Stickney was well educated and funny. In college he'd been something of a pothead, so we had that in common.

"Dude, my buddies and I were like culinary experts," he told me once. "We cooked every night. We would cook and get high and eat like crazy."

People end up in the Army for all kinds of reasons. I would not have pegged Stickney as an obvious soldier, but he turned out to be stellar. The thing is, he enlisted almost on a whim, after one of his best friends from high school died while serving in Iraq. Stickney said he really wasn't happy with the way things were going in college anyway and he felt the need to honor the memory of his friend. So he dropped out of school and joined the Army. And suddenly there he was, almost twenty-four years old and being trained by a kid who was less than two years out of high school. But he seemed to have no regrets.

"I only need one more semester," Stickney said on one of the many occasions when I told him he must have been crazy to enlist. "I can always finish up later."

Another newcomer was Jayce Holmes, a country boy from

Oklahoma. And Jonathan Santana, from Gaffney, South Carolina. And then there was Kevin Thomson, who would become my best friend in the Army.

Thomson and I clicked right away. He was a big, charismatic kid from Reno, Nevada, but when I say charismatic, I don't mean in a loud or ostentatious sort of way. He had one of those laid-back personalities that just made you feel comfortable whenever he was around. People were drawn to him because he was just so damn likable. You could talk to Thomson about anything; you could play pranks on him, and he'd laugh it off. He stood about six-foot-five, but he was kind of gangly and goofy. In high school he had been really overweight, topping out at around 300 pounds. Then he shed the weight, which left him with a hollow, sunken look. He was always slouching over and shuffling along, like he was forever uncomfortable in his own skin.

But he was a hell of a soldier, and I was struck right away by his maturity. You meet a lot of soldiers who are irresponsible; they're like children, really. Thomson was a little older. He'd already graduated from high school and held a job. He had a sense of the real world and what was required of him. When we first met, he said, "Just tell me what you need and I'll do it." And he was true to his word. I never had a single issue with Thomson. Fraternization is a tricky thing in the Army, but Thomson and I hung out together all the time. We went to bars and ball games. We worked out together. And when we got to Afghanistan and found ourselves sharing a mortar pit, eating three meals a day together and sleeping next to each other on tiny bunk beds, day after day, week after week, we were like brothers.

Thomson had been a butcher in civilian life. Metaphorically speaking, I suppose you could say that joining the infantry was a lateral move. I never really understood why Thomson enlisted. He had a good job, with a decent paycheck and benefits, and he didn't really seem like the gung-ho type. But appearances can be misleading. Thomson was proficient with his weapon and courageous in combat. The journey from adolescence to Afghanistan was a popular subject among the troops—"Bro, how the fuck did you get here anyway?" Thomson usually met that question with a shrug and a smile.

"Just got bored with the job, dude. Thought I'd try this for a while."

After a few months in Afghanistan, Thomson began to have second thoughts about the life he'd left behind. That hardly made him unusual. Most people found the Army to be a vastly different experience from what they had anticipated. Especially those who saw combat duty. This is not a comment on their professionalism, competence, or bravery. I believe the modern US Army is the greatest fighting force on the planet. I met some of the most uniquely talented and capable people I've ever known while serving in the military. I developed incredibly close and intense friendships, the kind that can be forged only under extraordinary circumstances. We all took our jobs very seriously and were proud to wear the uniform and to defend our country.

That said, it was a transitional phase of life for many of us. I joined the Army primarily to get away from something else. The other stuff—traveling, training, fighting—was almost like a by-product. I didn't realize that it would be as hard as it was, or as terrifying as it sometimes was. For most enlisted men and women, I think, the Army turns out to be less than the action-adventure movie we had hoped it would be. That's just reality smacking down fantasy. To this day I've yet to encounter anyone who joined the military and came away saying, "Man, this was everything I dreamed it would be. And more!" It was a job, and a damned difficult job at that. I was proud to do it, and to do it well. But less than halfway through my first deployment, I knew that I wouldn't be reenlisting. I was already thinking about the next phase of my life. In fact, that seemed to be the general consensus among the soldiers I knew. Some of them got out and moved on to other things. Some found a life in the Army. Others never came home from Iraq or Afghanistan. But all of them talked incessantly about what they were going to do when they got out.

Thomson and I talked endlessly about our plans and aspirations. I was going to go back to college and possibly resurrect my football career. Thomson? He just wanted to go back to being a butcher. It was precise, repetitive work, a craft that bordered on art. It seemed to suit his temperament.

The first time I met Thomson he was hanging out in the barracks at Fort Carson with Holmes, Stickney, and Santana. I stopped by to introduce myself one night shortly after they arrived, and they invited me in to have a beer. For the next hour or so we hung out together, shooting the breeze, getting to know each other. If this sounds like a breaking of the ranks, well, it was and it wasn't. My job was to supervise them, but I wasn't an officer or even an NCO. I was a specialist on the way to becoming a sergeant. And the fact is, sergeants and privates hang out together all the time in the military. So when the four new guys invited me to tag along that night when they went to a local bar to see a Sublime cover band, I jumped aboard.

"Hell, yeah," I said. "I love Sublime."

We stayed out till two in the morning, drinking, talking, listening to music, and just generally getting to know each other. It felt comfortable. It felt right. Would the Army have considered this to be "fraternization"? Probably. But like I said, it happened all the time. As a specialist or sergeant supervising privates, I was pretty easygoing. If you did your job and behaved in a respectful, professional manner, I had no problem with you. We could maintain the chain of command and still be friends. Hell, we were all so young. I had earned a supervisory position because of my time in combat and because my platoon sergeant trusted me. In a sense, I was his protégé.

The platoon leader's name was Sergeant First-Class John Breeding. He was from Amarillo, Texas, and he was one of my all-time favorite guys in the Army, irrespective of rank. Sergeant Breeding had a complicated and sometimes tumultuous personal life. But none of that mattered to me. I would have run through fire for that guy. (Come to think of it, I did!)

That's the thing about the military: you learn to distinguish between a man's personal life and his professional life. If you're a good soldier or a good leader, I don't care where you came from or what you do on your time off. Some guys would get off duty and put in their grills; other guys would spike up their hair and change into beaters. Some guys drank too much; other guys smoked too much weed. Some guys listened to rap, some liked country, and others listened only to metal and punk. Whatever works for you, dude. As long as you clean up in the morning and do your job, I'm cool with it. When we fall into formation, our differences melt away. We look the same, and we are expected to behave in a certain way. We are all part of the same team. If I had an issue with another soldier, it was never because of something superficial and trivial, like his taste in music or clothes, and it certainly was never because of his ethnic or religious background. Who gives a shit about any of that? At worst it was fodder for the endless teasing and trash-talking that went on in the barracks and on deployment. But it wasn't serious. The only time I had trouble with another soldier was when he failed to understand the responsibility that comes with wearing the uniform. You have to get the job done – lives depend on it.

Sergeant Breeding understood all of this, which is one of the main reasons we got along so well. He was a good ten to fifteen years older than me and far more experienced in the ways of the military, but our beliefs and attitudes dovetailed nicely. I wanted to work hard for Breeding, and he appreciated my effort and relative maturity. He was an old-school Army guy who didn't take shit from anyone. Everyone used to talk about how Breeding should have held a higher rank, but he'd supposedly been busted down a couple times for incidents both related and unrelated to his military service, including a bar fight stateside with a serviceman who held a higher rank than Breeding.

"How the fuck was I supposed to know?" Breeding once told me. "We were both in street clothes."

It's hard to make rank when you keep getting busted down, so Breeding was a comparatively old sergeant first-class. But nobody messed with him. If he told you to do something, you did it. Breeding could easily have been a sergeant major. He had the experience, the combat deployment, and the leadership skills. When he walked into a room, people naturally straightened up. The guy had a presence, and he had perspective: he knew what was important and what wasn't important. If we didn't need to be at work, we didn't need to be at work. And Breeding would point that out. He would say to our first sergeant, "Are we going to sit around here playing with our dicks, or are you going to let us go home?" That's the kind of man you want by your side when things get rough, and it's why I was grateful to have him as my platoon sergeant in Afghanistan.

We hung out together a lot when we were off duty; sometimes we'd take off for the weekend and go snowboarding together. "All right, fuckers," Breeding would say. "Up here, I'm not your sergeant. Call me John. We might run into some women, and I don't want them to know I'm in the military. Got it?"

"Yes, Sergeant. I mean . . . yes, John."

"Hey, John?"

"Yeah."

"How about if we call you JB?"

"No. I have a problem with that."

Okay . . . end of discussion.

It makes things much easier when you don't feel like you're working *for* somebody but rather *with* somebody. It takes a special kind of leader to walk that tightrope and build that kind of camaraderie and teamwork. Breeding had it.

There was never any question about whether or not we would be going to Afghanistan. It was simply a matter of when. We knew that it would probably be sometime in the late winter or early spring of 2009. As that date grew near conversation naturally became more focused on what we could expect overseas. The younger guys who had never deployed had a lot of questions about combat in general. I hadn't been to Afghanistan, but I had been to Iraq. I had fired my weapon. I had killed people. I had witnessed the slaughtering of American soldiers.

Practically speaking, I had experience, and they wanted to know about that experience. At first I was a little reluctant to talk about my deployment, but it's natural and understandable for younger guys to feel anxious. As one of their leaders, I was expected to help quell some of that anxiety, but it's a tricky business, deciding how much to share. You want them to be prepared. You want them to understand that it's going to be messy and dangerous. You want them to know what the job will really be like. At the same time, you don't want to scare them.

Although, ideally, a soldier entering Iraq or Afghanistan would be well trained and equipped with a healthy dose of respect for the assignment and the risks involved, I went to Iraq with virtually no mental or psychological preparation. I was sent straight from basic training to Baghdad: *Here's your rifle, son. Good luck!*

I wish somebody had given me some insight before I left. Of course, there are limits to what anyone could have told me. It's one thing to hear about combat; it's another thing to see it. But even worse is seeing it without having had any idea that it was coming. I had no idea what I was getting into; if someone had at least given me a quick crash course, it might have helped. No, it wouldn't have changed anything, but I think it would have been beneficial.

So when the new guys asked questions, I answered them. I shared information in small batches, usually with very little emotion. The one thing that would get under my skin was when some new private would start talking about how eager he was to get his first taste of the battlefield.

"I can't wait to shoot those motherfucking towel-heads! It's gonna be awesome!"

"Listen to me," I'd say, trying to remain calm in the face of such ignorance. "Here's what you need to wish for. You need to wish for a deployment where we do not fire a single bullet and nobody fires a single bullet at us."

The private would invariably respond with disappointment.

"What are you talking about? We're fighters!"

"I'm telling you, dude, you might think you want all that shit, but until you see it and experience it for real, you have no idea what you're talking about. You know what I wish for when we go to Afghanistan? Nothing. I hope we have a mountaintop deployment and we get bored as hell. And then we can all go home."

I understood their eagerness. On some level it was probably even healthy. But I thought it was important for them to know that this wasn't going to be clean and easy.

I had no idea what to expect in Afghanistan, which was its own particular theater of combat. Almost none of us did. We had several guys who had fought in Iraq, but only one person who had been to Afghanistan. As we would soon find out, Afghanistan was a totally different type of conflict, and it was fought on terrain that was rugged, remote, and unforgiving. It was a far cry from the crowded, chaotic streets of Baghdad.

I had heard the basic comparisons: There would be more toe-to-toe fighting in Afghanistan than there had been in Iraq. There would be fewer roadside bombs and IEDs. Sniper fire would still be problematic, but more often than not it would signal the start of a small-arms battle. In Iraq we rarely saw the enemy. In Afghanistan we would have a clear and vivid image of the enemy. We would know who was shooting at us and where they were shooting from. They would engage and ambush. When you hear that, as a soldier, you're like, *Hell, yeah, that's what I want!* You don't say it out loud (I didn't anyway), but you think it to yourself. I know that if I have to die in battle, I'd rather go down fighting an enemy I can see, as opposed to getting blown up in a Humvee or shot in the back of the head by a sniper.

If you have to fight, you want a fair fight. Face to face. May the best man win. That was my philosophy. And I have to admit . . .

the Afghans? Those boys know how to fight, which is why they've held those mountains for centuries. Not that we wanted to take the mountains, of course. But I never got the sense that any of the Afghans – Taliban, insurgents, or civilians – wanted us there. If you want to fight with the Afghans on their soil, they're going to make it hard for you.

Even now I have friends in the military who are deploying for the first time and still don't understand the magnitude of the task in Afghanistan. I'm talking about college grads – officers – who have asked me for insight. "Do not underestimate them," I'll say. "Tactically, they're smarter than you think they are. It's their country. They know the terrain, and they know how to use it to their advantage. And they will fight you until the day they die."

A buddy of mine named Tim Kucala deployed about a year after I got back. We came from the same town. I had joined the Army, he became a Marine. He asked me point-blank what he could expect in Afghanistan.

"Think of it like this," I said. "Imagine someone trying to attack us in our hometown. The way we know our woods and our property, we'd pick them off even if they had more firepower. That's how you need to go into this. You're fighting in their backyard. Don't take any shortcuts. Go with your instincts. Never question your gut. If you get a bad feeling when you're out on patrol, get the hell out of there."

It's too bad no one said any of this stuff to me before I left for Afghanistan. Maybe it would have helped. Maybe not.

In late February 2009, I went on a thirty-day leave, at the end of which I would be deploying to Afghanistan. Before deploying this second time, I had come to the conclusion that I did not want a career in the military. I was comfortable with this decision. I wasn't sure what I wanted out of life, but I knew that I couldn't find it in the Army. The military had served its purpose. It had provided a bridge from high school to the adult world; it had allowed me to escape a traumatic situation. In a very real sense, it had forced me to grow up. But I was ready to move on. Maybe college. Maybe football. Who knew?

Before starting leave, I called two of my friends from back home, Stephan Batt and Nick Graves, and invited them to come out to Colorado for a few days of snowboarding and skiing. They knew that I was deploying to Afghanistan; they did not know that I was already making plans for when I returned.

"I'm leaving the Army when I get back from Afghanistan," I explained to them. "So rather than put my truck and all my stuff into storage while I'm gone for a year, I thought I'd drive it across country and leave it with my sister."

"Yeah, okay . . ."

"And I thought if you guys want to fly out one-way, we could shred some powder and then I'll drive everyone back. I really don't want to do this alone."

I can't say enough about Nick and Stephan, as well as a few other guys I've known since boyhood. They've been there for me through some really tough times, and they're with me now. That's the great thing about childhood friends: they know who you really are. And if you're lucky enough to maintain those friendships over time and distance, they become an amazing resource and a source of great strength.

We hit the mountains for a few days, did a lot of skiing, drank a few beers. Then we packed my truck for the 2,500-mile drive across the United States. It should have taken four or five days, but we did it in three, including a memorable stop in Kansas City for some beer and barbecue. It was one of the best road trips I've ever been on, and the funny thing is, not all that much happened. For the most part, we were just driving and shooting the shit, reliving all our youthful exploits (and stupidity).

One could argue that I was screwing with karma by planning so meticulously and so far in advance for the life I would have when I got out of the Army – the part of my life that would come after I got back from Afghanistan. A superstitious soldier (and there are a lot of them) would not have tempted fate in this way. Better to take it one day at a time, try to come back alive, and then worry about what happens next. I didn't care. I actually thought there was a reasonable chance that I might not make it home. But at least this way, if I died while in Afghanistan, all my stuff would already be in Virginia. A lot less work for everyone.

I hung out in Virginia for a few weeks before returning to Fort Carson and getting ready to deploy. There were no big emotional scenes with my family (my mom was living in New Mexico) or my friends. These guys were always pretty good about just playing cool, not making a big deal out of anything, even though going to one of the most dangerous parts of Afghanistan, as a member of the infantry, is by definition a big deal. But that's how it's always been between us: a lot goes unspoken. When I'd come home on leave, even when I was at my war-torn worst, we'd just retreat to the sanctuary of a driveway basketball court and play pickup ball on an eight-and-a-half-foot hoop, just like we had been doing since we were in grade school. We'd sweat and trash-talk and call each other names. And by the end of it I'd feel almost normal again.

So there were no tears or long, drawn-out good-byes when I left home. No dramatic sit-down during which Stephan or Nick told me to keep my head down and come back in one piece. We talked about more practical matters, like how the Redskins would do that year and whether I'd be able to follow the team. They promised to help my sister take care of the house.

"Stay in touch," they said. "Be safe."

I told them I would.

6

I N APRIL 2009, I arrived at Forward Operating Base Bostick, located in Kunar Province, in northeastern Afghanistan, on the Pakistan border. I was attached to Bravo Troop, 3rd Squadron, 61st Cavalry.

It took even longer to get to Afghanistan than it did to reach Iraq. First came the requisite weeklong layover in Kuwait, followed by another weeklong stint at Manas Air Base in Kyrgyzstan, which at that time was a primary transit point for US military personnel entering or leaving Afghanistan. Finally, we boarded a C-130 for the trip to Bagram Airfield in Afghanistan.

I should have known Afghanistan was a whole new ball game when I stepped onto the C-130. It's like a warehouse with wings, which is why it takes a couple days to pack the thing and get it ready for any given flight to Bagram. Ours was packed with not only soldiers but tons of supplies, communication equipment, weapons, ammo, even tanks and Humvees. Anyone will tell you that riding on a C-130 is an unpleasant experience under the best of circumstances; when you're flying into the mountains of Af-

ghanistan, under the cover of night, it's horrible. You might think
that a larger plane would be well equipped to handle rough air, but
the C-130 is so heavy and uncomfortable that you feel like you're
riding on a roller coaster without tracks. Everyone was nervous
and suffering at least to some extent from motion sickness.

As the engines roared and the plane slowly descended – so low
that it felt like I could reach out and touch the treetops – I heard
what sounded like hailstones rattling off the hood of a car.

Ping! Ping! Ping! Ping!

I'd been through something like this before, in Iraq, so I knew
what it was: we were taking small-arms fire. I looked around the
cabin of the C-130. Some guys were holding their helmets tight to
keep them from flying off; others were hunched over, dry-heaving
between their legs. Everyone looked scared shitless.

Well, almost everyone.

Sergeant Breeding, veteran of two Iraq deployments, was stone-
faced. Our eyes met. He shrugged, didn't say a word. I wouldn't
have heard him anyway over the din of the C-130.

I tried to take his cue. Most of the men on this plane, including Thomson, Holmes, and Stickney, had never been deployed.
I knew exactly how they were feeling – frightened, disoriented,
probably second-guessing their decision to join the Army. I was
in charge of these guys; they looked to me for leadership and reassurance. And the truth was, even though I could feel the adrenaline rushing through my body, I was not terribly worried.

Through luck or genetics, I've always been pretty good at rolling with various situations – throwing a switch and going into
whatever mode is necessary in order to deal with the current circumstances. I knew my deployments were going to be bad, but I
also knew that I wasn't built to fold. I don't mean to sound arrogant. It's not about toughness or courage; it's about something in
my DNA that allows me to cope with challenging or even dangerous situations without losing my shit. I've seen enough combat to
know that this is a gift. While experience and training are invaluable, the way a person responds to battle is largely a matter of

personal constitution. Doesn't mean I wasn't scared; I was scared all the time. But I was able to keep my wits about me.

Because of the small-arms fire, we did a combat landing, which means we came in a little faster and lower than usual. The idea was to get on the ground as quickly as possible. I closed my eyes for a moment to prepare for the worst. I remember trying to control my breathing, and then I started running through different scenarios in my head. If the plane was going down, I had to pull up my legs and strap in as tight as possible, in the hope of surviving the crash. I looked for the exit doors. I thought about how quickly I could retrieve ammo from the men who died. I was in survival mode, ready to put boots on the ground and do whatever was necessary to stay alive. At the same time, a strange sensation came over me, a feeling . . . almost like tranquillity. I would experience this numerous times in the next year – having a sense that I would do the best that I could, but that things were largely beyond my control.

If we go down, we go down.

I opened my eyes a few seconds before the plane touched down. I looked over at Thomson and the rest of my guys. They were terrified. I gave Thomson a little wink. And that's all it took. The fear almost instantly drained from his face. He smiled. Within seconds, the wheels of the C-130 touched the runway. We landed safely, spent the next few hours unpacking the plane, and prepared for the next leg of our trip.

A couple days passed before I boarded a Chinook for the ride to FOB Bostick. That too was an experience. I mean, the chopper ride itself was fine – a Chinook is much smoother than a C-130 – but no sooner had I stepped off the bird than we took incoming rockets. This was just at daybreak, maybe five o'clock in the morning. The insurgents had overshot us and the rockets crashed into the surrounding hillside without doing any damage, but still . . . it was one hell of a wakeup call.

It would take several days to transport everyone to Bostick, and it would be a few weeks before everyone reached our final destination: Combat Outpost Keating. Breeding and I were on the first chopper out of Bostick; we arrived at Keating in the middle of the night. COP Keating was located in the Kamdesh District of Nuristan Province, in the Hindu Kush Mountains, not far from the infamous Korangal Valley (dubbed the Valley of Death), a Taliban stronghold where many American soldiers had been killed or wounded. At full strength, Keating was staffed by forty-five to fifty soldiers; however, we were rarely, if ever, at full strength. Soldiers went on leave or got hurt or transferred. Most of the time, I'd say, we had thirty-five to forty-five men at Keating. My primary job location was a mortar pit at the northern tip of the base. There were four of us in a small compound – a shack, really – some 300 meters above the main base. We had four little bunk beds and a seven-foot ceiling. It was cozy, to say the least.

The transition from Bostick to Keating was a slow and painstaking process. Two or three men would leave Bostick and cross-train at Keating. When the new guys were deemed sufficiently prepped (a laughably short time), a like number of soldiers would transfer to Bostick to begin the long trip home. And so it went over a period of weeks, swapping two, three, maybe four soldiers every few days, until eventually an entirely new unit had taken over COP Keating. During the transition we got to know the men we replaced, which only made it even more shocking to hear about what happened the following November, when some of the soldiers in this unit were at Fort Hood, Texas, when thirteen US soldiers were murdered and thirty others were wounded in a mass shooting.

When we heard the news it was like, "Holy shit! We knew these guys." And it contributed to the feeling that Keating was truly a cursed place.

Everything about Afghanistan in general, and Keating in particular, was different from what I had experienced in Iraq. The Chinook ride from Bostick to Keating, while fairly calm, was still breathtaking. We came in at night, with a full bird and a sling-loaded hatch, meaning the bottom of the chopper was basically open (cargo was dropped into a giant net suspended below the belly of the chopper), giving passengers a view straight to the mountains below. So we were literally a foot away from falling out of the chopper for the duration of the trip. Again, in scenarios like this, you have to have faith that everything will work out, but you also have to exercise a good deal of caution and common sense.

I'd been on a Chinook before, but I'd never done any sling-loading over 15,000-foot mountains. It's one thing to fly into a city, like Baghdad. It's quite another thing to navigate the unforgiving terrain of Afghanistan. We were sweeping through narrow mountain passes, skirting rocky outcroppings. Incredibly, we took no fire coming in, but that hardly diminished the excitement.

I'll say this: These pilots, the guys who fly Chinooks in combat conditions? They are absolute beasts. You have to be somewhat crazy to want to do this; you also have to be incredibly skilled and confident. Brad Larson, a friend of mine with whom I served at Keating, and who received a Silver Star for his role in the Battle of Kamdesh, eventually became one of these beasts. Larson is a former college football player who joined the National Guard after our deployment and eventually became a helicopter pilot. This is a guy who has seen some serious shit on the battlefield, but he still describes the experience of piloting a Chinook as one of the hairiest things a soldier can do.

I don't doubt it. Everything about flying a Chinook into a battle zone is dangerous, and the setting at Keating only complicated matters. The helicopter landing zone at Keating was situated on a peninsula jutting out into the Landay-Sin River, a good distance from the actual outpost. As we hovered above the landing zone, I looked through the hatch while wearing my night-vision goggles. I swear I saw nothing but water.

Where is he putting this thing down?

A soldier ran out beneath the belly of the Chinook and began cutting away at the straps holding the sling load in place. This struck me as a job not for the fainthearted. Within a few minutes, though, the load had been released, and we went back up into the air. The Chinook hovered for a short time, until finally we settled over a tiny patch of grass – it looked as small as a putting green on a golf course – surrounded by massive, jagged boulders rising up out of the river.

No, he's not going to land there . . . is he?

Indeed he was. The pilot put the Chinook down perfectly on the smallest landing zone I had ever seen. I remember yelling, "Nice job!" and him saying, "Good luck." And then I was out the door and running away from the landing zone, over a bridge, with my head down, 150 pounds of gear on my back and in my arms. The landing zone was probably only 100 meters from Keating, but it was a treacherous, rocky sprint. I'd never felt so disoriented in my life. Arriving in Iraq had been strange and scary, but this was like being in another world altogether.

At an elevation of around 5,000 feet (and the surrounding mountains were twice that high), Keating was high enough that I could feel the altitude. Exhausted, I dropped my bags inside the COP, grabbed an empty bunk, and passed out. Less than two hours later, Breeding and I were woken up by two soldiers – the men who would be training us – and offered a tour of our new station.

"Come on," one of the guys said. "We'll take you up to the mortar pit."

I was surprised. In my experience, the mortar pit was usually part of or adjacent to the base. That's the whole point, really. Ideally, a mortar pit should be situated in the very center of the base so that you can defend against attacks from 360 degrees. But there was something about the way he said it – "We'll take you up to the mortar pit" – that hinted at a trek.

"Isn't it right here?" I asked. "Aren't we on the base?"

He laughed.

"Oh yeah, we're on the base. But we've got about a three-hundred-meter walk back up to our position."

I looked at Breeding. Again, he was stoic. Following his lead, I said nothing, but something about this arrangement felt wrong.

And when we stepped outside the building and I got my first look at COP Keating and the surrounding countryside in the light of day, it felt really wrong.

What the fuck?!

The COP was surrounded on three sides by mountains. In effect, the base had been positioned at the bottom of a bowl, at the lowest point in the valley. In the event of a confrontation, any opposition force would have the higher ground, which meant it would have a tactically advantageous position. The only possible support from above would be provided by Observation Post Fritsche, a smaller base less than half the size of Keating, located approximately two kilometers to the south. Fritsche was at an elevation 2,400 meters higher than Keating, but still well below positions held by insurgent forces; additionally, there was no direct line of sight between the two outposts, which made support challenging, to say the least.

It seemed incomprehensible that Keating had been deliberately constructed in this fashion, but apparently that was the case.

"Like we're in a damn fishbowl, huh?" one of our guides said.

I nodded.

"You'll get used to it," he said.

As I craned my neck and looked up at the jagged mountains above us, I wasn't sure. I could just imagine the Taliban gathering on the cliffs at night, laughing at the silly Americans who didn't know any better than to surrender the high ground before the fight even began. It was like spotting your opponent to a three-touchdown lead. Who would do that? Why would anyone do that? There was, of course, no good answer, and in light of what ultimately happened to COP Keating, it would be hard to make an argument in defense of its position.

Still, this was our new home, and we would do our best to protect it and to fight from it. We were, after all, the United States Army, the best-trained and best-equipped fighting force in history. We'd make do with what we had.

The mortar pit, as promised, was a nearly quarter-mile hike uphill from the main base, along a rocky, uneven path. South of the COP, it was easily the highest point on the entire compound, but it was still far below anything else in the vicinity. Even in the mortar pit, looking down on the COP, I felt highly vulnerable. It was obvious that all of our fighting would be done at an inopportune angle as we fired blindly up at the surrounding mountains. It was horrifying.

And it was beautiful.

I don't mind saying that. A lot of American soldiers hated Afghanistan, just like they hated Iraq. The circumstances of their visit precluded the possibility of any sort of appreciation for the natural wonders or ancient architecture either country had to offer. I can sympathize with that mind-set; it's hard to be moved by the beauty of the mountains when you know that they're crawling with insurgents who want nothing more than to flush you out of their country. In this setting, hatred very quickly replaces awe. But just as I had been left speechless by the blackness and brilliance of the desert sky over Baghdad, I couldn't help but be impressed by the topography around Keating. The way the mountains dropped effortlessly into the valley floor. The way the Landay-Sin River snaked through the region. And above it all, on that first morning, was the most brilliant blue sky imaginable.

It was raw and pristine and seemingly untouched. It was gorgeous.

The COP itself was another matter. Living conditions at Keating sucked. There was a little chow hall that had recently been hit by a rocket and was badly in need of repair. There was one aid station. The sleeping quarters were cramped and musty. We did have a fairly nice little gym, under the circumstances, with some weights and barbells. Nothing special, but functional, which was about all you could really ask for. Plumbing was a luxury we could not afford. There were a couple little pump showers that never seemed to work, so we relied mainly on baby wipes for hygiene. There were no toilets, just a shack some 100 feet from the base. We'd piss in tubes and shit in buckets, and at the end of each day we'd burn the accumulated waste. There was nothing scarier than using the latrine – knowing that you were not only isolated but an easy, half-naked target. It was every soldier's worst nightmare: to get shot or blown up while taking a crap. Not exactly a glorious way to go.

The mortar pit also was positioned in a manner that was tactically questionable. It was tucked into the mountainside, almost like a snow fort that a kid would carve out after a winter storm. The mortar pit was thus shielded from attacks emanating from the south and, to a lesser extent, the east, although it was wide open to fire from the north and west. That might sound like a reasonable compromise, but it really wasn't. When insurgent forces tried to fire from the south and east, the shells would explode just beyond the mortar pit, but the very same topographical quirks that prevented those attacks from reaching us also precluded our returning effective fire in those directions. We couldn't turn around and direct our mortars or guns to the south and east without risking deadly ricochets off the cliffs. The overhangs were simply too severe. When enemy forces attacked either the mortar pit or Keating from those positions, we could only respond with grenades and other handheld weapons. We had to be so careful that it almost wasn't worth the effort. We could return fire from the north and west ferociously, but the fact was, there rarely was any fire from the north, since the low point in the valley lay in that direction. So, in effect, the Taliban and insurgents held a massive tactical advantage over roughly 75 percent of the region.

The mortar compound itself was cavelike and decidedly less comfortable than the rest of the base (not to imply that anyone at Keating felt like they were staying at a four-star hotel). It was just a little structure built into the mountain, almost like a mud hut, with makeshift concrete walls. When standing in the doorway of the mortar pit, you were at eye level with the roof. Then you'd walk down a few steps into the living quarters. It was dark and dreary and subject to wild fluctuations in temperature: freezing at night, boiling during the day, especially in the summer months. We had a cheap little air conditioner to cool the place down, but it rarely worked properly. Water and mud constantly seeped through the walls – I worried that the entire pit might just collapse under the weight of the mountainside. There were four sleeping spaces – each was a plywood slab covered by a couple of yoga mats tied together to approximate a mattress. We slept completely enveloped in bug nets to reduce the likelihood of being bitten by a scorpion or camel spider. The nets were claustrophobic and hot, but they did their job reasonably well. Neither kind of bite was fatal – unless you had some sort of allergic reaction – but they could be mighty painful and unpleasant; it was best to take every precaution. Keating was miserable enough without having to fire a weapon with a hand bloated from a bug bite.

I don't know when or how the mortar pit came into existence. It seemed to predate Keating, which had been established by the Army in 2006 as a base for a provincial reconstruction team. The mortar pit looked like something the Afghans had used while fighting off the Soviets some thirty years earlier. It might have been even older than that, although it had been reinforced and tidied up by American forces.

If there was a mission statement for the troops at Keating (and I'm sure there was, somewhere), it was this: find and recruit allies among the local residents of the Kamdesh Valley, deter insurgents, and discourage illegal movement across the border with Pakistan.

There is some seriously vague verbiage there. "Recruiting allies" basically referred to winning the hearts and minds of the locals, but to be perfectly blunt, I didn't spend one minute in Afghanistan worrying about this particular aspect of the job description. Like most of my fellow soldiers, I was too busy trying to stay alive. Negotiating with the locals was best left to the officers. And anyway, it quickly became apparent that in Keating we had been assigned to one of the hottest spots in Afghanistan, and one of the most vulnerable bases in the entire country. We took fire virtually every day; under those conditions, you very quickly stop caring about anything other than protecting yourself and the men with whom you serve.

Which brings us to the other aspects of the mission statement: deterring insurgents and discouraging illegal movement across the border with Pakistan. Simply put, this referred to fighting. We "discouraged" insurgents by shooting at them and bombarding them with mortar fire.

We tried to use a military presence to prevent illegal movement across the border, which was presumed to be of a nefarious nature, and that ultimately led to more fighting. But the important thing to keep in mind is the way we were frequently asked to conduct this operation. For most of my deployment, the rules of engagement stipulated that we could not initiate contact; we could only respond to contact. And so we would spend hours patrolling, with no real purpose other than to attract attention and provoke the enemy into shooting at us; then we would respond with deadly force. Similarly, we would not use our mortars from Keating unless we were fired upon first.

This arrangement often instilled feelings of helplessness and agitation, but we learned to deal with it. There was no other choice.

I'll admit to having a visceral response to both Keating and, especially, the mortar pit, where I'd be spending the great majority of my deployment. I could tell instantly that the experience was going to be much worse than it was in Iraq, from the standpoint of both combat and comfort. You can tell a lot simply by looking at the unit you have been assigned to replace. These boys were filthy and ragged. You could just tell that their year in the mountains had sucked all the energy out of them.

"Man, we've got a whole fucking year in this shit hole?" I said to Breeding. I should have known better. He just shrugged.

"Whatever, man. We signed up for this, right? It's our job."

Shitty as it was, we quickly made the mortar pit our home. And once we got settled in, it was fun in a weird sort of way. We had a fat, old 27-inch tube TV in the corner and a stash of 500 DVDs, accumulated over the previous three years. Whenever a unit transitioned out, they'd leave everything behind, so we had an endless supply of movies and TV shows. We'd just leave the set running all day long. It was background noise whenever we weren't fighting. By the time we left, I think I had memorized every episode of *The Wire* and *24*. We also had a PlayStation and a handful of old video games. (I should add that we had access to these creature comforts only when our generator was in working order, which was often not the case; sometimes we'd go weeks or even months without power.)

It took a while, though, to get everything set up.

The first day we jumped right into training and procedure, working closely with the men we'd be replacing. The entire mortar pit was perhaps 500 square feet. This included living quarters, sleeping quarters, and the actual mortar pit itself, where our weapons were positioned. It was all one area, although the weapons, of course, were outside. You'd step out of the living quarters and directly into the mortar pit itself.

"See right up there?" one of the guys said, pointing toward a ridge roughly southwest from our position. "That's where they'll usually attack from."

There were two mortars: one that fired 120-millimeter shells, and another that fired 60-millimeter shells. (The size refers to the diameter of the projectile, which is basically a bomb loaded into the muzzle of the mortar; it's fired at a specific target and explodes on impact.) Mortars are actually fairly primitive weapons that have been used effectively for hundreds of years. They are relatively lightweight, portable, and capable of doing significant damage. They are also highly accurate – if you know what you are doing. Each system has its quirks and eccentricities, which are compounded by the topography of the region where they are being employed. Given how the mortar pit at Keating was situated, accuracy took on even greater importance.

The departing mortar unit explained all of this to us and showed us how to lay in the guns (shorthand for properly calibrating the weapons). To have maximum range and efficacy, we had to lay in our guns in an unconventional way. The insurgents often used mortar fire against us, but it was rarely accurate. They had inferior equipment and comparatively unskilled soldiers. If you don't take the time to become proficient in calibrating your gun, you might as well just be tossing long-range grenades and hoping for the best. And because the mortar pit at Keating was so tightly wedged into the mountains, we had to make all kinds of adjustments; we couldn't simply rely on textbook procedures.

And believe me, I knew the textbook. When we first got to the mortar pit and they introduced us to our weapons and began explaining protocol, I was nearly blinded by my own arrogance.

Man, I've been to school. I'm great with weapon systems! I'm fast, I'm a gunner — I can set up a mortar in little to no time, four or five seconds, all by myself.

But I was wrong.

"Forget about the textbook," they told us. "Forget everything you've learned. Up here, this is the way you have to do it. It's the only way that will work."

It was somewhat humbling to realize that even with all my training — even after a year in Iraq — there was still much to learn. At the same time, it was kind of badass, because when you tell stories and go back to other mortar units and teach them how to shoot, they look at you with a sense of awe and bewilderment.

"Listen, that conventional bullshit? Throw it out the window," I'd say. "You're going to have to use your instinct, and you're going to have to modify everything you do when you go fight in Afghanistan. The terrain changes everything."

Learning all of this stuff on the fly in our first couple days in-country was simultaneously thrilling and intimidating. Fortunately, the men who had been there before us (or maybe it was the unit before them, or the one before that) had come up with a system that seemed to work well.

How well?

The maximum range of the 120-millimeter mortar was 7,200

meters, or roughly four and a half miles. At this distance, if properly calibrated, a mortar would have a flight time of approximately thirty seconds and would be accurate to within a distance of ten feet.

I found that to be rather amazing.

At the same time, we had to be prepared to use every tool at our disposal, for while we were assigned to the mortar pit and spent virtually every day of our deployment in the mortar pit, combat protocol (if there was such a thing) dictated the use of other weapons as well. When the shit hit the fan, I would respond first by grabbing the nearest gun – usually a sniper rifle or an M4. We also had a 240 Bravo, a belt-fed machine gun capable of firing 700 rounds per minute. In a firefight, it wasn't unusual for the mortar to be the last weapon we used. The 60-millimeter mortar was small enough (the shells were roughly the size of a soda bottle) that one man could handle it by himself. You could pick up the tube and the shell, move them around the compound, and fire when ready. The 120-millimeter mortar was a different animal – the baseplate alone weighed ninety pounds. Moving it, loading it, and firing it safely was a two-man job.

Fighting from the mortar pit was pretty wild. During a firefight, we had the same responsibilities and the same weaponry as the men at Keating, but we also were expected to provide mortar cover. And it wasn't long before we got our first taste of action. In fact, it happened on the very first day, while we were in the middle of our first training session.

The thing about being a newcomer to Afghanistan is that you don't quite understand just how dangerous a place it really is. Both the appearance and attitude of the soldiers who have been there for any length of time contribute to the generally lackadaisical atmosphere. But that is highly misleading. Everyone at Keating was a seasoned combat infantryman. These guys were among the best the Army had to offer. But they had grown accustomed not only to the violence but to the shitty conditions as well. They were tired, hungry, and bored. They had let their hair grow out, and they hadn't shaved in weeks . . . or months. Their boots were unlaced. They wore T-shirts and shorts. They were gaunt and haggard, and they'd been there long enough. Everything about them seemed to say, *I have no fucks left to give. Just let me go home.*

And there I was, like a poster boy for the Army, all eager and properly dressed. Clean-shaven and well-fed. I had my sniper rifle in my hand, an M4 slung over my shoulder, and my helmet strapped neatly in place. I was good to go.

So why were these guys looking at me like I was an idiot?

"You know, we get attacked all the time up here," one of them said. "But lately it's been kind of quiet."

I swear, not more than two minutes after he said that, there was a thunderous explosion – I'd heard or felt nothing like it since I'd been in Iraq. All of COP Keating seemed to rumble from the force.

"What the hell is that?" I yelled.

There was no answer.

Suddenly bullets were flying everywhere. A rocket had landed in the middle of the base, and though we were nearly a quarter-mile away, the explosion rocked the mortar pit as well. I put a hand on my head to make sure my helmet was still in place. Then I did what everyone else was doing: I fired my weapon, almost randomly at first, just strafing the hillside. I saw what appeared to be people – yes, people! – their heads peering out above a small mountain ledge. It almost looked like a compound or a base of some kind. No more than a couple hundred yards away, just slightly above us. I could see them scrambling, maneuvering. They had dark skin and wore loose clothing. They had guns. They were shooting.

Insurgents . . . Taliban.

I didn't know what the hell I was doing. I'd been at Keating for only a few hours, and already I was involved in a firefight that surpassed in intensity and craziness anything I had experienced in Iraq. I squeezed the trigger. Bullets bounced off the rocks. The figures disappeared into the woodline, but the firing continued. Unable to see the shooters, I settled for simply firing at their muzzle flashes. I heard more gunfire, this time from a different location. I turned. There, almost directly across from the mortar pit, was a glowing gun barrel, an automatic weapon blasting away. Suddenly the firing stopped and the operator peered out above some rocks. He had a long beard, just like the others. I took aim. I had a clean shot. I squeezed the trigger again. The bullet cracked into the mountainside, missing by no more than a few feet. Bits of rock and rubble splattered into his face and knocked him down. He scrambled to safety, holding a hand over his face.

"What the fuck are you doing?" someone yelled.

"I'm shooting! What does it look like?"

"Not there. He's ANA!"

Oh, shit . . .

The fight ended within ten to fifteen minutes, after which it was explained to me that the man I had nearly killed was a member of the Afghan National Army force that manned a position near the perimeter of the base. There were roughly twenty ANA forces at Keating during most of my deployment; technically speaking, they were on our side, although they generally displayed a lack of both enthusiasm and expertise when it came to combat. Among the men at COP Keating, there was no great love or respect for the ANA; still, US soldiers did not typically go around shooting ANA forces during a firefight, accidentally or otherwise, as I had nearly done on my first day on the job. This became a huge source of amusement among the departing troops, and dogged me for the duration of the transition. Not that they would have cared if I had killed the guy; they just thought it was funny.

There was at least one American casualty that day. I don't know his name, but I saw him being airlifted out shortly after the firefight. He'd been hit by shrapnel from the rocket that had landed in the compound. I heard later that he made it home alive. I don't know the extent of his recovery.

I do know that he had been scheduled to leave Keating that very day.

7

NEVER FELT AS THOUGH we had a clear-cut goal in Afghanistan. In Iraq, at least we were given high-value targets and told to go after them. In Afghanistan, we had no specific mission. We were there to give the Taliban something to shoot at. And once they shot at us, we could return fire. We were there to draw contact. We were there to fight. Day after bloody day. If that sounds like lunacy, well, I guess it was. Like every other soldier in Afghanistan, I'd occasionally find myself wondering, *What the hell am I doing here?* But at the same time, I never lost sight of the fact that no one put a gun to my head and forced me to enlist. The United States has a volunteer army, and I willingly signed up. We all complained at one time or another, but basically this was my attitude: *Yeah, this is crazy, sitting around here getting shot at. But at least I get to shoot back.*

Isolation plays a role as well. The world is a much smaller place when you're at war. Global politics has no place in the mind of a soldier. Maybe it's a cliché, but it's also true: you care only about the guy fighting next to you and the bullets whizzing past your head. Nothing else matters. It doesn't take long to develop a very morbid and practical attitude about the whole thing. You end up with a bunch of guys – kids, mostly – growing out beards and shooting at anything and everything, trying to stay sane and live to see the next day. In this scenario, you develop friendships that are deeper and more intense than any you could possibly imagine.

The physical setup at Keating accentuated all of these things. Although we interacted on a somewhat regular basis with the guys at Keating, those of us in the mortar pit acted as a separate unit. We were the Four Horsemen: Breeding, Thomson, John Hammel, and me. While everyone else would go out on patrols lasting eight to ten hours, we would remain behind in the mortar pit. This could be frustrating and claustrophobic, but generally I preferred it. Sometimes, if the patrol was shorthanded, I'd volunteer to go out, just to break up the routine and try to pitch in. But the longer I was in Afghanistan the more I came to see the benefits of being part of the mortar crew.

For one thing, the autonomy was great. Adherence to formal military protocol and rank breaks down a bit during a combat deployment, but it disappears almost entirely when you're sequestered with only three other men in a mortar pit. Simply put, we had to put up with a lot less bullshit in the mortar pit than the rest of the guys at Keating. Our job was to fight, and if we did that well, we were left alone. Sergeant Breeding was a hell of a leader, and we took our jobs seriously. We'd work on our guns every day, making sure we were ready for the inevitable attack. And when it came, we fought ferociously. The immersion was instantaneous and complete: I was involved in five firefights during my first two weeks in Afghanistan – roughly the same number I saw during my entire Iraq deployment – and the intensity of these encounters was almost overwhelming. Like everyone else at Keating, we were expected to return small-arms fire. But we were also expected to use our mortars to devastating effect. If a team was out on patrol and came under fire, they would transmit coordinates to us and we would support them with mortar fire.

If you had to be in the infantry, serving in that region, the mortar pit was the best job available. And everyone knew it. There was a steady flow of traffic between the main base and the mortar pit. Guys would come down just to hang out with us, to get away from the rules and the COs.

As in Iraq, I served under and alongside some great people in Afghanistan ... and I served under some men who weren't so great. Among the former was Captain Stoney Portis, a West Point grad who was cool and confident and super fit, and who just seemed not only to understand the impossibility of our mission but also how to get everyone to buy into it nonetheless. The guy was a strong leader.

At the other end of the spectrum was Captain Melvin Porter, who seemed to fail to understand the severity of our situation and was frequently reluctant to use the tools at his disposal. We had a couple of nicknames for Captain Porter. First we called him "No Mortar" Porter, because he was so hesitant to use mortar fire, even when it was the perfectly appropriate response. Porter worried about collateral damage, which was honorable on some level, but the fact is, COP Keating was in an incredibly hostile location, at the foot of three mountains, in an area overrun with insurgents; tactically and strategically, the very placement of Keating was idiotic. At the very least, we should have been permitted to use maximum firepower to defend ourselves. Under No Mortar Porter, we often felt handcuffed.

Porter's other nickname was "Bunker Six." See, when communicating by radio, every person has a call sign. There is a pecking order: one is an officer, two is a platoon sergeant, and so on. Each number is tagged to a color or other description. For example, my call sign was "Green Seven." Captain Porter was "Black Knight Six," in part because the highest-ranking officer on the base is always number six. And Bravo Troop was "Black Knight."

So Porter proudly went by the moniker Black Knight Six. What he didn't know — or maybe he did (there are few secrets in the field) — was that most of his men, when they weren't calling him No Mortar Porter, were referring to him as Bunker Six, because he never left his little compound. He didn't go out on patrol, he didn't come to the mortar pit, and he rarely fought. Simply put, the guy was apparently scared of combat. If you think that doesn't have an impact on the men who serve beneath you, well, you're wrong. At best, it breeds cynicism and disrespect; at worst, it crushes morale.

Bunker Six was the kind of officer who was big on protocol and appearance. He made everyone walk around in full battle rattle (helmet, vest, weapon) at all times. If you simply left the hooch to smoke a cigarette, Porter insisted you put on your gear. I know how that probably sounds – like common sense, like an officer who is concerned about the safety of his men. But the guys viewed it as a colossal pain in the ass and as devotion to form over substance. In Afghanistan, soldiers would sometimes fight in flip-flops and T-shirts. They sure as hell didn't want to have to gear up just to take a smoke break, even if it might have seemed like the prudent thing to do. Porter was big on defense and squeamish when it came to offense. Like a boss who is more concerned about the office dress code than about actual productivity, he had the respect of almost no one under his command.

In the mortar pit, though, we rarely interacted with Captain Porter. He trekked up to see us maybe two or three times in the first three months. He left us alone, which was one of the reasons other people were always dropping by to hang out or play cards, or to just take off their gear and chill for a while. Sergeant Breeding was like the anti–Bunker Six. He rolled up his sleeves and fought alongside us. He understood what was important.

But here's the thing about a combat deployment: even in the most dangerous and hostile environment, there are great chunks of time when you have virtually nothing to do. As I said, we were involved in five firefights in my first two weeks at Keating, but most of those encounters were brief. It wasn't unusual for a fight to last no more than fifteen minutes. The rest of the day, if you weren't out on patrol, would be devoted to laying in your weapons and making sure all the equipment worked properly. In other words . . . being *prepared*. But even this task left huge holes in the day—time that we filled in a variety of ways.

In addition to a TV and DVDs, we had something known as a "whack shack," a small ammo holding area in the mortar pit devoted to, well . . . whacking it. This was hardly unique to Bravo Troop, or even to Keating. I doubt it is even unique to the modern-day soldier. Anytime you put a bunch of young men in an environment dripping with testosterone for months on end, with no female accompaniment, masturbation becomes somewhat chronic. It was a way to pass time, a sexual release, and a coping mechanism for dealing with unbelievable stress and violence.

It was also the source of endless amusement and jokes. No one even made the slightest attempt to hide their onanistic habits. Why bother? When you have four guys living in one tiny space, there are no secrets.

"Where you going, man?"

"Ah, I can't sleep. Going to the whack shack."

"Okay, cool. Try to keep it quiet, all right?"

Unlike Iraq, there was very little use of drugs or alcohol in Afghanistan. First of all, it was too difficult to obtain; more importantly, it was simply not worth the risk. Opium is a cash crop in Afghanistan, but that's grown more in the lower country, and we had very little exposure to it. Marijuana, interestingly, grew wild in the mountains, but the plants were female and thus did not have buds, so there was no way to smoke it. You could chew the leaves if you were desperate to get high (we used to watch goats eat the plants and then stagger around drunkenly), but it was an unpleasant experience. The Afghans would often chew qat, a flowering plant that behaves like a stimulant when ingested. I tried that once, got a real head rush, and felt sick to my stomach.

A few of my friends sent me liquor in Afghanistan. But it took forever to arrive; by the time I got it, I'd lost interest. In Iraq we drank on our days off. Strictly speaking, we had no days off at Keating. Every day brought the possibility of another fight. I decided very early in my deployment that I would need a clear head just to survive. We were so on edge and fighting all the time. I had enough common sense to realize that the risks associated with getting drunk far outweighed any short-term benefits. So I just didn't do it. In fact, hardly anyone did. Drinking wasn't an issue in Afghanistan. Staying sober was a matter of life and death.

It's easy to become fatalistic on a combat deployment, to presume that there is some sort of cosmic plan and that you will either survive or die through no fault of your own. Control becomes elusive. In an effort to inject some sense of normalcy into my life and to feel good about myself, I began working out while I was at Keating. That might sound strange at first. I mean, isn't every infantryman in Afghanistan by definition in pretty good shape? Isn't that part of the job description? Well, yes and no. It's true that simply getting through each day in such spartan conditions requires a certain degree of strength and conditioning. This was especially true for soldiers who were out on patrol for eight or ten hours a day.

I was in the mortar pit. I spent a lot of time sitting on my ass. Bursts of combat notwithstanding, it wasn't like the job required a ton of physical exertion. Moreover, there were risks beyond getting shot or blown up associated with living in this way – illness, spider bites, snake bites, rabid dog bites. (Yes, there were wild dogs everywhere, and many of them were rabid.) It simply made sense to try to stay in shape, and that required both effort and creativity.

For the first few months I mostly used the small but functional gym at Keating, taking nightly trips down to the main base to work out. In the summer and early fall, prime fighting season in Afghanistan, there was less movement between the mortar pit and the main base – it just wasn't safe or practical to walk around when you knew the enemy was watching and waiting for an opportunity to attack. Also, we had to be prepared to respond from the mortar pit on a moment's notice. So, once the fighting heated up, we had to create our own primitive little gym in the mortar pit. We'd fill empty ammo cans with sand and use them as dumbbells or barbells. We would do endless crunches, push-ups, and pull-ups. Multiple sets, hundreds of reps. It became not just a way to pass the time but almost an addiction. I can see now why prisons are filled with jacked-up inmates. It's not just about getting big and looking tough (although I suppose that's part of it); it's also about filling the endless hours with something productive, something you can control.

Believe it or not, I got into CrossFit while I was in Afghanistan. I was introduced to it by Captain Christopher Cordova, who was the senior medical officer at COP Keating. Chris is one of my best friends now. He's an amazing guy, super fit and talented and smart. His efforts to keep people alive during the Battle of Kamdesh were truly heroic; he was a physician's assistant (PA) and medic who displayed all the skill and patience of an MD and the courage of a warrior. It's no surprise that he received the Silver Star.

Chris and I were together throughout my time in the Army. We arrived at Fort Carson around the same time, and we deployed to both Iraq and Afghanistan together. Chris was probably a decade older and outranked me by a wide margin; he was also a medic and I was a private (soon to be staff sergeant), so we had completely different roles and responsibilities. Nevertheless, what with deploying together and our shared interest in sports and fitness, we were able to develop a strong friendship in the unlikeliest of places.

While I was a guy who had enlisted in the Army primarily to get away from a bad situation at home, Chris was a true believer. He understood the military and the political ramifications of the conflicts in Iraq and Afghanistan in ways that frankly didn't even interest me (or most other infantrymen, for that matter). He could have been a doctor or made significantly more money as a PA in the private sector, but he believed in the work he was doing; he felt there was nothing more important than supporting this country's fighting men and women, and he did it from the trenches.

It was impossible not to admire Chris, in part because, physically speaking, he was a monster. We used to go mountain biking and snowboarding together in Colorado, and I struggled to keep up with the guy. He's closer to forty than thirty now and still doing Ironman triathlons, where he routinely kicks the asses of guys ten and fifteen years younger.

I'd never even heard of CrossFit. It's insanely popular now, of course, but back in 2009? It was at best a novelty.

"What is it?" I asked Chris when he suggested I join him for a few CrossFit workouts.

"It's perfect for this place," he explained. "You hardly need to use weights at all. Ninety-five percent of the workout is about using your own body weight."

I was up for just about anything, and I figured that Chris probably knew what he was doing. You don't get into that kind of shape by accident. So we created a bunch of makeshift equipment: bars and rings, ropes and PVC pipes. We had a couple of forty-five-pound plates, but for the most part our workouts incorporated little in the way of traditional weights. It was primitive as hell, but we did the best we could. And every night we'd bang out one of the CrossFit workouts that Chris had looked up online. It was insanely difficult and exhausting. I loved it!

I was lucky to be sharing the mortar pit with three guys I liked. There's certainly no guarantee of that. Believe me, as much as you fight for the lives of your brothers, it's possible to have serious personality conflicts with soldiers in your own platoon. That happens more often than you'd think. And if you're unfortunate enough to have those types of issues when you're stuck in the mortar pit . . . well, life can be downright miserable. Our foursome was tight, though, even if we came from different backgrounds and had different interests.

John Hammel was a white kid who had grown up in a housing project in Portland, Maine. He had that inner-city swagger about him; he was quick-witted and short-tempered. You could tell that Hammel had been raised in a tough neighborhood, the kind of place where you didn't talk shit about people unless you were prepared to back it up with your fists. Stateside, I'd been out drinking with Hammel, and on a few occasions the night had ended with fighting. We even got into it with each other once. I forget the exact circumstances, but basically we were talking trash, which led to some harmless wrestling, and then, for some reason, it escalated quickly. We were rolling around on the ground, and Hammel hit his head on one of the empty ammo crates that we used to store clothes under our beds. Just like that — *wham!* — things got ugly. Hammel broke free and threw a punch that caught me right in the nose. I wobbled for a moment and hit him back. Next thing you know we were trying to rip each other's heads off. The whole thing lasted only about a minute or so before it got broken up. We stood there, chests heaving, shirts ripped, staring at each other, trying to calm down.

"Everybody good here?" our platoon sergeant asked.

"Yeah, I'm good," I said.

Hammel nodded in agreement. "Yeah . . . but fuck you, man."

"Fuck you too."

Then we both laughed.

And that was it.

Hammel was a gun nut, but not in a psycho kind of way; he just liked guns — knew everything about them, could break down his weapon and put it back together again in a heartbeat. He was a couple years older than me, had a wife and kid, and was on his third deployment. He'd been in the Army for a while and hadn't yet made sergeant (although he would be promoted while we were in Afghanistan), but the guy was a good soldier. When it came to fighting, he was squared away. Hammel knew his stuff and was willing to put bullets downrange anytime. We fought side by side every day; I couldn't have trusted him more.

Hammel was also one of the chattiest people I've ever met. Guy could talk your ear off, day or night. Mostly night, though. See, we took turns sleeping in the mortar pit. Even though we didn't have to pull guard duty, the way we did in Iraq, someone always had to stay awake to monitor the radio; there were no exceptions to this rule, no days or nights off. Fortunately, we had two guys — Hammel and Thomson — who both liked staying up at night, so they usually took turns on the night shift. Then they'd sleep for a few hours in the morning while Breeding and I monitored the radio. Hammel was such a social guy that sometimes he'd finish his shift and stay up to bullshit with the rest of us rather than go straight to bed.

Conversation kept all of us sane. The person with whom I shared the most was Kevin Thomson. We talked and talked and talked, until there was nothing we didn't know about each other. That's what you did on deployment — you told stories about where you came from, what your life was like before the Army, and what you hoped to do if you made it home in one piece. I told Thomson all about my dad dying and how I had fucked up academically in my last couple years of high school.

"When I get out," I told Thomson, "I'm going back to school."

I had the same long-range goal a lot of kids who grow up in northern Virginia have: to get a college degree, followed by a steady job with the federal government. Lots of paid vacation, great benefits and security, a fat pension.

Thomson found this perplexing. He had originally wanted to be a butcher, but not because he had any great interest in the profession. See, the guy loved smoking pot, so his big thing was finding a job where mandatory drug testing wouldn't be part of the equation. I guess "butcher" fell into that category.

"D-Rod, why do you want to work for the government?" he'd say, his voice always a flat, expressionless monotone. "You won't be able to smoke weed."

I'd just shake my head.

"Dude, seriously? Is that all you think about?"

Sometimes I'd let on about one of the great regrets in my life: that I had blown an opportunity to play college football. Like I said, we had a lot of time to work out in Afghanistan. At some point during my second deployment, I realized I was in the best shape of my life, and I found myself obsessing about the possibility of resurrecting my football career. And not just D-III ball. For some reason, I had this crazy notion that despite being only five-foot-eight and 175 pounds, I could play big-time college football. Division I. Maybe Virginia or Virginia Tech. It was crazy, but what the hell? There was no harm in dreaming big. And Thomson, good friend that he was, never tried to dissuade me.

"You should do it, man. Why not?"

Yeah, exactly. *Why not?*

Over time the fantasy took root in my head and refused to let go. I imagined what it would be like to suit up for a major college football team. I could picture myself running onto the field in front of 80,000 people. I could hear them. I could feel them.

"You know, if we get out of here," I told Thomson one day, "I'm really going to do this. I'm going to play college ball."

Thomson didn't say anything. He just nodded in that laid-back way of his.

"I'm serious," I said.

Thomson smiled.

"Yeah, I know."

8

THE FACT THAT COP Keating was the northernmost base in Afghanistan added to the sensation of being isolated. Since our fastest jets needed twenty minutes to make the trip from Bagram Airfield to Keating, that was how long we had to wait if we needed air strikes. To put that in perspective, consider that these same jets can fly across the United States, a distance of 3,000 miles, in roughly one hour. A simple Chinook ride from Keating to Bostick took at least forty-five minutes. In a very real sense, the soldiers at COP Keating and at nearby OP Fritsche are very much on their own. We were an island in the middle of the hottest death valley in Afghanistan. Consequently, if something went wrong, we were in big trouble.

On October 3, 2009, just about everything went wrong.

For the previous month we'd been hearing all kinds of crazy chatter on the radio — communication between Taliban members saying things that we knew were patently untrue, like claiming to have killed a certain number of American soldiers in specific encounters when in fact they hadn't killed anyone. This lent an air of incredulity to virtually anything that came across the airwaves. We continued to use interpreters to monitor everything – that was part of the process – but when we began getting intel about the Taliban gathering a force of 300 to 400 insurgents and freedom fighters in preparation for an attack on Keating, we dismissed it as so much bullshit.

"No way there's three hundred of these guys to attack us. That just doesn't happen."

And so it went, every single day for at least a month, careless and boastful radio chatter about an impending attack on COP Keating. Eventually we came to the conclusion that they were just screwing with our heads. Every night we would get the report from the intel guys at the bottom of the base, and it was always the same thing.

"Enemy forces are mounting up again."

"Yeah? How many this time?"

"Same as usual – a few hundred."

"Right . . ."

And then we'd laugh and go back to working out or playing cards or prepping our weapons. I can honestly say that despite all the chatter – or maybe because of all the chatter – we never saw it coming.

Maybe we'd grown complacent. Maybe we were arrogant. Maybe we just didn't give a shit. For whatever reason, I think we had started to believe that Keating was impenetrable.

Logically speaking, this was absurd. By this point the base had already been targeted for closure by General Stanley McChrystal, who was at the time commander of US forces in Afghanistan. Withdrawal from Keating was part of a broader plan to shut down outposts in some of Afghanistan's more remote regions and to consolidate troops in more heavily populated areas. This would presumably facilitate the US mission of protecting Afghan civilians, while simultaneously minimizing casualties among American troops. In retrospect, this was probably a good idea, as Keating was among the most remote and vulnerable outposts in all of Afghanistan. There was only so much that could be accomplished from that position, and the threat of attack was constant.

We had fought virtually every day during the summer and early fall, and yet we had incurred only one serious casualty: Sergeant First-Class Jeff Jacops, who took shrapnel to the head one morning when a rocket exploded into a nearby wall. Sergeant Jacops lost a bunch of teeth and had his face ripped wide open. He was taken out by medevac and underwent several hours of surgery, but he made it home alive. Six months later, he came back for more! Just showed up one day with a long scar running down his face. Only three or four months left in his deployment. I didn't know Jacops very well before his injury, but I got to know him a little afterward, and I can't tell you how much respect we all had for this guy. I mean, I'm sure some people thought he was nuts, but I admired the hell out of him. He could have stayed home for the duration of his deployment. He could have petitioned for a medical discharge and gotten out of the military altogether. But he didn't. He came back.

Boys like that . . . they keep you honest. They make you want to fight for them, because together you have an unbreakable bond. As miserable as it was to be in Afghanistan, I would have done the same thing. As long as my injury allowed it, I would have returned. I was going to stay until the bitter end. I think most of us felt that way.

As awful as it was, Jacops's injury was an outlier in the summer of 2009. Despite daily contact and firefights, despite a fairly steady barrage of rockets and mortars, COP Keating sustained little in the way of human or structural damage. Part of that can be attributed to the heart and skill and fighting ability of Bravo Troop 3-61. And part of it—maybe most of it, to be perfectly honest—was pure luck. Now that I've had some time to reflect on it, my personal opinion has evolved somewhat. I think the insurgent forces were planning the attack on COP Keating for a long time, and much of the fighting that preceded it was just to see how we'd react – it was one long, elaborate test.

They'd harass us night and day. At the time I presumed they were trying to kill us, no matter how haphazard and half-assed most of their attempts seemed to be. But now I can see that they were really trying to soften us up, to expose our weaknesses and gain a clear understanding of how we operated in a combat scenario. They'd pepper the base with rockets and small-arms fire and then watch as we assembled and returned fire. I can imagine them now sitting on the hilltops above Keating, recording our every move, taking note of the way we patrolled and how we ran to our positions. Over a span of weeks and months, they could easily have accumulated enough information to mount a devastating attack, learning everything from where to infiltrate our perimeter to where they would need to suppress fire.

I honestly believe that the summer was one giant rope-a-dope, a ploy to make us think that not only were they militarily incompetent, but we had nothing to fear. They were setting us up. So even though we didn't get hit hard all the time, we did get hit. And it was annoying as hell, like a ceaseless swarm of mosquitoes. It didn't matter if they shot one round or a hundred; it didn't matter if there was one rocket or five. Regardless of the intensity of the attack, we responded the same way every time. We'd mount our positions and return fire. It was almost like a game for them:

We'll launch a couple rockets, make them go out, deprive them of sleep.

And it worked every time. We were nothing if not well trained and professional. Every contact, however benign (although, really, there is no such thing as benign gunfire), sparked a full-scale response. Once engaged, we'd stay out there, firing back, until helicopters came in and quieted everything down. Then we'd go back inside, try to relax . . . and it would start all over again. Sometimes the fights would last for ten or fifteen minutes, sometimes they'd last for an hour or more. Didn't matter. We were fully invested.

If their plan was to tease and taunt us and to instill in us a deceptive sense of superiority, well, it worked. But it came with a cost. We killed a lot of Taliban (or insurgents, or whatever you want to call them) in the summer months, usually with mortar fire. As I said, the mortars were lethally accurate, and by simply monitoring intercom chatter or using chopper surveillance, we could easily pick up their positions, especially once the fighting began. And since we were far more technologically advanced, casualties on their side were frequent and numerous. Sometimes we'd go out and do a body count, but more often we would simply listen to the chatter, which frequently revealed as much information as we needed, including the number of enemy kills.

I rarely thought about the big picture: Why were we in Afghanistan in the first place? Did it make sense? What goals were we trying to accomplish? I did what I was told; I tried to help my buddies get home in one piece. You learn to live in the moment when you're on a combat deployment, to embrace the situation and take from it whatever positive things you can find. I built strong relationships and friendships. I learned to appreciate what I had, before I screwed everything up in the last couple years of high school. I forgave my mom while I was in Afghanistan, stopped dwelling on the anger I felt and tried to focus on everything she had done for me. For better or worse, I had a lot of time to crawl into my own head. Realizing that every day could be my last was a sobering experience; it put things in perspective. I had friends and family who cared for me. I had enough God-given ability to succeed in life. I just needed to put in the effort. And I kept telling myself that when I got home – if I got home – I would do precisely that.

I tried to stay positive, but the truth is, a steady diet of combat and death plays tricks with your mind. There were days when I would think about my own funeral, and I'd wonder how many people would show up and how they would react. Had I treated them well enough? Had I earned their friendship and loyalty?

· · ·

I woke around five o'clock on the morning of October 3. I was up before anyone else in the mortar pit – and probably before just about anyone else at the base – because I was scheduled to go on leave in a month and had to complete some paperwork. We were already down a man in the mortar pit, Hammel having gone on leave a few days earlier. (My leave would begin after he returned – that's the way it worked.) Well, technically speaking, we weren't shorthanded, as we'd received a temporary replacement for Hammel. His name was Janpatrick Barroga, and at first he did not fit in particularly well with our crew. Barroga was a sergeant and had an attitude and arrogance that were unwarranted, especially considering that he had never been deployed. He didn't understand the job or the rhythm of life in Afghanistan, or what it was like to be involved in a firefight. Unfortunately, he would soon find out.

It seemed like a typical morning: quiet, in a way almost beautiful. What we did not know was that Taliban and insurgent forces had spent the previous night forcibly evacuating most of the village of Kamdesh and preparing to mount a massive and simultaneous assault on both COP Keating and OP Fritsche. In other words, they had assembled and executed precisely the plan we had heard them discuss on countless occasions. And while we never did get an exact head count, the Army's official report on the Battle of Kamdesh estimated the attacking force to have been roughly 300 strong. A tiny village of maybe a dozen little mud huts was less than 100 meters from the entrance to Keating. By daybreak, the occupants of these homes had been chased away, their places taken by at least fifty well-armed enemy soldiers. Groups of similar size were stationed at various places around the perimeter of Keating and Fritsche. It was a remarkably well-coordinated attack, and one of the largest ever mounted against US forces in Afghanistan.

I knew none of this as I walked the 300 meters downhill to the aid station so that I could use the only computer on the base. Along the way I passed Specialist Stephan Mace, who was in the turret of an armored Humvee, smoking a cigarette, pulling an overnight shift on guard duty. Mace was another guy I liked a lot. He was funny, friendly, and competent as hell. He used to joke about how his mom was a veterinarian and his father was an avid hunter.

"So I love animals," he'd say. "But I like to shoot 'em sometimes."

Mace used to come up to the mortar pit and hang out all the time. As I passed his position he smiled, we exchanged a few words, and I kept right on going. Nothing out of the ordinary. It was still pretty dark outside when I walked into the aid station. All the lights were off, all the medics were asleep; there was no reason for anyone to be awake yet. I took a seat at the computer station, logged into Facebook, checked a few e-mails, and then started filling out forms for my leave. I was planning on visiting the Gold Coast of Australia, getting in some beach time, maybe doing some surfing. (It's funny — I never did get that leave, and I never made it to Australia. But my girlfriend now is from the Gold Coast. We joke sometimes about how it's fate and how we should have met four years earlier.)

I was in the middle of filling out my paperwork when the first rocket whistled in. I could hear it approaching. At first I thought nothing of it. *Just another day at Keating.* But then it hit, and it hit close.

Boom!

Now, this happened with some frequency. Rockets landed inside the wire all the time, so there was no reason to believe that this particular rocket was the first volley in what would turn out to be a massive and protracted strike. But then there was a second blast. And a third. After about the sixth explosion, all inside the wire, I started to wonder what the hell was going on. Not only were there more rockets than usual, but they were coming from all different angles, a clear indication that the enemy was firing from multiple positions, something that required a large degree of manpower and organization. Then there was another crash, louder than the others, and much closer. The aid station shook.

Shit . . . this is not normal.

The timing couldn't have been worse. I had to get back to my position in the mortar pit as quickly as possible to provide cover for the whole base. As it was, we had a new man in the pit, and with me down here in the aid station, that left only two experienced gunners, Breeding and Thomson. I wasn't exactly dressed for an assault of this magnitude either—just Army shorts, Puma sneakers, and a lightweight vest. Thinking back on it, though, I was probably lucky. Being underdressed made me more mobile and allowed me to get back up the hill safely.

By now the medics had been roused. Morning attacks were not unusual—in fact, the insurgents typically engaged us just before sunup and just before dark. But it was impossible not to recognize right away the difference in the severity of this attack. The first medic to emerge from his hooch was Staff Sergeant Shane Corville. Like Chris Cordova, Shane was unusually fit for a medic, and he had earned massive cred with the guys in our unit because he was more than willing to pick up a gun when things got hot. It wasn't part of his job description, but he did it anyway. As Shane walked into the computer area, still rubbing the sleep from his eyes, another rocket hit.

"What's going on, D-Rod?"

"Not sure, man. They're fucking with us again."

It was crazy. We stood there talking for a minute or so, with rockets coming in every ten to fifteen seconds. I clipped up my vest and put a round in my 9-millimeter handgun.

Boom!

Another rocket. Again the aid station rumbled.

"Shit, that's close!" I said.

Shane nodded.

"What are you doing?" he asked.

I didn't know how to respond. I didn't really have an answer, since I didn't know what I was doing. I knew only that I had to get back to the mortar pit.

"Gotta run, Doc. Wish me luck."

I opened the door, stepped outside, pulled it shut behind me . . . and immediately felt an overwhelming sense of regret. I froze for maybe half a second, then ran around the building and found myself faced with at least twenty-five meters of completely exposed ground. As I sprinted uphill I could feel dirt and rubble kicking up all around me, lashing my bare legs. Small-arms fire, and it was coming from someplace close. I'd never felt anything quite like that before. It was harrowing in a way that rocket fire wasn't. There's something eerie about running away from gunfire, knowing that the enemy can see you well enough to put bullets at your feet. I remember thinking, *Holy shit, these are close.* I could feel my ankles bleeding from the spray of rocks.

While sprinting up the hill, zigzagging back and forth in the hope of presenting a more elusive target, I glanced into the woods just outside the wire. Muzzle flashes popped and sparked all around. They were so close, and there were so many of them—it was unlike any attack we had ever experienced. Out of sheer desperation, I began firing my 9-millimeter into the brush, peppering the muzzle flashes in a feeble attempt to dissuade the insurgents. But with only sixteen shots available (fifteen in the pistol's magazine and one in the chamber), there wasn't much I could do. Within what felt like no more than a few seconds, I was out of ammo. And I still had roughly 100 meters to cover before I reached the mortar pit.

I kept running as fast as I could, past the Humvee, where someone—I presumed it was still Mace—was perched in the turret and spraying the mountainside with a 50-caliber rifle.

"Mace! Mace! Friendly coming! Friendly coming!" I shouted, in the hope that he wouldn't confuse me with the Taliban. I don't think he heard me. I'm not even sure he saw me—he was so focused on fighting. And the Humvee was taking so much fire. As I ran past it, I could hear the bullets ricocheting off the armor.

Ping! Ping! Ping!

For a brief instant, I thought about taking cover beside the Humvee, but just as I was about to duck in, a rocket-propelled grenade came screeching in from above and ripped into the side of the Humvee, just above one of the tires. The concussive force of the explosion knocked me to the ground, but not before I saw Mace drop like a rag doll into the turret.

Shit . . . Mace is dead.

It's amazing how quickly you can process something like that. One minute you're talking to one of your buddies, and the next minute he's gone. And you have to keep moving, keep fighting, trying to stay alive.

As I scrambled to my feet I could see flames rising from the twisted wreckage of the Humvee.

"Mace!" I yelled. I heard a muffled response, or thought I heard something anyway, but I didn't have time to go check. Everything happened so fast.

What I would not find out until many hours later was that Mace's guard shift had ended just a few minutes after I had seen him in the morning and his place in the Humvee had been taken by Brad Larson. It was Larson rocking the 50-caliber, not Mace, and it was Larson who had disappeared into the turret. But he hadn't been killed. He'd been hit in the head by an armor-piercing round, and somehow his helmet had saved him. Larson later told me that as he fell he was certain that the bullet had pierced his skull.

When I reached the mortar pit, the first thing I saw was the massive frame of Kevin Thomson, coming out of our hooch (where we lived and slept when we weren't fighting), trying to pull his boots on while he walked. Thomson was still half-asleep, having only been roused a minute or two earlier by the crack of gunfire. It felt like the fight had already been going on for an eternity, but the truth is, we were just getting started. No more than five minutes had passed since the first rocket crashed into the COP. As I entered the compound on a dead run our eyes locked. Something about my demeanor must have told Thomson that this was no ordinary day.

"Shit!" he said. "Where they at?"

"RPG Rock! RPG Rock!" I shouted. "We gotta get fire down there!"

RPG Rock was a well-known enemy landmark, so named because insurgents would frequently gather at that position and use it as cover while launching rocket-propelled grenades. The two of us scrambled around the mortar pit. I grabbed our 240 machine gun and began to run, with Thomson, rifle in hand, beside me. The plan was simple: take our positions in the mortar pit and fight back. But we hadn't taken more than a couple steps when, out of the corner of my eye, I saw Thomson's rifle slip out of his hand.

Fuck!

I turned just in time to see his knees buckle. He hung in the air for a second, as if suspended by invisible wires. Thomson was a big guy, and to see him like that, nearly motionless in midair, was beyond comprehension. Finally he dropped and lay perfectly still on the ground.

I had seen a lot of men get shot, and I had seen a few get killed. There is a distinct difference between the two. When a man gets shot, he screams. He responds to the pain and the shock. This is usually a good thing, for it means he is still alive. But when a sniper's bullet perfectly finds its mark, there is quite a different result. The victim falls, quietly, without histrionics. When someone gets shot, the last thing you want to hear is . . . nothing.

Without saying a word, I unloaded roughly 300 rounds on the surrounding hillside, squeezing the trigger so hard that my hand started to go numb. I kept firing, letting up only when the barrel of my 240 got so hot that I thought it might melt. Enemy fire weakened briefly, giving me just enough time to check on Thomson, who was covered with empty shell casings from the 240. He hadn't moved since getting hit, so I feared the worst. I rolled him over. A bullet had shattered his cheekbone, just beneath the eye, and exited through his shoulder. He was dead before he hit the ground.

I felt a surge of anger and panic as I ran back into the living quarters and screamed at Sergeant Breeding, who was on the radio, trying to gather information and get enemy coordinates so that we could begin firing mortars.

"Thomson's dead," I told him.

Breeding said nothing at first. He seemed shocked. Later he would tell me that he had presumed that Thomson was the one who had been firing the 240. When the rockets had started coming in, Breeding had gotten on the radio and noticed that I was gone. He thought I was still down at the main base when he heard the 240 outside.

"Are you sure?" Breeding asked.

"Yeah, I'm fucking sure."

As I said, rank frequently goes out the window in the heat of combat, as does decorum. It was absolute chaos, and I was torn between doing my job and retrieving Thomson's body while it was still in one piece. He was my closest friend, and there was no way I was going to leave him out there. I also knew in my heart, although I couldn't really process the ramifications, that Thomson had taken a bullet that otherwise would have killed me. He had stepped between me and wherever the sniper had been located an instant before the shot was fired. To this day I think that bullet was meant for me. I'll never get over that.

I went back out, hooked Thomson under the arms, and tried to drag him a few feet. But then his body sort of turned sideways and got stuck just beyond the doorway. He was so big, and there was so much fire. An RPG came ripping into the compound and exploded only a few meters away. For a moment I lost my hearing and thought I might pass out. I realized then that I had screwed up. Thomson was gone, and by focusing on trying to retrieve his body, I had failed to provide adequate cover for my unit. So I went back inside.

We continued to fight. Well, some of us anyway. Barroga, at first, totally froze. As Breeding worked the radio and returned fire and I ran back and forth from the hooch to the doorway, shooting my weapon and then ducking for cover, the new guy just sat there, a blank look on his face.

"If you're not going to fight, you need to at least stand at the door"—to be clear, there wasn't an actual door, just a tarp we hung over the entrance—"and make sure nobody comes up behind me," I said to Barroga. "Can you at least do that?"

He nodded, but I had little faith in him. At the time I was so angry with Barroga that I almost wanted to kill him myself. I know that sounds crazy, but when you're under siege, your buddy has already been killed, and one of the three remaining men in your mortar pit refuses to even fire his pistol (he wasn't even sure how to remove the safety!), you sort of lose your mind. Looking back on it now, I realize that Barroga was shell-shocked. Here he was, less than a week into his first deployment, having been exposed to only a minimal amount of gunfire, and he finds himself in the middle of one of the bloodiest battles in the Afghanistan conflict. The guy was in way over his head. I get that. I just wish he hadn't been in our mortar pit when it happened.

From that point on we fought primarily from the hooch. We were totally isolated. For a good twenty to thirty minutes all we could do was hunker down and wait for a lull in the action. Anytime I would try to stick my head out to shoot or to get a round off, it was just like, *Ping! Ping! Ping!* Right on top of us. They couldn't have been more than thirty meters away.

Breeding worked the radio, communicating with First Lieutenant Andrew Bunderman at the tactical operations center (TOC). Through a series of events, Bunderman had been placed temporarily in command of Keating. Captain Porter had been reassigned, and Stoney Portis, the new commander, had yet to arrive. Both of them were at FOB Bostick taking part in a formal ceremony marking the change of command. That left COP Keating without a captain. Now, I'm not saying this is relevant in terms of what happened that day. It's not like we were lost without a captain, or that we didn't know how to do our jobs. I liked Lieutenant Bunderman. He was an unpretentious Midwesterner who knew his job. But the fact remains that in the event of a catastrophic invasion and loss of life, you'd better be able to demonstrate that all precautions were taken and that a proper chain of command was in place.

We took a lot of flak for not having a captain at COP Keating on the day of the Battle of Kamdesh. Bunderman, though, was solid. He tried to remain calm as he spoke with Breeding, but it was clear he needed our help.

"Can you get anything out there?" he shouted over the radio. "We need cover."

Breeding turned to me.

"Can we shoot?"

I shook my head.

"No fucking way. I can't even poke my head up, man. I'm sorry, I'm trying, but I can't even load the 240, let alone get out there far enough to use it."

Breeding calmly translated.

"Listen, we have no room. We've already taken one casualty. We have one KIA."

I shouted from the doorway: "We can't even drag his body in! He's getting lit up! We cannot support fire!"

The feeling of helplessness, of being unable to help our brothers when they were pleading for our assistance, was the worst of all. We wanted to fight, we wanted to help, but for most of the first hour we were completely pinned down. Any attempt to leave the hooch and go outside would have been tantamount to suicide. Forget about mortars—they were too far away and took too long to set up; it would have required at least forty-five seconds of prolonged exposure for two men just to fire a single mortar. In that time, under these conditions, both men would have been killed. Hell, I couldn't even go out and fire my M4 without being tagged at least three or four times. All I could do was reach up from my little hobbit-hole and take a few blind shots with my arms extended from beneath cover. We had sandbags surrounding the entrance to the hooch, and as soon as we tried to peer above the bags they'd start firing at us. For most of that first hour I didn't think there was any way we were going to survive.

And at some point I stopped caring. I just wanted an opportunity to go down fighting.

Things went from bad to worse when a rocket hit our generator and knocked out all internal communications. We were left with nothing but walkie-talkies. And that mode of communication was cut off shortly thereafter. I never found out exactly what happened, but one of our devices was hot-miked: the push-to-talk button was held down for a prolonged period of time, effectively preventing anyone else on that channel from talking. All anyone could do was listen to that one device. It's possible that the walkie-talkie was hot-miked when one of our soldiers was killed and fell on his device, engaging the push-to-talk function. Or it's possible that one of the Taliban gained possession of the device. Regardless, the loss of the walkie-talkies, coupled with the dead generator, left all of Keating in blackout mode. No one could talk to anyone.

From the mortar pit I could only imagine what had happened to COP Keating, but even my imagination was insufficient. By the time we lost communication, I'd later learn by reading official Army accounts of the battle and talking to my buddies, the insurgents had breached Keating's perimeter defenses in multiple places — including the main entrance, where civilian Afghan security guards were overrun, and the eastern side of the base, where Afghan National Army forces were stationed. A word about that. We later heard that the ANA troops responded with utter cowardice. When urged to stand and fight and to help provide support to the American troops at Keating, the ANA soldiers (if you can call them that) simply ran away. In video footage of the battle, you can actually see them fleeing, like rats from a sinking ship. Some of them even stole items from the base, both before retreating and during the actual battle.

I'd had little respect for the ANA troops before October 3, 2009 — they were sloppy, undisciplined, poorly trained, and disinterested in the fight, even though it was their country we were supposedly protecting. After that day, though, I had only contempt for them, even hatred.

Again, I didn't have a bird's-eye view of anything that was happening at this time. But here's what I know. Once inside Keating's perimeter, the insurgents set fire to much of the base and continued to push toward the center. Our soldiers pulled back and established a smaller perimeter deep within the compound. And from there, despite being vastly outnumbered, they fought heroically over the course of several hours. They gradually expanded the perimeter and regained control of much of the outpost. But it was a long and bloody effort.

Luck, fate, coincidence – all of these play a major part in any battle. I believe Kevin Thomson intercepted a bullet that was meant for me. He didn't do it intentionally, but it happened nonetheless. And I don't think that was the only time he saved my life that day. As maddening as it was to see Thomson's body stuck outside for most of the battle, I think it's quite likely that the very sight of him prompted the insurgents to overlook the fact that there were three other soldiers hunkered down in the mortar pit. While the perimeter was being breached, the Taliban literally walked right over the top of our compound on their way down to the main base. We could hear them laughing and cheering as they went by. There were probably two dozen of them – far too many for us to fight in close quarters. We couldn't come up and shoot, so we basically hid until there was a lull in the action. I can't say for sure why they didn't stop and investigate the mortar pit. They knew it was there. And they knew we had been firing randomly from that position when the attack first started. For some reason, though, they just ran right over us and kept going. My best guess is that they saw Thomson's body and figured that either the mortar pit had been abandoned or everyone inside was dead.

A few times I could hear them scurrying over the roof of our hooch. I could have almost reached out and grabbed their legs with my hand. And I wanted to do that. But it would have been suicidal. We were heavily outnumbered and outgunned. All we could do was wait until the heaviest waves passed and we regained communication with the TOC so that we would have some idea what was happening. We sat there motionless, quietly waiting for one of them to peer into the pit. If that happened, well ... we'd be dead almost instantly, but at least we'd be able to return fire. More frightening was the possibility that they would just toss a grenade into the pit.

But neither scenario transpired. Maybe we have Thomson to thank for that.

Here's another strange thing: I could hear the insurgents talking as they went by, and while I did not speak Farsi, the language most commonly spoken by the Afghans, I had picked up enough to recognize it when I heard it and to occasionally grasp the gist of a conversation. Much of what I heard being spoken was completely foreign – a different dialect, perhaps, or maybe even a different language. As it turned out, there was a reason for this. Many of the insurgents were probably not Afghan. One of our Afghan interpreters had gotten caught outside during the attack and ran for cover in a latrine. He spent the entire day hiding in a bathroom, praying that the bombs and gunfire would somehow not find their way into his meager shelter. And they didn't. He survived. Afterward he said that he had overheard a great deal of conversation among the enemy forces during the attack, and that much of it was unrecognizable. This is a guy who understood multiple tribal dialects. The only explanation?

"They were not Afghan," he said. "Probably Pakistani."

What does the possibility of Pakistani involvement mean? Well, it suggests a degree of organization and coalescence behind the attack that we simply had not anticipated. It also is just one more example of how unprepared we were for an ambush of this magnitude. When you're not taking casualties, when fighting becomes almost normal without being lethal, you stop thinking about worst-case scenarios. You figure everything will work out just fine because the enemy obviously does not have its shit together. But nothing could have been further from the truth. On more than one occasion that day I thought about how quickly the battle might have ended if Keating had been constructed in a more traditional manner. I thought back to my first day at the COP, when I'd been so surprised to discover that the mortar pit was 300 meters away from the base, tucked into the mountainside. Had the mortar pit been in the middle of Keating, we would have been able to fight back from the very beginning, and the outcome might have been different.

At Keating we had given the enemy every tactical advantage. And now there was a price to pay. What should have happened instead? When all hell broke loose, we should have been in the middle of the base, hunkered down in a true mortar pit where nothing could get us, even from the tallest mountains. We should have been dumping mortar rounds in all directions, just hanging hundreds of rounds anywhere they were needed. If that had been the setup, we would have had a chance. At the very least, we would have taken fewer casualties. But since we weren't set up conventionally, we were completely exposed – and thus helpless. A base that comes under heavy attack needs mortar support. Without it, the base is doomed. And this realization was what led me to do something really stupid.

"Hey, I'm going to make a run to go get the 60," I said to Breeding, referring to the smaller of the two mortars. Both guns were outside, no more than ten to fifteen meters from the hooch, which was normally a short distance but under the circumstances they might as well have been a mile away.

"No fucking way!" Breeding shouted.

"We can hang 60s from the hooch!" I pleaded. "It'll work!"

The 120 was too big and too heavy. There was no way to move it. And as I said, it was a two- or three-man job to set up and fire the thing anyway. But the 60-millimeter could be carried and operated by one person. It seemed worth the risk. Breeding disagreed.

"You stay right here!" he ordered.

Fear washes over you in waves during battle. There are moments of complete shit-your-pants terror, and there are moments when you so thoroughly don't give a damn that you do crazy, irrational things. The moment Breeding turned his back I ran out of the hooch, unarmed, and sprinted toward the mortars. It was one of the scariest feelings I had the entire day. I didn't even look around, just twisted the gun off its baseplate, grabbed a can of ammo, and started to run back. As I turned to face the hooch, however, I found myself not forty feet from one of the insurgents. With his back to me and a gun over his shoulder, he was moving his hands, clearly directing a group of people some distance away. I remember thinking, again, how lucky I was: if he had been facing the mortar pit when I emerged, he could have easily mowed me down. But he never saw me. I ran back into the hooch, got chewed out by Breeding, and went back to fighting.

At least two hours passed before partial communication was reestablished using a backup generator. After that, we were able to get a better sense of what was happening throughout the base. I had feared at first that Keating had been completely and quickly overrun. Was it possible that there were dozens of dead American soldiers? Yes. That seemed like a legitimate outcome. But it soon became apparent that the men of 3-61 were putting up one hell of a fight.

"We've got men moving!" someone shouted through the intercom. "We're trying to get ammo and recover a dead soldier!"

The fight became semicoordinated, with small groups responding simultaneously from different positions.

"If anyone can hear this, give fire on three! One ... two ... *three!*"

And then everyone would spring from their positions, blazing away with whatever weapons they had at their disposal. I would simply reach out and spray the area around the mortar pit, hoping to hit something, anything.

Every so often the enemy fire would briefly subside, and I'd take another run at Thomson, low-crawling out to his position and trying in vain to pull him back. And then I got an idea: I knew that Hammel had given Thomson his M203 grenade launcher when he went on leave. And I knew that Thomson had been carrying it with him when he went down. We had a couple hundred rounds of 203 ammo in the pit; if we could get the launcher, it would greatly enhance our fighting position. If we couldn't fire mortars, 203 rounds were the next best option. And they could be fired easily by one person, almost like using a gun.

So I crawled out, unhooked the 203 from Thomson's shoulder, where it had been slung, and retreated back to the hooch. Suddenly I heard a blast and felt something tear into my shoulder. It was high, near my neck. Everyone does an instinctive self-triage when they get hit, or even when there is a blast in the vicinity. For me, it was always the same thing: assuming I hadn't been knocked unconscious, which would mean a head wound, I'd wiggle my fingers and toes. So I did that. Everything worked.

Great — no paralysis.

But then I felt the white-hot sting of shrapnel on my skin. I put a hand under my shirt and withdrew a puddle of blood. For a moment I started to freak out, but the bleeding did not get any worse and I never became light-headed. Once again I'd been lucky: I'd only been grazed.

I grabbed the bucket of 203 rounds and low-crawled back toward the entrance, closer to Thomson's body, where I'd have some minimal cover but also some clearance for the grenade launcher. I was sitting down, back against a wall. The 203 is a shoulder-fire weapon, but there wasn't room for that. I would have had to stand up and lean out into the line of fire. Instead, I shoved the butt of the 203 into the ground, and pointed the muzzle at roughly a forty-five-degree angle. Then I fed some ammo and pulled the trigger. Just like a mortar.

Fwoomp!

The grenade exited cleanly. A few seconds later came a loud report.

Boom!

I had no idea whatsoever where the grenade had landed. For all I knew it might have killed two or three Taliban. Or none. It was an act of desperation. I loaded another. Pulled the trigger again.

Fwoomp!

Boom!

I loaded a third . . . and a fourth. I kept launching. Over and over, hoping to hit something . . . anything. Hoping that a barrage of grenades, even if launched blindly, would have some sort of deterrent effect. I don't know exactly how many I launched in that initial volley. Probably fifty or sixty. At the time it seemed feeble, hopeless . . . a waste of ammunition. In retrospect, though, I think it helped. Whether my grenade attack diminished the size and strength of their force, I don't know. But I'd like to think it sent a message: we're here, we're armed, and we're fighting.

The battle began to turn in our favor after several hours, when OP Fritsche was stabilized. Finally we'd have mortar support! But it wasn't that simple. Mortar systems have become increasingly sophisticated, utilizing advanced computer technology to achieve a ridiculous degree of accuracy. Once the guns have been properly calibrated, all you have to do is plug the proper coordinates into something known as a light handheld mortar ballistic computer (LHMBC), and you're good to go. Unfortunately, the LHMBC at Fritsche got knocked out during the attack, leaving them with two options: fire blindly in the general vicinity of Keating's perimeter and hope for the best, or withhold mortar fire entirely.

Neither option was acceptable.

"Tell them to give me their grid," I told Breeding, who was still working the radio. "I'll plug the info into our system."

"You talk to them," Breeding said.

It made sense. Breeding was in charge of the mortar pit, but he had never been trained on the new system. I got on the radio with Lieutenant Jordan Bellamy at Fritsche, and we began walking through a complicated and risky process in which I would use our LHMBC to try to figure out the proper coordinates for their gun system. I would be directing rounds at Keating, from Frit-sche.

"I need a ten-digit grid to your baseplate at Fritsche," I said. "If it's not yours, just get me within like ten feet of your baseplate. Get me as close as possible."

Bellamy gave me the ten-digit grid, I wrote it down, plugged the info into my LHMBC, and began setting up the gun system from a remote location.

"Where's Stickney?" I asked. Stickney was stationed at Frit-sche. Breeding and I had trained him. He was my boy. I trusted him. "I need to talk to him."

I asked Stickney exactly how he had laid in his gun, meaning how he had calibrated it. That information would allow me to provide a more accurate target setting. The slightest variation and Fritsche's mortar fire, designed to take the heat off Keating, could instead end up killing a number of our own troops. I entered the information, the LHMBC spat out a new code, and I relayed it to Stickney. The goal was to have mortar fire all around us, but not within fifty to seventy-five meters of our compound. It was an in-exact science, though, to put it mildly.

"If this thing comes in on top of us, we are fucked!" Breeding said. He almost seemed to be smiling. We had reached the point of lunacy.

"Put the first one on delay," I told Stickney. That way, if the mortar landed too close to our hooch, it would burrow a foot or two into the ground before detonating, rather than exploding on impact. That would ensure a smaller spread of shrapnel.

Within seconds the first round came in. It landed almost ex-actly where we wanted it to land, approximately seventy-five meters away. And then there were more, crashing all around us. With the help of a forward observer at Keating, we kept relaying coordinates to Fritsche and they kept hammering the perimeter with mortars. Eventually their support allowed us to get back in the fight.

"Hey, Sergeant, cover me," I said to Barroga. "I'm going to go get some more rounds." For whatever reason, Barroga snapped to life and began fighting. He fired his gun repeatedly, covering me while I ran to grab some more 60-millimeter rounds for the smaller mortar.

And then we did something really unconventional. We put the baseplate of the smaller mortar inside the hooch – right where we slept – and fired mortars out the door, downrange toward Keating. I got on one knee and tucked behind the gun. Then Sergeant Breeding crouched behind me to hold me in place so that the recoil wouldn't knock me on my ass. I put the barrel of the mortar at an angle and fired. If my aim was off by a foot or more, I'd blow off the roof of the hooch and kill all of us.

There was a familiar sound . . .

Fwoomp!

And then . . . nothing. The mortar cleared the hooch, sailed downrange, and exploded. My goal was to hit the ANA compound, which I knew had been overrun by the Taliban. But I misjudged the distance and nearly killed one of our own guys.

"We've got indirect!" he shouted over the intercom.

"No, that's us!" Breeding explained. "It's friendly!"

"Make the next one fifty meters farther!" came the order.

And so we did. Or we tried to, anyway. I loaded the mortar and fired.

Fwoomp!

As the shell sailed I felt terrific pain in my calf, like someone had hit me with a sledgehammer. The baseplate had come loose when I fired the gun, and the recoil had driven it into my leg.

"Fuck!"

"You all right?" Breeding asked.

Not really. I'd have a deep-tissue bruise that would leave me with a limp for months to come and could have developed into a blood clot. Comparatively speaking, though, I was fine. By this point, of course, we had revealed our position. If the enemy had thought the mortar pit was deserted or lacking firepower, they no

Daniel on Christmas Day. A future football star—and lifelong Washington Redskins fan.

Young Daniel, with his father, Ray Rodriguez.

Rodriguez, fresh out of boot camp.
U.S. Army Photo

All photos are courtesy of the author unless otherwise noted.

A lighter moment on the streets of Baghdad. Daniel (front row, center) with (going counterclockwise) First Lieutenant Luke Pereira, Sergeant Josh Emanuel, medic Tomas Rivera, and Jeremy Snell.

On patrol in Baghdad, Daniel hoists an AT84, an antitank shoulder-fire weapon.

Sergeant Josh Emanuel, on patrol in Baghdad.

Daniel gets a warm greeting from his mother, Cecilia, and his sister, Veronica, at Fort Carson, Colorado, after returning from deployment to Iraq.

Daniel with his weapon, preparing to go out on patrol, with the mountains of Afghanistan looming in the background.

Half a world away from home, a group of US soldiers plays a game of pickup football in Afghanistan on Christmas Day.

Kevin Thomson and Sergeant John Breeding in the mortar pit at COP Keating.

Kevin Thomson works on laying in his gun (in this case a 60-millimeter mortar) while Daniel offers instructions.

Daniel and John Hammel react to the force of a 120-millimeter shell being fired.

In the aftermath of a firefight, the ground in the mortar pit is littered with spent shells. Pictured (left to right) are Daniel, Kevin Thomson, and John Hammel.

A sleeping barracks still smolders the day after the attack on COP Keating.

General George W. Casey, chief of staff of the US Army, shakes hands with Daniel after presenting him with the Bronze Star with Valor during a ceremony at Bagram Airfield. *Photo by Sgt. Elizabeth Raney / Defense Video & Imagery Distribution System*

Daniel hugs his sister, Veronica, at Reagan International Airport after returning from Afghanistan.

Daniel holding the Purple Heart and Bronze Star with Valor, the two medals he received following the Battle of Kamdesh.
Brownie Harris / ESPN

Daniel looks out over the Aquia Creek near his home in Virginia, and contemplates his future after coming home from Afghanistan.

Daniel pushing himself to the limit while training for a shot at playing Division I college football.

Legendary television journalist Dan Rather poses with Daniel in the hallway of Brooke Point High School. Rather was among the first journalists to bring Daniel's story to a national audience.

Daniel celebrates another Clemson victory with his good friend Stephen Batt as fans gather nearby.

Daniel holds the American flag while leading his teammates onto the field before a game against Virginia Tech on Military Appreciation Day in October 2012.
Corbis/AP Photo, Rainier Ehrhardt

Daniel in his Clemson University football uniform.
Clemson Universoty/Ashley N. Jones

longer labored under such illusions. Before firing each mortar, we had to pull the tarp to the side. As the shell left the hooch the tarp would flap in the breeze, another clear signal of activity.

No sooner had the tarp fallen back over the entrance after one of our volleys than an RPG came screeching into the compound. It crashed into the dirt just outside the doorway, exploding on impact and sending debris and shrapnel through the tarp. The force of the blast knocked me back into Breeding. I lost control of the mortar tube and watched in horror as a round fell to the ground and wobbled across the floor. Mortar rounds are not supposed to detonate when dropped in this manner, but . . . you never know.

I was dazed, still trying to process what had happened, when I felt something hot on my neck. The pain increased, as if someone was holding a flame to my skin. I reached up and touched something strange – a large patch of rough skin, burning hot – and I started to panic.

"Oh God!" I yelled. "God, no!"

I was holding my neck, afraid to let go. I thought if I just kept my hand over the wound, everything would be okay. If I let go, my carotid artery would immediately begin pumping blood like a fire hose, and I'd be dead in minutes. Or so I thought. I'd held it together reasonably well until that moment, but for some reason I was now gripped by fear and anxiety. I thought for sure I was dying.

Breeding knew otherwise.

"Move your hand, goddammit!"

"No, no, no!"

"Let me look at it."

Breeding pried apart my fingers and immediately assessed the damage as unworthy of such a display of histrionics.

"You're going to be fine."

Only a small piece of shrapnel, maybe the size of a dime, had slipped through the tarp, and although it lodged in a vulnerable spot, it had been so hot that it immediately cauterized the wound. There was actually very little blood, but it hurt like hell. I ran my hand over the wound again; a portion of the shrapnel protruded from the skin.

"You pussy," Breeding said. Then he grabbed a pair of Gerber pliers, put a hand on the side of my head for leverage, and quickly extracted the piece of metal, like it was a giant splinter. He held it up for me to see.

"You think that's shrapnel, bitch? This is shrapnel!"

He lifted his pant leg to reveal a calf that was shrunken to half its normal size. This was not a surprise to me. I knew that Breeding had nearly lost his leg to a roadside bomb in Iraq. I'd heard the story, and I'd seen the evidence. But I guess, under the circumstances, he thought it was appropriate to remind me. A little heavy-handed, perhaps, but that was Breeding. Like I said, the dude was old school.

Hours passed—hours in which we launched more 60-millimeter mortars and threw dozens of hand grenades and fired thousands of rounds of ammunition. We were doing our best to provide as much support as we possibly could, even though we remained pinned down the entire time.

There were multiple times when I thought we wouldn't make it out alive. At one point I cooked a grenade ("cooking" is the terrifying practice of pulling the pin from a grenade and holding it for a while before throwing it, in the hope that it will explode as quickly as possible after release) because I knew there were insurgents close by. I peeked up over the sandbags and spotted two men, just standing there, talking. And then they stopped talking. One of them turned and looked right at me. He couldn't have been more than thirty feet away. At that moment I remembered that I had already pulled the pin on the grenade, so I just chucked it. It exploded in the air, virtually on top of them, killing both men instantly. I remember having the strangest reaction as I watched their bodies disintegrate. I wasn't appalled or disgusted. I was thrilled. I had killed two men with one grenade. Usually that only happened in video games.

If you think that sounds cold or harsh, well, so be it. War makes us all something less than human. And something more.

Eventually the Apache helicopters and the A-10 and F-14 jets came in and lit up the hills outside the wire. At first they were wary of firing, out of concern that they might hit American troops. But we were all trapped inside the wire. I remember hearing the communication over the intercom, listening to Bunderman as he talked with the fighter pilots.

"Are you sure all the Americans are inside the wire?" one of the pilots asked.

"Roger. There are no friendlies outside. Everything you see is danger," Bunderman replied.

"Are you 100 percent sure?"

"Yes! Just drop the bomb! Please! Drop the fucking bomb!"

There was silence for a moment. And then I remember distinctly hearing Bunderman say, "Godspeed. God be with you."

I'm not sure how much time passed before the bomb hit. Maybe twenty seconds. I'd never felt anything like it. The entire mountain valley seemed to shake. Our hooch rattled and rumbled; I worried that it would collapse on top of us and that we'd be buried alive. More followed, and each time I heard the order to drop one of the bombs, I ran into the hooch and slid underneath my bunk and gripped the legs for stability. I'd count down from twenty, gritting my teeth and praying it wouldn't land too close to our position. The fighter jets had been instructed to bomb only locations outside the wire, but of course the mortar pit was as close to the perimeter as any position at Keating.

Later in the day two massive B-52 bombers arrived on the scene. There is a military term for what happened next: "going Winchester." It basically means to deplete all ammunition. Going Winchester in this context meant that the B-52s dropped an entire payload – thousands of pounds of bombs – at one time, in one place. It was a fairly common tactic in World War II and in Vietnam. But it had happened only once in Afghanistan since US involvement began in 2001.

On October 3, 2009, in the Battle of Kamdesh, it happened twice.

The Afghans made videos of the fight in which you can see the Taliban forces funneling from the east side of the base like ants. If that bombardment had made it through, I wouldn't be writing these words right now. We would have been outnumbered inside the wire, with air support unable to safely provide assistance. In all likelihood, none of us would have survived. But the Apaches opened fire and instantly killed thirty to forty people, giving us enough time and space to defend our position until reinforcements from the 10th Mountain Division arrived and helped secure the perimeter.

Not that there was much left by the end of the day. Keating looked like something out of Armageddon. Nearly every structure had been either blown up or burned, thanks to the RPG-7s employed by the Taliban. Manufactured by the Chinese with maximum devastation in mind, the RPG-7 is a truly nasty fucker: the tip of its shell is filled with kerosene, so that it not only explodes on impact but also spits flames in all directions. Hours after the fighting had ended, fire smoldered throughout what was left of the COP.

There were bodies everywhere, inside and outside the wire. We lost eight American soldiers; another twenty-seven were wounded. My buddy Mace was among the men who did not make it out that day. He and three others had joined Larson in the armored Humvee shortly after the attack began, in an effort to protect the outpost from the insurgents. With RPGs strafing the side of the vehicle, the men separated. Mace was shot and hit by shrapnel and nearly bled out on the battlefield. He was rescued by Specialist Ty Carter, who, under heavy enemy fire, applied tourniquets and pulled Mace under cover. (Carter would later receive the Medal of Honor for his heroics.) Mace eventually made it back to the aid station, where Chris Cordova employed a rare battlefield transfusion in an effort to save his life. Cordova stabilized Mace and, against all odds, got him onto a chopper, still talking, still very much alive, more than twelve hours after the fighting had begun. Not until early the next morning did we hear that Stephan Mace had died on the operating table.

As for the Taliban, well, we counted at least 125 dead. We left the corpses where they were. The next day we were given the green light to shoot anyone deemed an unfriendly; it was all we could do to refrain from firing at those who were merely trying to collect bodies, using bags that we had supplied.

Within seventy-two hours, COP Keating had been evacuated. What remained of the base was bombed and burned by American forces to prevent the Taliban from recovering any of our equipment. Our footprint was essentially wiped away.

9

A T FIRST I COULDN'T sleep. Later, I didn't want to sleep, because sleep became the enemy.

Let me explain . . .

The heavy fighting at COP Keating ended around sundown on October 3, although sporadic bombing and gunfire would continue for several more hours. Sometime well after midnight I lay down on my bunk in the mortar pit and closed my eyes. I'd never been so exhausted, but sleep would not come. My heart beat furiously. I put a hand over my chest; it felt as though my ribs were going to separate and my heart would spill out. This was not a panic attack. This was the residual effect of twelve hours of combat—an adrenaline rush so severe that my body was still in fight mode. And it would remain in that state for the better part of forty-eight hours. I did not sleep at all that night, or the next day. I staggered around the base, trying to pitch in with cleanup. I started hallucinating. For a while I wasn't sure whether I was awake or dreaming.

"Dude, take a nap," one of the boys from the 10th Mountain Division said to me. "We've got you covered."

They knew we were fucked up, physically and emotionally,

and they wanted to ease some of our burden. But there was only so much they could do. Keating had become almost like a mass gravesite; simply being there, where our friends had fallen, was too much to bear.

When my body finally gave out and I fell asleep, there was no relief. The unconscious mind is a formidable foe, capable of capturing and projecting horrific images and thoughts. It started for me immediately after the Battle of Kamdesh and did not relent for months . . . even years. Most common were dreams involving some type of explosion. I'd be fighting, or just hanging out with my friends – with Thomson and Mace – and suddenly the bombs would begin falling. RPGs would whistle into the compound. Or, in my mind's eye, we'd be sitting together in a Humvee that had rolled over an IED. Suddenly there was chaos, carnage everywhere. Body parts floating in midair, people screaming and crying. I'd hear Mace and Thomson wailing, pleading for assistance, but I couldn't find them, couldn't help them. And then I'd look down and realize that my legs had been blown off. There was so much blood. I'd try to put myself back together, scooping blood and gore like water from a sink. I'd try to call for help, but no words would come out. I was frozen, paralyzed by a fear that was every bit as real and consuming as what I'd felt in combat.

I'm dying . . .

And then I'd wake up, sometimes quietly, sometimes whimpering, always drenched in sweat, my heart pounding.

There was another recurring dream, even worse, involving a sniper's bullet. Sometimes I'd get hit in the face, sometimes in the back of the head. There was never any pain. I'd be sitting there alone, feeling fine, and then there would be the crack of a rifle and a blinding flash, and suddenly I'd be facedown in the dirt, unable to see, but aware that I'd been shot. I could reach around and feel the entry wound, wet and sticky. Sometimes there wouldn't be an entry wound, and then I knew the bullet had entered through my eye. Waves of red would flood across an imaginary screen. I was drowning, unable to move, choking. Dead but alive.

Dreams can mess with you regardless of setting. They come out of nowhere, long after you've returned stateside, and grab you by the throat and toss you right back out onto the battlefield, squirming and scared. I still have them sometimes, and they are no less terrifying now than they were four or five years ago. But I've learned to deal with them. Worse are the nightmares that come while you're still on deployment. Those can lead to madness. You go to bed one night and dream about getting shot while on patrol, and then you wake up the next morning thinking maybe it's not such a good idea to go out that day.

Intuition . . . bad juju . . .

Call it what you will, but it can destroy your spirit and damage morale throughout a platoon.

"Man, I got a bad feeling about this one," someone will say just before boarding a truck to go out on patrol. "Had a dream last night that—"

"Shut the fuck up! Don't bring that shit over here."

I tried not to say anything like that. I tried to swallow my nightmares and keep them to myself. But the truth is, I wandered around in a fog for the rest of my deployment, and for much of the next couple years, overwhelmed by guilt and confusion. I still have my duffel bag from Keating. It's riddled with so many holes that it's almost like a sieve. I keep it in my closet, with the gear I wore that day—the vest and helmet and the blood-spattered Pumas. Sometimes—though not as often now as when I first returned—I'll go through the bag, and I'll find the occasional piece of shrapnel, and I'll think, *How the hell did I survive? Why am I still here?* I look at this gear now more out of a sense of gratitude, to remind myself of how lucky I am to have gotten through that day and to have a second chance at life. If ever there was a day to go, that would have been it. For some reason, though, the angels did not call my name. I don't know why. There is no explanation for it. I understand that now. But for the longest time I couldn't deal with the randomness of it all—the fact that there was no reason for my being alive when so many others had been killed.

Why had I been granted a reprieve? What had I done to deserve it?

Not a damn thing.

In the wake of a lethal battle, the Army has several obligations, perhaps none more pressing, and certainly none more sobering, than notifying the next of kin that they have lost someone in combat. Thanks to the nature of social media and the twenty-four-hour news cycle, the military no longer has the luxury of waiting until the details of fatalities have been sorted out. So, for better or worse, controlling the flow of information means getting the information out as quickly as possible. When a serviceman is killed, there is an immediate and urgent need to inform his family, and sometimes that urgency can lead to mistakes. The risk of error is naturally compounded when the fight is as complicated and catastrophic as the Battle of Kamdesh.

For roughly ten to twelve hours, I was dead.

Officially, I mean. Somewhere along the line, as the battle unfolded and casualties were reported, my name had been added to the list of those who had fallen.

"Rodriguez?" someone had said to me the next morning. "We have you down as KIA."

"What?! Did you tell my mom? My sister?"

"I'm not sure."

I had heard stories about this sort of thing happening – of loved ones being told prematurely, and incorrectly, that they had lost a son or a husband in combat – but I figured they were just that: stories. I mean, the Army couldn't really screw up that badly, right? Well, in my case they very nearly did. Fortunately, the Army insists on breaking the worst possible news in person; phone calls and e-mails are unacceptable. The men assigned to tell my mother and sister of my death had already left their base and were well on their way. Thankfully, they were recalled before reaching their destination, and I was able to contact my family and let them know that I was safe. They had been worried, of course, because by now news of the battle at COP Keating had gotten out. Details were sketchy, but there were fatalities. It was only natural for anyone with a friend or family member stationed in that part of Afghanistan to fear the worst.

I didn't feel the full weight of the battle until a couple weeks later, when the Army held a ceremony at Bostick to honor the men who had been wounded or killed while distinguishing themselves on the battlefield. The Battle of Kamdesh would eventually (because the long and complicated process for recognizing valor on the battlefield involves arduous and exhaustive investigation) produce dozens of medals: twenty-seven Purple Hearts, thirty-seven Army Commendation Medals with "V" devices (for valor), three Bronze Stars, eighteen Bronze Stars with "V" devices, and nine Silver Stars. In addition, Staff Sergeant Ty Carter and Staff Sergeant Clinton Romesha would both receive the military's highest honor, the Medal of Honor, for their actions at Keating.

The ceremony at Bostick, though, was not about the awarding of medals; it was simply to recognize those who had made the ultimate sacrifice, to remember the friends we had lost:

Sergeant Justin T. Gallegos
Specialist Christopher T. Griffin
Sergeant Joshua M. Hardt
Sergeant Joshua J. Kirk
Specialist Stephan L. Mace
Staff Sergeant Vernon W. Martin
Sergeant Michael P. Scusa
Private First-Class Kevin C. Thomson

In the days and weeks after Keating was overrun, I had kept mostly to myself. A lot of soldiers went immediately into counseling, trying to talk through things with psychologists and clergymen, both available at Bostick. I felt neither the need nor the desire to do that. I told myself I was fine. This was not true, but it was easier to deny my feelings than to endure the grieving process.

A couple days before the ceremony, Sergeant Breeding stopped by the gym while I was working out to explain how the ceremony would be conducted. Each of the fallen soldiers would be eulogized by one of his fellow soldiers.

"The other guys are all in agreement: they think you should do Thomson's eulogy," Breeding said. "Are you up to it?"

"Sure. What's involved?"

Breeding shrugged.

"Just speak from the heart."

I have an uncomfortable relationship with emotion, and especially with grief. I don't like to show it, and most of the time I'm pretty good at not showing it. I've been this way as far back as I can remember. Under most circumstances, I can talk about my father's death, or a friend's death, and it doesn't damage me. It doesn't really even hurt. If I'm speaking to a reporter or standing up in front of a classroom, I can get outside my own body and just tell the story. It flows naturally and comfortably. But as soon as I go to Arlington to see my friends' gravesites, or to Quantico National Cemetery to visit my dad's grave, I lose it. If I have to talk on behalf of somebody, in front of a like-minded audience – in front of people whose suffering is similar to my own – I start crying.

I walked up to the podium at my father's funeral thinking that everything was okay and that I was in control of my emotions. I couldn't even get through the eulogy.

My father could be tough, but I never doubted his love for me; I never doubted that he considered being a father the most important role in his life. He talked about it often.

"You only have one time, one chance to raise your child," he'd say. "And I'm going to do everything I can until the day I die to make sure I did it the right way."

I relayed that anecdote at my father's funeral. Or I tried to anyway. By the end I was too choked up to convey much of anything.

It was the same way with Kevin Thomson. I had written some notes down on a sheet of paper, inside jokes and personal references – things that would make the other guys laugh, help us remember Thomson the way he was: funny, quirky, good-hearted, simple. A lot of soldiers at Keating were high-strung and anxious; it was a by-product of the job. Not Thomson. Give the guy a cigarette and a blueberry Pop-Tart and he was good to go. He was as low-maintenance as a soldier could be. I was going to talk about all the mundane, goofy stuff that goes into a friendship rather than the heartbreaking events of October 3. I wanted to keep it light.

The ceremony was outdoors, in the middle of the compound, with probably seventy-five people in attendance. With a whole speech outlined, I started off well, sailed through the first couple jokes, got a few chuckles ... and then I looked up at the audience, at all the guys who had been with us at Keating. Some were smiling. Some were crying. And my throat tightened. My eyes watered. Suddenly I could barely speak. Every word triggered a flood of emotion. I barely got through it.

Setting is important. Context is important. I'm in control most of the time and present to the public an image of stoicism and survival, of adjustment. But it's an ongoing process. Sometimes, when nobody is around, I lose it. I just do. The first time I ever saw my father cry was while we were watching *Saving Private Ryan* together. I was just a kid who thought it was a badass movie. Made me want to be a sniper or storm the enemy beach under withering fire. I remember looking over at my father and seeing him cry and having no idea what was bothering him.

Then I came home from two tours of duty, in Iraq and Afghanistan, and one night I turned on the television and there was *Saving Private Ryan*. Talk about a different perspective. I sat there alone, slumped in a chair, letting the images wash over me, sobbing like a baby. Honestly, I don't think I had ever cried so hard. For the first time I knew the suffering behind the movie, and why it was important. I felt the burden of service, of having been to war, of having seen my friends killed, of having taken lives myself.

The hardest part, still, is acting like there is no burden. Regardless of what I have become, or what I will become in life, I will always struggle to shed that vest of negativity. Like anyone who has been in battle, I carry the scars forever, whether they can be seen or not. I'm trying so hard to be something positive to people who have gone through what I've gone through, or who are struggling in some way, but it's hard, because I have my issues too.

I've cried about my father twice since his funeral: the first time, as I said, was one starry night in Iraq. The second time was only about a year ago, when I visited his gravesite and talked as if he could hear me:

"I wish I could show you what I've become. I wish I could tell you that you raised your son the right way. I was a fuck-up when you were alive, and I'm sorry about that. I am so sorry. But I've learned . . . I've learned. You didn't fail, Dad, in what you tried to do."

It's true that we don't appreciate what we have in life until it's gone. I know my father would be proud of me, but it still hurts not to be able to share things with him. It hurts knowing that he died before I had a chance to tell him that he meant the world to me. And it hurts to know the truth: that in the last year or two of his life I was too busy getting high and hanging out with my friends to spend time with my father, to play one more game of catch. I was too busy, too selfish.

That's why I am so ambivalent about the medals I've received. I understand what they represent. I understand that they give strength and hope to others, and that by accepting the medals with humility and respect, I honor those who have fallen. The medals represent something larger than me.

But I would gladly trade them in for a chance to talk with my father once more, or to see any of my buddies who died at Keating and tell them, "You guys are the heroes! I get credit on your behalf. I get medals and awards and praise because of your deaths. It's not right. I didn't do shit. You guys paid the ultimate sacrifice. Why should I reap the benefit?"

· · ·

Several months later, after my deployment had ended and I had returned to the United States, there was another ceremony at Fort Carson. This one was for the families of the fallen soldiers. By this point I thought I was doing pretty well; I thought I had come to terms with what I had seen and done in Afghanistan, and with the loss I had experienced. And then suddenly there I was, in a room with children who had lost their fathers, with mothers who had lost their sons, with wives who had lost their husbands. And it was the saddest thing in the world. Our names were called, and one by one we stood up. And at the end they called the names of the missing . . . the dead.

"Private First-Class Kevin Christopher Thomson . . . Private First-Class Kevin Christopher Thomson . . . Private First-Class Kevin Christopher Thomson."

Just like that — three times. A somber pause between each pronouncement.

"Specialist Stephan Lee Mace . . . Specialist Stephan Lee Mace . . . Specialist Stephan Lee Mace."

This was done for each of the missing soldiers from the 4th Infantry Division. Why the repeated calling? I don't know. Out of respect and admiration, I suppose. But I couldn't help but wonder about the families in attendance, and the children hearing the names of their fathers. What were they thinking? Had Daddy not been paying attention? Was he in a back room somewhere? Would he magically appear on the second or third try?

No, he wasn't coming back. Not now. Not ever. None of them were. As I looked out over the room and heard the muffled sounds of grief, the crying and the sniffling, I couldn't help but think that there had been some sort of cosmic mistake.

Why them? Why not me?

10

ADOG HELPED SAVE ME.

She was a Chesapeake Bay Retriever that I raised from a pup. This was the fall of 2010. I'd come home in September and officially separated from the Army on October 10, a little more than one year after the Battle of Kamdesh. I lived with my sister and her husband, but they both had busy lives and traveled a lot for work, so I was alone most of the time. Alone with my thoughts and regrets. Alone with my anger and depression.

As is true with a lot of vets, the first few months back home were the hardest for me. I spent a lot of time sleeping and drinking, feeling sorry for myself, questioning what I could have done differently to help the friends I'd lost overseas. Post-traumatic stress disorder? Yeah, I guess so. I don't know what else you'd call it. I passed the day hanging out at home, watching television, supporting myself mostly with the money I'd saved when I was in the Army, but also collecting unemployment. For a while I felt entitled. Until one day I started thinking about my father and found myself imagining how he'd react to the idea of his son taking a handout. Jesus, he would have punched me in the face.

I don't want to make any of this sound easier than it was. The truth is, PTSD is a very real and serious problem facing many veterans, and it hit me hard. When I got home, I felt totally empty and alone. I was in a relationship but probably shouldn't have been, because I was an extremely confused and difficult person to be around.

Alexis and I had known each other for years; we'd gone to Brooke Point High School together. We were friends, got along great, but that's all it was: a friendship. Until I came home on leave from Afghanistan in late November 2009, roughly six weeks after the Battle of Kamdesh. We ran into each other one night, started talking and reminiscing and connecting in a way that I had not anticipated. Alexis was a senior at Virginia Tech at the time, as confident and friendly as I remembered; she hadn't really changed much since high school. I, on the other hand, had undergone an enormous transformation. I'd experienced combat deployments in both Iraq and Afghanistan. I'd lived through one of the worst battles in either place. I had only a few minor physical scars to show for it, but I was deeply and profoundly screwed up from an emotional standpoint. I was drowning, and Alexis threw me a lifeline. I grabbed it and hung on.

I want to be fair to Alexis, to acknowledge how much that relationship meant to me, and how important it was at the time. I don't want to demean her by understating what we had together. It wasn't just a fluke. There were good times and bad times, as there are in most relationships, and I definitely fell in love with her. But the truth is, ours was a more tumultuous relationship than most, for the simple reason that I was not a stable person. At the time we reconnected I was on a two-week hiatus from hell. I was absolutely certain that I was going to return to Afghanistan and die. So the relationship didn't exactly start from a healthy place; it started from a place of fear and desperation.

It happened so fast. A two-week romance, followed by six months of sporadic long-distance communication. Alexis was great. She would write long, heartfelt letters and send care packages to Bostick, where I spent the remainder of my deployment. I went on a lot of patrols those last few months, and every day I was sure that I wouldn't come back. I had convinced myself that by surviving the Battle of Kamdesh, I had used up whatever good karma was due to me. I wasn't alone in feeling this way, incidentally. It's a fairly common experience for soldiers who avoid death in one setting to presume that their luck has run out. And it wasn't like I freaked out about it; I just figured my time would come. I didn't deserve to be alive anyway. I should have died alongside Mace and Thomson and the others.

Alexis did her best to provide a counterpoint to that argument. She cared about me, she loved me. And I loved her. She was a reason to come home, a reason to live. I needed that in the worst way. But things went downhill really fast after I returned, when the full scope of my PTSD became apparent. I still have guilt about that. I deprived her of her last semester in college, which not only is supposed to be one of the most enjoyable times of your life, but is also a time when girls – contemporary Southern girls – are usually trying to connect with someone who might be a viable lifelong partner. A husband, in other words.

I wasn't that man.

I knew she wanted marriage out of me; I knew she wanted me to go back to school and follow a traditional path, one that would quickly include children and a solid career. I had certainly led her to believe that this was what I wanted as well. I would be leaving the Army in the summertime, and then, I said, we could get a place together and begin planning a wedding, and I'd enroll in community college and everything would be rainbows and sunshine. Except that once I got home, we both discovered that I wasn't even much of a boyfriend or roommate, let alone someone who should get married. We fought constantly, broke up at least half a dozen times. Each little separation would end with me running back, tail between my legs, deeply apologetic for being such an asshole.

"I'll treat you better," I'd say. "I promise."

And I would . . . for a while. Then I'd go back to being distant and depressed and generally more concerned with self-medicating through marijuana and alcohol than with figuring out how I was going to get on with my life. The fact is, I was not ready to be in a relationship, and both Alexis and her family (who were all there for me) deserved better. I should have been honest; I should have been stronger. At the time, though, I was damaged; I needed some type of security, a bridge from one life to the next, so I held on far longer than I should have. That wasn't fair. To her credit, she stuck by me for a while when she didn't have to, but there wasn't much she could do to pull me out of my depression.

We understand much more about post-traumatic stress disorder today than we did a generation ago—or even ten years ago, when vets began returning from Iraq and Afghanistan. It's a very real, very painful, and deeply troubling condition. It's a term that encompasses a spectrum of emotional and psychological issues—in my case, all related to battlefield trauma (and probably the loss of my father). PTSD has also become something of an epidemic, afflicting to some extent just about everyone who experiences combat. I don't think it's possible to be involved in a firefight and not be changed by the experience. And I sure as hell don't think it's possible to see your friends killed and walk away unchanged.

I started going for counseling through the Veterans Administration shortly after I came home, in part because I knew how messed up I was, but also because others around me could tell that I was struggling. My personality had changed. I was drinking way too much. I have to be honest about this. While I'm sure that counseling is a valuable resource for a great many returning vets—and I certainly wouldn't want to discourage anyone from seeking help—it didn't provide a lot of comfort for me. Truthfully? The more time I spent in a counselor's office, discussing shit that I wanted to forget, the worse I felt. My depression and anger deepened. I left every session filled with sadness and self-loathing.

I know counseling and therapy help some people, but for me it seemed like a pointless exercise in self-abuse.

Why am I sharing these stories, these feelings, with someone who has no idea what I've been through? You're going to diagnose me and treat me based purely on what you learned in school? How can you possibly have any idea what I'm feeling?

It might have been different had my therapist been a combat veteran as well as a PhD. I don't know. Probably not, actually. I was not in the right frame of mind to accept help. One of my counselors was a very pleasant and thoughtful young woman, just a few years older than me. In all fairness, she did nothing wrong; I'm sure she wanted to help me. But I went in with the wrong attitude. I was combative, hostile, reluctant.

"I know I'm supposed to be here, but you should understand from the outset that I don't believe in any of this bullshit. I'm just trying to get the VA off my ass."

She nodded, no doubt having heard exactly this type of rant before.

The first session was devoted to merely getting acquainted. I didn't say a whole lot. She tried to be sympathetic, threw some academic jargon across the room that supposedly explained and rationalized my current frame of mind. The next time I came to her office, I was armed with an assortment of "memorabilia" from my time in Afghanistan.

"What do you think of this?" I said, placing a photo on the table between us. The image was startling, if not repulsive. It showed the body of a man – probably a man anyway – shredded by a hand grenade. The counselor tried to hide her shock and revulsion. She said nothing.

"How about this one? Maybe you'll like this better."

I showed her another photo, another fresh kill. A body with its face sheered off.

She was ashen now.

"What does your textbook say I should do when I see this at

night?" I asked. "When I remember what I did to this guy? What do you have for that, Doc?"

She remained impressively calm, although I'm sure she was thinking, *This dude is a total head case.* And she was right. I had a tenuous grip on sanity at that point. But counseling did nothing to make it better, and I never tried meds, even though they were recommended. I had seen that backfire with other vets. That's why I'm ambivalent about the role of therapy and psychiatry in treating PTSD. I know it has value for some people – maybe a lot of people. It just didn't work for me. I don't feel that the best way to help soldiers with PTSD is to make them get in a room and talk about the ghastly things they've experienced. What good does it do to sit on somebody's couch and relive that shit . . . over and over? Get out there and do something with your life that is meaningful and use the negativity in a positive way. That's what worked for me.

It just took a little time to figure it out.

Valor was a big help. See, that's what I named my pup – *Valor*. She came from a breeder in North Carolina because I wanted a purebred bird dog for duck hunting. She was about two months old when I got her, and while she required an enormous amount of work and effort, she was exactly what I needed at the time: she represented responsibility; she represented love. I trained her and cared for her and did all the little things that come with owning a puppy. Nothing special about it, except that, without her, I'm not sure what I would have done. She gave me focus and helped with my sanity. No matter how bad I was feeling, there was work to do. This little puppy had to be fed and walked and trained. I know – she was just a dog, but she was literally a lifesaver for me. And here's the crazy part: I picked her up when I was at my lowest point.

While getting ready to drive to North Carolina one morning, I posted a message on a friend's Facebook page, telling him that I was going to be passing through his neighborhood.

"Let me know if you want to meet up and have a beer."

The guy's name was Edward Faulkner. He was a private in my unit, and he also was wounded at Keating. I had not seen him since October 2, 2009, the day before the Battle of Kamdesh. Like a lot of guys, Faulkner brought the war home with him. Not five minutes after I posted that Facebook message, my phone rang. It was one of my former platoon sergeants. I figured it was a hell of a coincidence, him calling right after I'd reached out to Faulkner, but there was nothing coincidental about it.

"Hey, Sergeant, I just wrote something on Faulkner's wall," I told him. We had all served together in Afghanistan.

"Yeah, I know," he said. His tone was quiet, serious. "I guess no one told you, huh?"

"Told me what?"

There was a pause.

"Faulkner killed himself. Happened a few weeks ago."

I don't know if it was officially deemed a suicide or an accidental death. It almost doesn't matter. Faulkner was a quiet kid, sort of walled off and emotionally isolated. You just knew he was going to have trouble when he got out. Apparently he'd been self-medicating with drugs, and one night he overdosed. I was speechless, partly because I felt an instant pang of guilt at not having reached out to Faulkner. Maybe I could have done something. I should have tried anyway. But there was something else . . . I knew that I was capable of the very same thing. In fact, I'd been close on a couple occasions. I was drinking too much, smoking too much weed, battling the same demons and finding with increasing frequency that the idea of nothingness held a strange appeal. It's very difficult to explain to anyone who hasn't been there, who's never experienced the emptiness and pain of serious depression.

A wave of anxiety washed over me as I hung up the phone. And then . . . despair. It was ten o'clock on a September morning, and my sister was at work, so I was home alone. I thought about calling her. I thought about calling my mom, or one of my friends. I thought about calling Alexis. But I didn't. Instead, I just sat there for what felt like an eternity, thinking about Faulkner and how much pain he must have been in right before he died. I won't presume to know what was going through his head, but it had to have been similar to what I was feeling. He was gone now, and in some crazy way I envied him, because for him the suffering had stopped.

He was free.

I started telling myself, once again, that I wasn't meant to live, that I should have died on October 3, 2009, with my friends and fellow soldiers. I had cheated death. I had let them down. With all that I had done — the people I had killed and the things I had seen and survived — there was no way that I had any right to be alive. I didn't deserve another day.

All the same voices and messages I'd heard a thousand times before, echoing in my head.

An hour passed. Maybe more. All this shit rattling around in my brain, eating me alive, until finally there was a moment of clarity.

Time to go . . .

I stood up. I walked upstairs to my bedroom and began rooting around in my closet, through all the gear I'd brought back from Afghanistan. There was so much stuff, but I wasn't interested in a trip down memory lane. I found a pistol, a 9-millimeter semi-automatic Glock, and lifted it out of the bag. I walked down the hallway and into the bathroom. I had a plan. My father had died in the bathtub in this very same house. *Maybe,* I thought, *I can be closer to him by dying in the same spot. I'll just lie down in the tub and swallow the barrel of the Glock, and everything will be over. My sister will have to deal with the mess, but at least if I blow my brains out in the bathtub, it'll be easier to clean up.*

That was my state of mind. That's how far gone I was. Suicide for me was no longer some abstract thing, an exit considered but quickly dismissed. I was ready to die. I *wanted* to die. Or at least, I wanted release from the torment.

For some reason, I went back downstairs and pulled up a chair at the kitchen table. I started playing around with the pistol, breaking it down and putting it back together, marveling at what a beautifully designed instrument of death and destruction it was. I had no fear at that moment. I was empty. I felt . . . nothing.

I put the gun together one more time, inserted a round in the chamber, and charged the handle. I thought again about Thomson and Mace . . . about Faulkner and so many others. And then, for some reason, I thought about my dad.

Like most families, I suppose, we had unofficially assigned seats at the dinner table in our house. From the time I was a little kid, I had always sat in the same chair, at the same position. There were four chairs around a rectangular table. My father would sit at one end, my mother at the other end. My sister and I would occupy the two other seats, directly across from one another. I realized at that moment, while fondling the Glock, that I had taken my designated spot at the table, and that realization struck me as odd.

Why had I done that?

Why did it matter?

I looked straight ahead, through the kitchen and into the living room, where I had spent far too much time in recent weeks, splayed on the couch, watching television. To my left was a large window with a view of the backyard. I stared at it for a few moments. The lawn was overgrown and thick with dandelions and weeds. The shrubs were asymmetrical and desperately in need of trimming. My father had died more than four years earlier, and in that time I had hardly been home at all. It struck me suddenly that he would have been terribly disappointed by the way his property had fallen into . . . not disrepair, but unsightliness.

Nothing had meant more to my father than providing for his family. He had spent his entire life trying to ensure that we had a stable roof over our heads and a life free of worry. I'd barely even noticed this while I was growing up, but Dad took great care of our house and the yard. I took it for granted that our home and property would always be in pristine condition, but as I look back on it now, I can remember my father spending endless hours outside, mowing and seeding and fertilizing, weeding flowerbeds and grooming shrubs and bushes. He didn't hire anyone to do this work; he did it himself. It was a source of immense pride and pleasure.

This, I realized, was what he worked for, this house and home, and the family who lived here. Yes, his marriage had dissolved by the end, but he still insisted on meticulously maintaining our home, preserving a facade of domestic bliss and tranquillity. Given his roots – the fact that he had grown up in poverty – this home represented the American Dream for him. When he was a kid, he had never imagined living in a beautiful house in a nice neighborhood. It was a fantasy. But he had succeeded in transforming that fantasy into reality. In many ways this was the pinnacle of his life.

After my father passed away, though, the inevitable erosion began. I ran off and joined the Army. My sister and my mother had clung to the house despite tenuous financial circumstances. Mom moved back to New Mexico. My sister and her husband moved in, but they had problems in their marriage and they were both busy; for whatever reason, the property became neglected. It wasn't falling apart or anything, but it lacked the charm of childhood. It just wasn't the same.

I rolled the Glock, locked and loaded, in my hand. I set it on the table. I stood up.

"I gotta cut the fucking grass."

I said those words out loud, knowing and not caring whether anyone could hear them. It was a measure of my madness that I was going to tend to landscaping issues before killing myself.

I'm going to leave this yard the way Dad would have wanted it.

Of course, Dad would not have wanted his son to eat a pistol in the bathtub (or anywhere else, for that matter), but for some reason that didn't concern me.

I walked out of the house and into the garage, stopping long enough to lace up my black Pumas from Keating. I had taken to wearing these shoes almost every day, despite the fact that they were falling apart and speckled with the blood of my friend. These were the sneakers that had saved my life, I thought. More than that, they were a totem of sorts: a daily, tactile reminder of the friends I had left behind – the friends I had failed (that's the way I saw it anyway). Unlike, say, a rubber bracelet or pink ribbon, the Pumas were not intended to signal to the outside world any commitment to a cause or to honor someone lost. No one else knew. The sneakers were my own silent reminder of the worst day of my life, and so they were both a lucky charm and a cross to bear.

It was an unusually hot day, more like summer than fall, so I stripped off my shirt and fired up the lawn mower wearing only green Army shorts and the Pumas. Mindlessly, almost without being aware of what I was doing, I began to mow the lawn. Back and forth, subconsciously cutting in the same pattern my father had always preferred, the one he had taught me. I did the back lawn. Then the front lawn. This took a couple hours. Despite the fact that we had a substantial amount of yard to tend, my father had never invested in a lawn tractor. He favored a simple push mower, one that would guarantee a bit of a workout as well as a neatly manicured lawn.

When I finished, I put the mower away.

And while I was in the garage, I noticed the weed whacker hanging on a wall.

Might as well do it right.

For the next half hour, I trimmed around the foundation and sidewalk. Then I walked back into the garage and traded the weed whacker for a set of hedge clippers. I began pruning the various shrubs and bushes that my father had planted years ago and nurtured to maturity. I raked and bagged the clippings and swept the driveway. I put everything away, started to walk back into the house, and as I stepped up onto the back porch I glanced overhead and noticed the gutters were starting to sag.

Should probably clean those out too.

I went back into the garage, got a ladder, and proceeded to

sweep the gutters, which were clogged with leaves and dirt, with dead insects and bird crap. Another hour passed. By the time I had finished cleaning the gutters and putting everything away, it was midafternoon. Tired and drenched with sweat, I sat down on the back deck. I looked out over the yard, admiring my handiwork. The place hadn't looked this good in years.

I looked through the window and into the kitchen, where my pistol remained on the table. Everything was in its proper place. My work was done.

All right, Dad. Here I come.

The rain came out of nowhere, one of those afternoon showers you typically see only in the middle of the summer, when the sky wrings itself out like a giant sponge. The sky was still mostly clear. There was no thunder. No ominous clouds. Without any warning, it just started raining. A thick, tropical kind of rain, hot and heavy, each drop exploding like a miniature balloon. I sat there on the deck and looked up at the sky, and let the rain wash over me. It fell harder and harder, until everything was soaked.

I just sat there. Didn't move a muscle.

For probably twenty minutes the rain fell from a nearly clear sky, and as it fell I began to cry. It was less a cry of anguish than one of relief. And when the rain stopped, so too did my tears. I had a sense of having been cleansed, of a burden lifted. I looked into the house, to the kitchen table and the waiting Glock.

What the fuck are you doing?

I am not an overtly religious man. I have faith, in a vague sort of way, but I do not regularly attend church. And I certainly have never believed in divine intervention. But something weird happened that day, something I can't quite explain. A torrent of rain from a nearly cloudless sky, at just the right moment, providing enough of a distraction to prevent me from taking my own life. I know it sounds crazy (which is why I have shared this story with only one person – until now), but maybe there was a reason for it. Maybe my father was looking out for me.

Maybe it was mere coincidence. Maybe I got lucky.

Who's to say?

For whatever reason, the crisis passed. I remember walking into the house and going into the bathroom to towel off. I looked into a mirror. My eyes were hollow, my cheeks sunken. I looked tired and weak.

"What are you doing?" I whispered. "This isn't you."

Somehow, just like that, all the shit — all the guilt and self-loathing — had been wiped away. Or at least some of it. Enough that I could pull back from the abyss and see that another death was not the answer. Killing myself would be an affront to my father, and to everyone who had died at COP Keating. They had given their lives for a cause. Whether you choose to believe that the cause had something to do with freedom or a vaguely defined "war on terror," that's fine. But I know the real truth. I know this much for sure: they died so that the rest of us could live. That's what it always comes down to in battle: fighting for your buddies. Did Thomson and Mace die so that I could come home and put a bullet in my brain? I don't think so.

I walked out of the bathroom, down the hall, and into the kitchen. Then I unloaded the pistol and put it back where it belonged, tucked away with my gear in the bedroom.

This . . . stops . . . now.

I didn't drink that day. Or the next day. I didn't smoke any weed. That probably doesn't sound like such a big deal to you, but to me, at that time, it was a significant accomplishment, as the only way I could get through the day was with the help of one chemical substance or another. Just for the record, I do want to say that of all the drugs used by vets suffering from PTSD — prescribed or otherwise — I think marijuana is the most benign. Drinking made me feel horrible, both while I was doing it and the following day. I know guys who were addicted to painkillers or were walking around in a trance because of antidepressants. By comparison, marijuana didn't seem so bad. It allowed me to sleep and to feel less anxious and sad. I'm not surprised that the federal government (specifically, the Department of Health and Human

Services) recently signed off on a formal study investigating the effectiveness of marijuana as a treatment option for veterans suffering from PTSD.

That said, I realized I had reached a point where it was time to regain control of my life. I'm not sure how much time it took – a couple weeks maybe – but I forced myself to live in a completely clearheaded and sober space to see if I could cope with all the anxiety and anger and sadness. And for the most part, I found that I could. It wasn't easy. It hurt. But I discovered that the condition wasn't fatal. I accepted my own mistakes and shortcomings. Eventually, I would learn to live with the scars.

Change was necessary. That much I understood. Perhaps the biggest challenge facing vets who return from combat is the loss of identity . . . the loss of purpose. For all its depravity and violence and discomfort, life on a combat deployment is pretty simple. Distilled to its essence, the job is this: try to stay alive, and while you're at it, try to kill the enemy. You come home and find out that life in the civilized world is a whole lot more complicated. People expect you to behave in a certain way, and it bears little resemblance to the way you behaved on a mountainside in Afghanistan. You're supposed to throw a switch and become someone different. You're supposed to forget about all the appalling shit you've done and seen and now get on with your life. And it's not easy. Look, I don't have all the answers. Hell, I don't have any answers. I only know what worked for me: finding something to fill the hole, something to which I could devote all my time and energy.

For a while, during this transitional phase of my life, Valor was the answer.

I drove to North Carolina and picked her up a week later. She was a tiny, curly-coated bundle of energy. We bonded immediately. I can remember picking her up, holding her close, and feeling the warmth of her body, the rapid beat of her heart. She nuzzled against me, licked me, did not try to get away. For the next few months we were practically inseparable. If you've ever owned a dog, and especially if you've ever raised a puppy, you know how quickly you become attached and how deeply you fall in love. I was totally devoted to Valor. My entire life revolved around her and her schedule – on feeding and housebreaking and walking and training. If I went out with my friends, I would always head home early because I knew she would have to go out. She became a deterrent to unhealthy behavior at a time when one bad decision might have led me down the wrong path. She was forced responsibility. And of course, she was unconditional love.

Yeah, I know, I'm making a big deal about a hunting dog, but at that point in my life this dog was critical to my health and psychological well-being. The crazy part is, I couldn't tell her any of this. I mean, it's not like you can sit down with your dog and say, "Thanks, girl, you literally may have saved my life." But that's the way I felt. Just a week before I picked her up, I was on the verge of killing myself. I honestly don't know what would have happened if I hadn't found something else on which to focus. Bringing a puppy into your home not only imposes certain restrictions on your lifestyle but forces you to become less egocentric. Suddenly, there is something else that requires your full attention, something that depends entirely on you for its very existence. Simply put, Valor needed me. And it had been a long time since I felt that anyone or anything needed me in quite that way.

She gave me hope.

This little dog, this tiny, adorable creature, did not care whether I was in a bad mood, or whether I hadn't gotten enough sleep the night before. She was there every morning, at 6:00 AM, bouncing around, licking me in the face, demanding to go out.

Let me pee, all right? And then I'll be cute and cuddly and we can play all afternoon. I love you, Daniel! No matter what you did.

There is no magic formula for reclaiming your humanity and finding purpose beyond the battlefield. What works for one person does not necessarily work for another. Having a new puppy around the house compelled me to get out of bed every morning and trudge through another day, whether I felt like it or not. I started working out consistently again – running, lifting weights – and while I wouldn't exactly call it "serious" training, even those initial sessions reminded me of the body's enormous potential to heal itself. The flood of endorphins that accompanied each workout had a curative power – both physiological and psychological – that I couldn't find anywhere else.

Eventually, the fog of depression lifted ever so slightly, and I began to focus on what I wanted to do with the rest of my life, or at least with the next chapter. I realized that one of the things I missed the most was sports: not just the training but the competition and camaraderie. If I could recapture some of the intensity and focus that had served me well as a high school athlete, maybe I could play college ball. Shit, I wasn't that old yet, and I was still in reasonably good shape. Even if I didn't make it, at least I'd have a goal, something to work for, and a way to shed the negativity that had been poisoning my system for months.

You see, it's not that all veterans come home so disgruntled and war-torn that they're unfixable; it's that too often they have nothing to focus on. Instead, the government pumps disability into them like a form of welfare, allowing them to curl up on the couch all day, replaying in their heads the horrible highlight reel of their deployment, until they're too tired or sick to do anything else. I was headed down that road. I could feel it, and I could see where it would lead.

I came to the conclusion that if I didn't do something with my life, then the Taliban would have won the war and my friends would have died in vain. I knew that what I had survived was far worse than anything I would experience in the States. So what if I failed in my attempt to play college football? So what if it turned out that I wasn't a great student? At the very least I had an obligation to try. I'd been given a second chance. I owed it to my friends to act on that opportunity. I thought about Thomson and the hours we had spent in the mortar pit. I thought about my father and how I had assured him that eventually I would get a college degree. I thought about the promises I had made and how they had fallen by the wayside.

And suddenly it all seemed so clear.

11

N JANUARY 2011, I enrolled at Germanna Community College. At first I just wanted to see if I could handle college classwork. It had been a few years since I'd cracked a textbook, and there was nothing about my high school transcript that would have predicted a smooth transition to the college level. But I knew in my heart that I was a more capable student than I had previously demonstrated.

The hardest part was simply getting started – acknowledging that I was going to make a dramatic change in my life and taking the necessary steps to achieve that goal. It was humbling in so many ways, if not downright humiliating. It had been four and a half years since I'd been in a classroom. It never occurred to me that anyone at Germanna Community College would consider my undistinguished high school career to be of any relevance whatsoever. Imagine my surprise when I was informed that I could not even take a single class without evidence of having graduated from high school. Documentation was required, which meant I would have to obtain and submit a copy of my high school transcript.

The day I walked into Brooke Point High School to pick up my transcript was among the hardest days of my life. And that's saying something. I had called ahead of time so that everything would be in order when I arrived. I don't know what I expected, but the entire process was far more daunting and emotional than I'd thought it would be. I hadn't walked back into that school since the day I graduated, and yet it seemed as though time had stood still. Everything looked the same – the hallways, the classrooms, the parking lot – and many of the teachers and administrators remained on staff. I was nearly five years older and a profoundly different person than I had been when I graduated in June 2006. But I felt as though everyone I spoke to that day – and there weren't many, as I tried to get in and out as quickly and quietly as possible – still saw me as an eighteen-year-old fuck-up.

This was simply my perception, and it was demonstrably untrue. The counselor in the guidance office remembered me, and I remembered her. She could not have been nicer or more pleasant.

"It's so good to see you, Daniel," she said. "We heard about what happened in Afghanistan. Thank you for your service."

I smiled politely and thanked her for the kind words, trying very hard to mask the unease in my heart. I think it's common for soldiers who have lost friends in combat to feel ambivalent about this type of recognition, regardless of how benign or well intentioned it might be. I've come to terms with it, but even now, five years removed from the Battle of Kamdesh, I still feel awkward when I hear the word "hero" attached to my name. I will never get accustomed to that. And at that point in my life, the wounds were still far too raw. I had gotten past the critical phase of self-loathing and self-destruction, but I still questioned why I had been permitted to live while my friends had died. It haunted me, and each time someone thanked me for my service, I was reminded of the myriad ways in which I had failed. I preferred to fly under the radar.

There were times in the first six months after I came home from Afghanistan when I did not handle these interactions graciously. Someone would thank me or call me a hero, and I would feel a flush of anger or discomfort. Usually I succeeded in choking back the rudeness, but a few times I actually did snap.

"Please don't call me that," I would say before quickly walking away.

I had become a coldhearted person, bitter and filled with hatred. Again, I think it's important to acknowledge that not all veterans are this way. Some handle the stress and strain of PTSD better than I did. Some handle it worse. I had to work through the anger and sadness and get to a place where I could accept the support and appreciation that so many people expressed. I understand now that when people interact with a veteran in this way, they aren't merely trying to be friendly; their words come from a place of genuine respect and gratitude, and I have an obligation to respond accordingly.

But on the day I picked up my transcript from Brooke Point High School, there seemed to be a gaping chasm between the boy I had been and the man I hoped to be. Here was a counselor thanking me for my service – for a job well done – while handing over a transcript littered with Ds. The juxtaposition was jarring. I had to stifle the urge to apologize for having been such an uninspired and uninspiring student. Despite her words of appreciation and encouragement, I couldn't help but feel that everyone at Brooke Point must have wondered what I was doing. I had barely graduated from high school. What made me think I could ever get through college?

I was so ashamed of that transcript, which represented irrefutable evidence of laziness and irresponsibility, but if I was going to make something of my life – if I was going to get a college degree and maybe even play college football – I had to take ownership of my past. No excuses, no spin. A transcript does not lie.

At the same time, it doesn't tell the entire story. I had been, at best, an indifferent high school student, one who preferred getting high to studying, who skipped classes and doctored report cards. But I wasn't stupid, and I knew it. I suppose in some ways that's even worse – the squandering of ability and resources – but at least I had a chance now. I knew that if I applied myself, I could be a successful college student.

It was all part of the process of putting my life back together. I'd gotten a dog, stopped self-medicating, and cleared up a lot of things with my mother and reestablished a close relationship with her. I'd reconnected with friends. I had always intended to get a college degree; now it was time to put in the hard work required to meet that goal. My father loomed in the background. That transcript was written proof that I had let him down in the past.

"Hit the books . . . study hard," he always said. "Once you have a degree, nobody can ever take it away from you."

My father had finished his college degree while working full-time and with a newborn in the house. He took most of his classes at night. And here I was feeling sorry for myself? Collecting unemployment? I realized that things had to change, and that change began with school. So I swallowed my pride, picked up my transcript, filled out the application for community college, paid the fees, and enrolled at Germanna, nervous but buoyed by the belief that I was capable of doing college work. It would just take some serious effort.

On the first day of classes I was twenty-three years old, and I felt like I was forty. The other students all seemed so young! They looked like high school kids, which of course is exactly what most of them had been just a few months earlier. But not all of them. At any community college, adults returning to the classroom are a common sight. And while I was significantly older than most of my peers, I still had something of a baby face. So I could blend in. But I felt like everyone could tell. I felt . . . different.

Before class started, I was sitting at my desk, fidgeting anxiously, trying to look over the course syllabus. A girl took a seat near me and started talking to another student. Their conversation was light and trivial. Turned out, they had attended the same high school but graduated in different years.

"I got out in 2009," the first girl said.

"I'm 2010," came the reply.

I just sat there, thinking about how long it had been since the last time I was in a classroom.

2006 . . .

A couple days later, in another class, a student raised her hand and then proceeded to explain to the professor that she had been having trouble with her computer and thus had fallen behind on an assignment.

"You don't understand," she said. "I can't even log onto Face-book. It's awful!"

Awful . . .

Not really. If the biggest problem you have in life is not being able to log into your Facebook account, then things are going pretty well. I had to laugh a little at that one. But you know what? It helped me feel more secure about this whole adventure. Okay, so I hadn't been much of a student the first time around. I was older now, more experienced. I had a greater sense of who I was and what was important. If my academic credentials were less impressive (and a bit moldier) than those of my fellow students, well, I had other attributes that might serve me well. I knew how to work hard, how to push myself. I knew how to compete. Practically speaking, the pressure of a classroom pales in comparison to the pressure of a firefight in Afghanistan. What was the worst that could happen? I'd fail. Okay. As long as I gave it an honest effort, I could deal with that.

I didn't expect it to be easy, and it wasn't. Things that are second nature to most college students (and high school students) presented significant challenges. I hadn't cracked open a textbook in years, and I found myself nearly dozing off two or three pages into most assignments. The brain is not just a muscle – it's more like a vast network of muscles, all of which have to be appropriately exercised in order to function in a given environment. You know that feeling when you hit the gym for the first time in six months or a year? When everything aches and you can barely get through a workout? Well, that's the way I felt in the classroom. I had to train myself to handle the rigors of academia.

It's mostly about focus, of course. I found that I worked best if I blocked out all distractions. No phone, no Internet, no television. Just me, the text, and a yellow highlighter. Endless hours of reading and note-taking. It was painfully tedious and arduous work. The first time I sat down to write a paper, I couldn't believe how daunting it was to stare at a blank screen, watching the cursor silently flashing, mocking me with each blink.

Come on, let's go! What are you waiting for? Type something . . . anything!

I would hunt and peck, one excruciating letter at a time, stopping after two or three words to make sure I hadn't lost my train of thought. I'd run spell-check at the end of each paragraph and nearly send my laptop into convulsions.

There is a certain amount of wisdom that is gleaned from serving in the military, but at the level of an infantryman it's a very specific type of wisdom. You learn about life and death. You learn how to survive and how to get along. There are tests, of a sort, but you don't have to write a lot of papers. I found that whatever limited knowledge I once possessed on things such as grammar and syntax and spelling had withered and nearly died. It's funny too, because people in the Army always used to comment on how well-spoken I was. But when I went back to college, I discovered that there is a big difference between speaking fluently and writing fluently.

In that first semester of community college, I leaned on friends who had already graduated from college and were settling into the workplace. My buddy Stephan was generous with both his time and his red pen, which he would use to liberally mark up any paper I asked him to proofread. Nobody did the work for me, but they gave me honest – sometimes brutally honest – feedback, and I accepted it and did the necessary rewriting. I studied for tests rather than merely cramming for them the night before, as I had done in high school. I made it a point to get to know every one of my teachers, both in and out of the classroom. I would raise my hand and try to answer questions. I would participate in classroom discussions.

Before any of that, though, I introduced myself to each of my teachers, in the very first week of classes. I explained that I had enlisted in the Army after high school and was therefore a little unsure of my academic footing.

"I'm very serious about this, and I want you to know that I will try my hardest. But it might be a rough transition."

I kept it simple — no details about where I had been or what I had done. I wasn't looking for sympathy or a pat on the back. I just wanted to make a connection, to let my teachers know that there might be some context to what I presumed would be a rocky start.

It is a small world, though. The husband of my math teacher, as it turned out, was a high-ranking Army officer. The way it works in the Army is that a wife in this position often becomes the equivalent of a team mom: she hosts dinners, bakes cookies, and generally acts as a surrogate. After I said that I'd been in the Army, she told me about her husband, and then she lifted her sleeve to reveal a thick rubber band around her wrist. I recognized it instantly as a KIA bracelet. They're worn by family members of fallen military men and women, by soldiers, and sometimes by soldiers who have lost friends in combat. I wore several for a while, with the names of my buddies who died at Keating. They kept breaking during football practice, and eventually I stopped wearing them. But I still have them.

"This is for men from my husband's unit," the teacher said, running the bracelet between her thumb and forefinger. They weren't friends exactly, but she knew all of them. They were boys, roughly the same age as her children, which of course was roughly my age. She thanked me for my service; I thanked her for the support. She was very kind and patient with me throughout that semester, and I did my best to be worthy of her compassion.

The bond between military people is strong and endures well

beyond the time of service. You never know when you will encounter a kindred spirit. Certainly it has become more common
in the past decade to meet someone who has either served in the
military or lost a loved one who served in the military.

There was another teacher, during a different semester, who
revealed to me one day after class that her son had been an Army
Ranger. He was killed in the line of duty while serving in Afghanistan. The context of this discussion was that I had begun to get
some publicity related to my interest in playing college football.
There had been reporters and television cameras at the school. I
had become a "story."

"I want you to know that I think what you're doing is wonderful," she said. "And I admire the way you present yourself."

That really hit me. She was so genuine in the way she said it.
But it got me to thinking about the price of fame, however small,
and the responsibility that comes with it. I couldn't stomach
the thought that anyone would ever suggest that I was using my
friends' deaths to in any way glorify myself. That kind of behavior ran counter to everything I believed. I had set out to honor
my friends by doing something productive with my life. I wanted
to be a good student. If possible, I wanted to play football. Regardless of whatever else might come of those efforts, I needed to
maintain a sense of dignity and humility. I couldn't imagine doing
anything to disrespect my friends or the families they left behind.

So when she said that to me—"I think what you're doing is
wonderful"—it was kind of an eye-opener. I had to remember that
as much as I felt like I had pulled myself up by my bootstraps, I
hadn't done anything on my own. I was here for only one reason:
because others had given their lives.

I shook my teacher's hand and looked her in the eye.

"I'm sorry for your loss."

"Thank you," she said.

One of the best days of my life was the day grades were posted
following my first semester at Germanna Community College, in

May 2011. I wasn't expecting to see any As, and indeed there were none. But there weren't any Ds or Fs either. Nor were there any Cs. I took four classes and got straight Bs.

I remember actually letting out a triumphant little yell: "Hell, yeah! I'm a B student!"

I was so happy. I called my mom and my sister. I called a couple of my friends. I only wish my father could have been there to share it with me, to see a report card that hadn't been fabricated and that contained legitimately decent grades. But I felt like somehow he could see it anyway and that now he knew: his son wasn't a dumbass after all.

12

I N THE SUMMER OF 2011, I took off on my own and back-packed around Europe and South America, just to clear my head and figure out what I would do next. At some point on that adventure I decided that not only would I try to transfer to a four-year college and play football — I would try to do it on the biggest stage possible.

I remember revealing my plans to my friends Kendall and Joseph one day late in the summer while we were working out. I'm very fortunate to have maintained close relationships with several of my childhood buddies. We're as close today as we were in middle school. But these guys weren't exactly encouraging when I broke the news. Joseph, especially, can be a sarcastic and cynical guy. But I'm sure he would claim that there is a method to his madness — that he uses negative reinforcement as a motivational tool.

"I think I'm going to try to walk on at Virginia Tech."

At first they said nothing. Then they started to laugh.

"Dude, are you nuts?" Joseph said. "You'll get crushed."

I shrugged. "Maybe so."

What started as a dream – a fantasy – quickly became an obsession. I started watching football recruiting videos on YouTube. (Just about every high school athlete who hopes to play a sport at the collegiate level will put together some sort of video package – game highlights, training footage – that can be easily accessed and analyzed by college coaches; it's all part of the recruiting process.) Some were laughably amateurish and uninspiring; others were amazing. One in particular caught my eye. It featured some jacked-up kid going through his daily routine, from sunup to sundown. The kid worked like crazy, putting in hours of gym time every day, honing his skills and his physique through endless hours of training and preparation. But what really made the video special was the narration – some faceless person with the power and inflection of a Southern preacher, speaking in the background, demanding that the viewer take notice.

Over the top?

Maybe, but it worked for me. (And a lot of others too, I suspect – the video had been viewed more than a million times.) I'd watch it every morning before I went off to the gym, just to get pumped up. To me, the video was both an inspiration and a challenge. I'd been working out for months, but not with any clear purpose or vision. Just an hour or two of cardio and light weights a few times a week, which is fine if you're merely trying to maintain a degree of health and fitness or hoping to keep certain psychological demons at bay. But if the goal is to reshape your body into something capable of withstanding the rigors of Division I college football (when you are only five-foot-eight), then a slightly more ambitious program is required. This video put everything in perspective for me. If this was what other people were doing – and surely he wasn't the only one working that hard – then I would need a completely different approach. I had to commit myself fully to a program and a lifestyle. That meant putting myself out there and making my intentions known, just as this kid had done.

The value of making a recruiting video and posting it on the Internet for all the world to see (or ignore) is that it sort of forces your hand. Once you publicly declare your intentions, there is no turning back. It would have been easier, and less risky, to keep the whole crazy scheme to myself. That way, I'd have an escape clause at any point in the process. If I got tired or discouraged or simply changed my mind, I could quietly go back to being just another student at Germanna Community College.

Nothing ventured, nothing gained . . . or lost.

On some level, though, I wanted the pressure. I needed it.

At the end of the summer I traveled to San Diego for the wedding of a high school classmate. The night before I left I couldn't sleep at all. I tossed and turned, got out of bed, fired up my laptop, and watched that kid's recruiting video again and again. Around one o'clock in the morning I picked up my cell phone and called my friend Kyle Otto. Kyle is another of the guys from our Brooke Point gang. He is perhaps the smartest of all of us, and definitely the most creative. Kyle is now living in California, finishing up a degree from Columbia University, and pursuing his dream of working in Hollywood. At that point, though, he was trying to figure out what he wanted to do. I knew I could count on him for some positive feedback (he was the least caustic and skeptical of our entire crew) and maybe an interesting approach to achieving a goal that, admittedly, might not even be realistic. At the very least I knew he'd be awake – the guy hardly ever slept – and willing to talk. I didn't need to have my balls busted at that moment; I needed some friendly reassurance.

"Dude, I'm leaving town for a couple days for this wedding, but when I get back, I need your help."

"Okay. What's up?"

"I'm serious about playing football. I know you guys think I'm crazy, but I am not kidding."

There was a pause on the other end of the line.

"I know, Daniel. I really think you can do it. How can I help?"

I told him about the video on YouTube and how the Internet had completely transformed the recruiting process. This was a good thing for me. I was five years removed from high school and organized sports. It wasn't like college coaches were lining up to offer me a scholarship. Moreover, there was no opportunity for them to see me play. There were no more games, no showcase events. There wasn't even much of an athletic résumé.

I was invisible.

But the Internet could change all of that. Aspiring college athletes now had an opportunity to interact with coaches differently – directly – and to control the flow of information. This represented not only a shift in the balance of power but, in my case, the only avenue of hope. At that point in time Kyle was preparing to enter Columbia. I knew he was interested in film and figured he might have some ideas about how to put together a recruiting package.

"I need a video that shows me working out," I said. "I mean, shit, I haven't played football in a long time. I have to convince coaches that they should take a chance on me. Maybe we could do something like that?"

"Sure," Kyle said. "Why not?"

And so it began. All of my buddies were, and continue to be, helpful and supportive to some extent, but Kyle was the most deeply involved in the beginning, and the least judgmental, both because of his nature and because he was into the idea from a creative and technical standpoint. Kyle was part of the crew that lived in Hawaii after high school, and while there he helped coach a high school football team and got to know some of the players on the University of Hawaii football team. He even provided some technical support for ESPN during broadcasts of U Hawaii games. Kyle is very football-smart and football-savvy, and even though he wasn't in the greatest shape, he embraced the role of "trainer." It was kind of funny, actually. Kyle would be out there wearing a headband, holding a stopwatch, and giving me pointers while I'd be running drills. I'd run routes, and he would throw passes to me. And you know what? He had a decent arm, pretty good zip on the ball, reasonably accurate. I was surprised. Then we'd go to my basement and he'd work me out. He'd sit there with a whistle, blowing it in my ear and screaming at me.

"Come on, pussy! Is that the best you've got?"

I love the guy, but he did take the job a little too seriously. Every time he'd show up for a workout, Kyle would have a new piece of equipment just to mess with me, to see how much I would tolerate. But I was committed to my goal and I appreciated his enthusiasm, so I didn't say much.

"You're the boss, Kyle."

We were in this together. Unfortunately, when it came time to create a record of my supposed athletic prowess, things did not go quite as well as we had hoped. Neither one of us owned any sort of high-tech video equipment, so I went out to Best Buy and picked up a little handheld camera for sixty bucks. The quality was probably inferior to just about any camera you'd find on a smartphone today, but it took basic video and photos. What more did we need?

Quite a bit more, as it turned out.

I'd set up the camera on a rickety little tripod in the corner of my basement and crank out a hundred push-ups and crunches. Or Kyle would shoot video of me running sprints on a football field. Then I'd come home, plug it into my laptop, play it back, and . . .

Wow, this looks like crap . . .

The lighting was bad, the focus was bad. It bore almost no resemblance to the recruiting video I had seen on YouTube. That video was impressive; this just looked like . . . me. I didn't want coaches to see me – a short, older guy who hadn't played football in five years. I wanted them to see the man I was trying to become: a serious, shredded athlete.

My body was changing. I had begun by working out with some friends but had slowly, steadily progressed to the point where they could not keep up with my workouts. Two hours became three . . . three hours became four . . . four hours became six. Every day, seven days a week.

Sometimes I'd go to a local gym, but just as often I'd work out in my basement. It was dark and austere, but perfectly adequate for what I was trying to do. Hell, I'd managed to get in pretty good shape by lifting ammo cans in Afghanistan. I could make do with the free weights and pull-up bar and the old universal machine that my father had purchased decades earlier. I bought a speed ladder and resistance belt and created an assortment of push-up benches. I hung a heavy punching bag in the corner to help with cardio fitness. And I continued to work out on the football field, because of course, I hoped to become a college football player. There was no free time whatsoever, and I didn't mind. If I wasn't training, I was at school. If I wasn't at school, I was in the gym. I even took up yoga to improve my flexibility and concentration.

The hardest days were also the best days. More than once I felt like quitting. You can't spend that much time training intensively and not have a few rough moments. When the lactic acid accumulates in your body and you feel like you're going to pass out or puke all over the gym floor . . . that's when you find out how much you really want it, how much you're willing to work and sacrifice. The true reward comes from pushing through the pain, from refusing to give up. Each time I made it through a particularly grueling session I felt better about myself. I felt stronger. In some weird way, I felt like I had earned the extra time on this planet that I had been granted.

Needless to say, I was no longer much of a party animal. I've learned to accept the fact that I have an addictive personality. For better or worse, I develop habits quickly. This was beneficial in both training and schoolwork – in both cases, I was immediately all-in. No half-measures. But the same chemical and genetic quirks that allowed me to spend hours in the gym or the library had also played a role when I became a pothead and borderline alcoholic. There's no denying that. In my case, the pendulum swings wide.

When I returned from San Diego, not only did I begin serious training, but I also gave up alcohol and marijuana. I'd already cut way back from the dark days of a year earlier, when I first got out of the Army, but now I felt like a total commitment was necessary, and part of that commitment involved living as cleanly as possible.

It really wasn't all that hard, not when I measured what was important in my life. When you're eighteen years old, you can get away with almost anything. I'd sit around with my friends on a Saturday night, blazing and eating an entire family-size bag of chips, and there were no physical repercussions. My eighteen-year-old legs and lungs always forgave me. Now, knowing that being older put me at a disadvantage, I wasn't willing to take any chances. I suppose that's just part of growing up. I never doubted my athletic ability. I knew in my heart that I was athletic enough to play college football. It was just a matter of whether anyone would give me a chance. There was every reason to believe they would not. I understood the stakes and the odds. I knew that if I wanted to get there, I had to change. So I completely quit everything — cold turkey. One day I just said, "I'm not going to drink anymore, I'm trying to get my body in perfect shape."

Then, whenever we'd go out, it became almost a game among our friends.

"Who can get Daniel to drink?"

That wasn't a lot of fun. We'd go out to a sports bar, watch a game, and while everyone else was knocking back beers, I'd sip a glass of water. The more inebriated they became, the less likely they were to respect my abstinence.

"Come on, man. One beer won't kill you."

I'd just laugh.

"Dude, I'm not drinking."

Roughly three or four months in, they stopped trying to pull me off the wagon and learned to appreciate the fringe benefits of having a sober friend — like the fact that they no longer had to take turns serving as designated driver. I'd been permanently appointed.

It was actually an eye-opening experience, and one that made me realize how my father must have felt. I never saw my father drink. Not a drop. He had worked in a bar while he was growing up, and he used to tell me how disgusted he'd get at the sight of grown men passing out or pissing themselves, getting into fights or throwing up on their shoes.

"Why would anyone do that to themselves?" he'd say.

Now I knew what he meant. When you see a bar late at night, through the eyes of sobriety, it's not very attractive.

Almost worse were the inevitable fast-food pit stops on the way home. Everyone else would gorge on cheeseburgers and French fries, in the hope of mitigating the hangovers they would feel the next day. I'd think about them in the morning, when I was at the gym or in my basement: I was two hours into a workout, and they were just rolling out of bed. I liked feeling strong and healthy. It was empowering.

My diet was radical as well. You can't work out six hours a day without taking in a lot of fuel, and if you want to add lean muscle, the best fuel is protein. I would go to the grocery store and buy a giant carton of eggs – three dozen at a time. I'd hard-boil the entire stash, throw away the yolks, and save all the whites. I'd keep them in a plastic container in the fridge and eat them pretty much around the clock: on breakfast sandwiches, mixed into salad with tuna fish, or just plain, as a snack. I would go to the deli, get a couple pounds of sliced turkey, thickly cut, and then I'd roll egg whites into a turkey wrap. Bread was a rarity, although sometimes I would eat peanut butter and banana sandwiches before a workout, using only a single slice of bread, cut in half. Just enough to hold the contents in place. Dinner would be chicken breasts and salad, maybe some plain brown rice – the only concession to carbs. And water. Gallons of water.

For the better part of a year, I ate protein bars and protein shakes and protein supplements – protein, protein, protein – until one day I looked in the mirror and realized that I probably couldn't get much bigger or stronger without sacrificing speed and agility. I wasn't trying to become a bodybuilder, after all; I was trying to become a football player. From then on, it was all about maintenance.

By that point, though, my world had been turned upside down — in the best possible way.

Despite our best intentions, it had become apparent that Kyle and I lacked the expertise and the equipment to create a professional recruiting video. I had one opportunity to do this right. First impressions mean a lot. In my case, first impressions meant everything. If I was going to post a video and then try to steer traffic in its direction, it had to be a provocative and compelling piece of work. I didn't know where to begin. But here, again, my friends bailed me out.

"You should get in contact with my cousin," Stephan suggested.

"Which cousin?"

"Ryan. You remember him, right?"

I did in fact remember Ryan Smith. We'd hung out together a few times over the years. A good guy. Smart too.

"He just started a production company," Stephan explained. "They've done some weddings and some other stuff. They're brand-new, so he might be able to give you a good deal."

The company was called Wandering Hat, and after viewing a sample of their work, I had to admit that they did indeed seem to know what they were doing. Maybe they were a little too good at it, in fact. I was worried that I wouldn't be able to afford to hire them.

I had $1,500 in a savings account and had to drain every penny to defray the cost of making a professional video. Truthfully, it was a bargain. Stephan's cousin wanted to help me out and charged me far less than the usual rate — just enough to cover his expenses. And what an amazing job he did! We shot the whole thing in one day over the course of seven or eight hours. There was lots of workout footage: lifting weights and doing pull-ups and push-ups in the basement, running sprints and routes on the field, catching passes. All the usual stuff you'd see in a recruiting video. But Ryan also brought an element of real artistry to the project.

"I want these coaches to understand who you are," he explained. "I want them to know that you were in the military, and that you haven't just been sitting around for the past five years. You were a wounded veteran coming back from Afghanistan. We want to tell your story."

My story?

At first I was reluctant. Most of what had happened in Afghanistan (and Iraq) I had kept to myself. I didn't like talking about it. That didn't really do any good. I wanted to get past it, move on.

"I think he's right," Stephan said. "It's important that coaches understand what you've been through."

We shot the video on November 23, 2011, the day before Thanksgiving. It was a cold, dreary day. I'd been working out hard-core (I mean, even more than usual) for the better part of a month in advance of the filming. I'd tweaked my diet, almost like I was getting ready for a bodybuilding competition. The idea, of course, was to look as good as possible on camera. Ryan arrived around 9:00 AM, with a couple extra guys to help with lighting and sound and other technical stuff. We worked all day and into the early evening. I had arranged to use some space at an indoor facility that hosted flag football leagues. I told them I was working on a recruiting video and just needed an hour or two to run some routes and catch a few passes while a small film crew recorded everything.

"As long as the field is free, no problem at all," they said.

We also shot footage in my basement and at the gym, which was a bit more problematic, since the place was always pretty busy. It was somewhat awkward, working out in front of a camera crew while the whole gym stopped and stared. Even more unsettling was the footage at my home. I'm pretty comfortable in the gym or on a football field, but once we left those settings, it was apparent that Ryan had something much more ambitious in mind than the usual recruiting video.

"We want to do some artsy shots of you around your house," he said. "The whole story needs context."

I live in a rural area, less than a mile from Aquia Creek, a tributary of the Potomac River, so in addition to filming scenes in my basement gym, Ryan took footage of me running on Government Island, near the water. It was a beautiful setting. Then we went back to the house and conducted an interview. I had no experience with this sort of thing at the time; I could not have been less media-savvy. But I tried to give straightforward answers. It was all a little unnerving, but I trusted Ryan. At the end of the day he packed up his equipment and went home, promising to begin work that very night.

The very next day he called me from Stephan's house, where he was having Thanksgiving dinner.

"Hey, Daniel. We have some of the footage edited."

"Already?" I was legitimately surprised. Not that I knew anything about filmmaking or videography, but I presumed that I wouldn't hear from Ryan for at least a couple weeks.

"Yeah, it's pretty cool. You want to come over and check it out?"

Stephan lived about a mile from my house, so I was there almost before the line went dead. I don't know what I expected, but what I saw that day was beyond my wildest imagination. From the opening scene, with musical accompaniment, I felt like I was watching a professional documentary rather than a simple recruiting video. The notion that I had attempted to pull this off on my own, with a $60 video camera, seemed ridiculous now. Whatever money I had spent on Wandering Hat was clearly a great investment.

About two weeks later, I saw the finished product. It was breathtaking. As Ryan had promised, my backstory, my narrative, had become the spine of the film. I was totally blown away. It wasn't just a video; it was like some incredible cinematic production, including raw combat footage from Afghanistan. It was so polished and compelling, and so accurate in its depiction of what I had seen and experienced, that it was almost difficult to watch. I thought about others seeing it, and the response it might provoke. And suddenly I got a little nervous.

Oh, man . . . what have I gotten myself into?

• • •

Within a few days I began e-mailing different coaches, providing a link to the video, which had been registered with an online service. In order to view the video, coaches had to set up an account and provide a password. Response was slow. A representative from Virginia Tech wrote back to tell me the video should be more accessible – they were worried about the viruses that are sometimes contracted when establishing an account.

In an effort to boost traffic, I decided to reach out to my friend Jake Tapper, who at the time was senior White House correspondent for ABC News. I'd gotten to know Jake pretty well because he was researching and writing a book about COP Keating and the Battle of Kamdesh. (*The Outpost,* which truly captured what it was like for all of us who were there in October 2009, would become a bestseller.) I told him what I was doing and asked if he had any suggestions for getting my story out there. Jake had a Twitter account with more than a quarter of a million followers. I figured maybe one of them would have some kind of advice.

Jake graciously agreed to look at the video and mention it on his Twitter account. "I don't know how many of my viewers follow college football, but we'll give it a shot," he said.

So I sent him the link that night – this was maybe a week before Christmas – and went to bed around eleven o'clock. When I woke the next morning, I had more than forty text messages and twenty missed calls and voice-mail messages on my phone. But that was only the beginning. I signed in to my e-mail account and was stunned to find nearly a thousand messages! You have to understand – I was not in any way a public figure. On a busy day I got maybe ten or fifteen e-mail messages, and most of those were spam.

Holy shit . . .

The video had gone viral while I slept. And at the end of the video I had foolishly, or at least naively, included my e-mail address. The video had already registered several thousand views. And that was just the beginning. With each passing day, it fed on the fuel of social media . . . 100,000 views . . . 200,000 . . . 300,000.

It was referred and re tweeted everywhere, until it became an Internet sensation. And because my e-mail address was included with the video, anyone who saw it could reach out to me personally. I tried to respond to each and every one of them over Christmas break, even if it meant just dashing off a quick sentence or two. There were messages from parents who had lost children as well as messages from veterans, thanking me for my service and wishing me well. Some people even sent money – cash! – in the mail, with no return address. Others sent me workout videos with a simple message: "Good luck, Daniel!"

And there were messages from college coaches. Lots of them.

They were thoughtfully and carefully written, and virtually all of them opened the door at least a little, which was nice, given the gap on my athletic résumé. Most coaches wanted to talk to me about the possibility of playing football; they also wanted to see my transcripts. I figured this wouldn't present much of a problem since, with two semesters of college coursework under my belt by now, I had an overall GPA of nearly 3.5. (I got all B-pluses and As in my second semester.) Over the next few months, though, I got a crash course in dealing with the sometimes mind-numbing bureaucracy of the NCAA. Despite having demonstrated that I was more than capable of handling college work, I was considered ineligible to play Division I college football. Why? Because my high school transcripts and SAT scores were not satisfactory; apparently those numbers superseded my more recent productivity. The only way around this rule was to complete a two-year degree and then transfer to a four-year college. In all likelihood, I'd lose a year or two of eligibility along the way.

This was unacceptable. I wanted to enroll in a four-year university in the fall of 2012, and I wanted to play football right away. If not for the power of the media, I might not have gotten the chance. As the winter months passed and my story was picked up by the *Washington Post* and *USA Today*, by Dan Rather and Fox News and countless others, interest from college programs intensified. But only one was willing to suggest that it would apply to the NCAA for a waiver on my behalf. That school, and that football program, was Clemson.

The Clemson coach, Dabo Swinney, had first contacted me in late February. I was sitting in a class at Germanna at the time, with my laptop open, taking notes, when his message hit my in-box. It's so weird to think about it now, because the moment I saw the address, which ended with "clemson.edu," I had what can only be called a vision. I literally saw myself in an orange football uniform, in a packed stadium. I suppose it might simply have been the excitement of the moment – Clemson was the most prestigious program to have contacted me – but it felt like more than that. It felt like . . . destiny.

Whoa . . . Clemson . . .

I still have that e-mail; I never killed it. It was a single sentence:

Hey, Daniel, this is Coach Swinney at Clemson. We would love to talk to you about a walk-on opportunity down here.

That was it. Simple and to the point.

I felt a rush of adrenaline as I stood up to leave the classroom. I had been a model student for two semesters and didn't want to appear rude, but I simply couldn't wait to respond. As I packed up my gear I looked at the professor and just sort of sheepishly said something about having an emergency. I didn't know how to explain it or what to say. I just knew that I had to make a phone call. Right away.

Two minutes later we were on the phone, chatting comfortably. Coach Swinney was friendly and energetic and positive. He invited me to come down to Clemson and tour the campus and the athletic facilities. He also asked me to forward copies of my transcripts to the athletic department. I didn't feel like he was giving me a sales pitch, but rather presenting an honest opportunity, and I felt like I owed him the same degree of transparency in return.

"About the transcripts, Coach?"

"Yes."

"I've been going around in circles on that with some other schools. I'll send everything, but I have to be straight with you: my grades in high school were horrible. I have a 3.5 GPA in college now. I'm not the same person I was. But my transcripts from high school are bad. Like . . . embarrassingly bad. And I've heard from some other schools already that the NCAA will not grant me eligibility right away. They want me to graduate from community college first."

"How much time do you have left?" he asked. "Is that what you want to do?"

"No, sir. I can't wait."

That was the truth. I was already twenty-three years old. By the time I finished my associate's degree, the following December, I'd be nearly twenty-four. And I wouldn't be able to play in college until six months later. I was ready now.

Coach Swinney did not even hesitate.

"Well, all right, then," he said. "Send us your credentials anyway, and we'll see what we can do. I'll take your file to my compliance officer, and we'll see how it goes. In the meantime, I still want you to come visit. You should check out our facilities . . . just in case."

The argument was simple and straightforward: I was five years removed from my shitty high school academic career. I had a B-plus average in college. I was a grown man who had served his country on the battlefield. I neither needed nor wanted an athletic scholarship, as the GI Bill would pay for my tuition. All I wanted was an opportunity.

The NCAA is not exactly known for exercising logic in its deliberations, but in this case common sense prevailed. Throughout the process I was in constant contact with Coach Swinney, e-mailing back and forth, chatting on the phone. His reassurance meant the world to me and solidified my interest in joining the Clemson Tigers.

"We're going to get you in, Daniel," he said repeatedly. "Just be patient."

I visited the Clemson campus in March, during spring break, and immediately fell in love with the place. In fact, I liked the coaches and campus so much that I decided I'd attend Clemson even if it meant waiting another year. In July, however, I got a call from Coach Swinney. The waiver had come through! I could enroll in the fall, and I'd have four full years of Division I football eligibility. It was the first time the NCAA had ever granted such a waiver without penalizing the student-athlete at least one year of eligibility. It was a groundbreaking decision.

Now all I had to do was make the team.

See, that was still the most important thing. I tried very hard not to get caught up in all the publicity. Our culture has become so obsessed with celebrity that it's easy to confuse fame with success. They are not the same thing. People gain a degree of notoriety for all kinds of reasons; the Internet and social media have turned the proverbial fifteen minutes of fame into fifteen seconds of fame. I was overwhelmed by the attention I received, but I was careful not to be swayed by it. In my own eyes, I hadn't achieved anything yet. Anyone can post a video on YouTube and with a little luck (and often a willingness to humiliate themselves) accumulate thousands of views. If you think that's success, well, it isn't. For me, the video was a means to an end. I was careful about that. Before making the video, I contacted some of my old Army buddies, as well as the families of some of the guys who had been killed at Keating. Even though I did not expect much to come of the video, I wanted them to be aware of what I was doing; I didn't want it to be a surprise.

I'm making a recruiting video because I want to play college football. And I'm going to talk about my experiences in Afghanistan. I want you to know that I have no intention of capitalizing on your pain, or exploiting your suffering. I am not trying to benefit through you (or through the death of your son). I want you to know that by talking about this, I hope to honor everyone who was there.

Everyone was incredibly supportive; I did not receive one word of discouragement. If I had, I can assure you, I would not have gone through with it.

But that's the way it's been through this whole crazy journey. There have been so many people who have offered support and encouragement. Among those who deserve special acknowledgment is Nick Wallace, a speed and agility trainer who reached out to me after the video first appeared. Nick had played Division I college football at Maryland and Towson State. Although he was a kicker, that role is misleading – the guy was incredibly fit. He also happened to be the head trainer at a little place in my hometown called East Coast Strength and Power. Nick is now a very successful trainer in Florida, working with a lot of professional and Division I athletes. At the time, though, he was still working on a degree and just getting started as a trainer. We clicked right away – first by e-mail, then on Facebook, and finally in person.

Nick's gym was almost as dark and austere as my basement, but I didn't care. It had all the necessities: bars, weights, squat racks, mirrors, tires. Everything you need to bust your ass. We'd meet at the gym every morning and sometimes again in the afternoon. I couldn't afford a membership, so I'd give him what I could – fifty, maybe seventy-five bucks a month, under the table, which was a ridiculous bargain. Nick knew I didn't have any money; the thing is, neither did he. But he had played college football and he understood what was necessary. He wanted to help.

"Dude, you have it," he'd say. "I'm telling you – you can play. Your work ethic is unbelievable."

We started working out shortly after Christmas and kept at it throughout the winter and spring. We'd meet and do strength drills, speed drills . . . everything. Nick wouldn't just stand there and yell. A lot of the time he worked out right by my side. I'm not exaggerating when I say that he transformed me. In the previous year I'd gotten into what I considered to be really good shape just by working out on my own, but I had nowhere near the knowledge and experience that Nick had. I was self-taught. He put me on a precise workout schedule and taught me more about the importance of diet: it wasn't just about stuffing my face with protein, it was about eating the right type of protein, and at the right times. For the first time I felt like I understood at least some of the science and physiology behind the training.

By the time I visited Clemson, I was legitimately shredded. I weighed perhaps 165 pounds, but I could bench 315. I'd never approached that number before. I was faster, leaner, stronger. When I walked into the locker room — into a shirtless sea of ripped football players — I did not feel out of place. Yes, I was older. And I was smaller. For some reason, though, I believed that I would fit in.

13

W HEN I PACKED MY truck and drove to Clemson in late June of 2012, I did so with confidence, but with no guarantee that I'd be playing football the following season. I'd been working closely with the athletic department's compliance officers to ensure that I had met every academic standard required for admission. Obtaining a waiver from the NCAA was difficult enough; I couldn't afford to make things even more complicated by getting a bad grade or neglecting to take a required course. So I loaded up on classwork in the first summer session at home (actually, I took courses at two different community colleges, just to make sure I covered all the bases), did well on everything, forwarded my transcripts to Clemson, and headed south down I-95.

Officially, I arrived as little more than a long-term visitor. I was not yet enrolled in classes, I was not a member of the football team, and I didn't even have a place to sleep. For the first few days I lived out of my truck. Through a friend of a friend, I found an apartment. It was close to campus, the price was right, and the landlord was willing to give me a short-term lease, so I snatched it up. The hope was that I'd be there only a month or two, until my waiver came through and I could find something closer to town or on campus as a bona fide Clemson student-athlete.

It wasn't like I was completely naive or deluded. I had put in a lot of work and truly believed that I had a chance to make the Clemson football team as a walk-on, despite my lack of size. But I also saw the bigger picture. By the time I got to campus in the summer of 2012, my story was widely known. There was a fair amount of buzz on social media about my coming to Clemson. Tigernet, a high-traffic website devoted exclusively to Clemson football, had already reported on my arrival, pending approval by the NCAA, so it wasn't like I was a complete stranger when I got to town. It was more a case of being in limbo.

I was grateful for the opportunity and determined to show the coaching staff and my teammates that I was a legitimate college football player and that my presence was more than just a publicity stunt. Look, I get it. Clemson is a Southern school, and there is a strong military tradition in the region. I don't doubt for a second that everyone associated with the football program and the university recognized the potential for a public relations windfall. They really had nothing to lose: give the decorated Army vet a uniform and let him take classes. Everybody wins. I suppose they never expected that I'd become anything other than a practice player and a goodwill ambassador for Clemson football. But I aspired to something more than that.

The ball began rolling very quickly. Within a week the NCAA approved Clemson's waiver request on my behalf, clearing the way for me to enroll in classes for the second of two summer sessions. (It's common, if not mandatory, for football players at major Division I programs to takes classes over the summer, as time constraints during the season often result in a reduced academic workload.) This represented the clearing of a significant hurdle, but it was not the end of the race. In order to be fully eligible to play football at Clemson, which was a member of the Atlantic Coast Conference, I had to wait for the ACC to approve my eligibility. In all likelihood that would happen, Coach Swinney assured me, but we would have to be patient; we would have to let due process run its course.

In the meantime, since the NCAA had given its approval, I could begin taking classes. If I wasn't yet a student-athlete, I was at least a student. And I felt pretty good about that; after all, I'd spent the previous eighteen months proving to both myself and my teachers that I could not only handle college coursework but actually excel at it, and that, to me, was every bit as gratifying as being offered a chance to play college football. Let's be honest: six years earlier, neither one of those accomplishments had seemed even remotely possible.

Because I'd been waiting on the NCAA's waiver approval, I missed the first couple days of summer classes, which put me in a big hole. Each summer session lasts only a little more than a month, so the pace is dramatically accelerated; by necessity, the material covered in each class is mountainous. On the first day I was disoriented and disorganized, lacking even the required textbooks. Fortunately, my teachers were familiar with the circumstances of my late arrival, and all exhibited extraordinary patience and compassion. Within a few days (coupled with long nights of studying), I had caught up and adapted to the academic routine.

The athletic routine was a little more complicated, as I was pretty much on my own.

Without approval of the waiver from the ACC, I was not permitted to work out with the football team in any official capacity whatsoever. But there was nothing to prevent me from attending the workouts as a spectator, or from working out alone. So that's what I did.

If the team had a 6:00 AM training session, which it often did, I would set my alarm and make sure that I was at the gym or the practice field when they arrived. I would watch and take mental notes. Eventually I started mimicking the workouts. If they were running suicides on one field, I would go on the opposite field and run by myself. If they did five sprints, I'd do five sprints, separated by fifty or a hundred yards . . . or more . . . but, in my head at least, right alongside them.

At first they probably thought I was crazy, but after a while I got to know some of the guys, and they all seemed to appreciate my effort and commitment. I had summer class with a couple guys on the team, including Adam Humphries, who, like me, was a wide receiver. Adam would become one of my closest friends.

The guys on the team were very cool about welcoming me into their ranks, even before I was officially a member of the team. You might think it would have been somewhat awkward. After all, I was twenty-four and a half years old, and some of the players were still in their teens. But I've always been a little bit of a chameleon when it comes to fitting in socially. And anyway, football was our bond. We were all putting in the same amount of sweat and sacrifice. We all wanted the same thing: to be part of the Clemson football program. A college football team has much more of a family atmosphere than you might expect. It just happens to be a very big family. And I was in the odd position of being almost a member of that family, but not officially a member.

But slowly the circle opened.

I remember a rainy Friday, at 5:30 in the morning, standing on the sideline, watching the team warm up. It was a miserable day, deep gray skies, the rain falling sideways, the wind howling. It was so dark the stadium lights were on. I was wearing a raincoat, unsure of what to do or how to fit in under such odd circumstances. As the players peeled off sweats and began to run I felt a surge of adrenaline. NCAA rules precluded my taking part in workouts with the team, but there was nothing that said I couldn't work out *near* the team . . . or at the same time as the team.

They're really going to think I'm nuts this time. And I don't care.

I unzipped my raincoat and pulled my T-shirt over my head. I was wearing nothing but a pair of shorts and sneakers. I glanced to my left to see what they were doing. I started to run . . . and I

kept running, every step of the workout. When it ended, as I prepared to walk away, I could hear someone call my name.

"Hey, Daniel! Over here!"

The entire team had gathered around the coaching staff for a
little post-workout pep talk. This is bonding time in college football. No one wants to be at a predawn workout in lousy weather,
but sometimes it's necessary. It isn't unlike basic training, where
the sheer misery of the experience brings you closer.

The coaches didn't say much at that point – technically, I suppose, they weren't allowed to say anything. But several of the
players offered words of reassurance and welcome, including Taj
Boyd, our star quarterback.

"You're with the team now, dude," he said. "Even if you can't
practice with us just yet."

That was one of the defining moments for me, knowing that my
teammates had my back. We were all in this together.

In August the ACC announced that it had accepted the NCAA's
recommendation that my waiver be approved. That same day I
got a call from Coach Swinney. He congratulated me on the waiver
and on becoming a full-time student at Clemson University. Oh,
and one other thing.

"Daniel, I'm inviting you to the one-fifteen," he said. "Hope you
can make it."

The "one-fifteen" referred to training camp, as that was the
number of players – 115 – who would try to make the roster of the
Clemson Tigers. Only seventy-two would make the travel squad.

"Yes, sir," I said. "Thank you."

"You've earned it."

We had a week off between the end of the second summer academic session and the official start of training camp on August 1. I
remember walking into the locker room on that first day and seeing my nameplate above one of the stalls. It's almost a misnomer to
refer to it as a "locker room," for the space in which Clemson football players dress and prepare for games and practice is as nice as

any locker room you'd find in the National Football League. There is no scrimping on amenities when it comes to Clemson football. I knew that already, of course; I'd been in the locker room before. But until that day I hadn't really felt like I belonged there.

I walked up to my locker, picked up my practice gear, and just sort of stood there for a minute, trying not to smile too broadly. After all, I didn't want to seem like a complete rookie. Not at my age. But I can't lie. That was one of the best days – one of the best moments – of my life.

Wow . . . this is really happening.

Everyone comes to camp with a designation: blue chip recruit, regular recruit (players in either of these categories are on full athletic scholarship), recruited walk-on, and nonrecruited walk-on. As someone whose tuition was being paid by the GI Bill and who was known but not actively pursued, I fell into a gap between the last of those two categories.

It's common for a major college football team to have walk-ons; the season is long and hard, and injuries routinely require that rosters be bolstered. However, walk-on status encompasses a range of levels of involvement. Some walk-ons never play or even dress for games, only going to practice and meetings. If that sounds like a lot of work with no reward, well, it is. But you'd be surprised how many athletes welcome the chance to be part of a college football team, if only for a couple hours at the end of each workday.

I aspired to something more. I knew in my heart that I was good enough to contribute to the team in some way, beyond merely being practice fodder. Whether anyone else anticipated that I would contribute, I can't say for sure. I never asked. I was grateful simply for the opportunity and didn't want to push my luck. But in all honesty, I think it's unlikely that anyone expected much of me. I was by far the smallest guy on the roster – smaller even than the kickers and the punters, and yet I was a wide receiver, a position typically populated by some of the best athletes in the sport. The prototypical wideout in major college (or professional) football is six-foot-four and weighs 210 pounds. Think Randy Moss or Terrell Owens . . . or Calvin "Megatron" Johnson, who at six-five and 236 pounds is built more like a tight end. But if you're fast enough and smart enough, and if you know how to run a route and hold on to the ball even after you get hit, there is a place for you in the game. Wes Welker is five-nine and 185, and he's done all right.

Look, I'm not comparing myself to one of the game's all-time greats, but when you're a little guy trying to carve out a place for yourself in a sport dominated by beasts, it's nice to have someone you can point to as a role model – someone whose physical stature is not much more impressive than your own.

I was five-foot-eight, 175 pounds, at the start of camp. I was so far down the depth chart at wide receiver that I knew I would have to find other ways to get noticed. I couldn't do anything about the fact that I was the smallest guy in camp, or that I hadn't played organized football since the fall of 2005. The only thing I could control was my own effort and attitude. I'd been working out four to six hours a day for the better part of a year. I was in phenomenal physical condition. There was no reason for me not to win suicides, and there was no reason why I couldn't hold my own in the weight room.

I had become a solid B-plus student in the classroom as well, and the skills I had developed there would prove beneficial when it came time to memorize playbooks and study film. You might think that football is a fairly simple game: pass, catch, run, block, tackle. It is a game of violence and reaction. But it's actually an incredibly complicated game, and if you don't put in the proper time and preparation, you will be revealed as a poser. At this level, there are no shortcuts. Believe me, I know. I used to be the king of shortcuts. But not anymore. If I failed to make the team at Clemson, it wasn't going to be from lack of effort. I had every intention of outworking every other guy in the locker room.

There is a place on a roster for someone who is fit and fast and, preferably, fearless, even if he is small. As often as not, that place is on special teams. It takes not just athleticism to run through a wall of people at full speed on a kickoff or punt, knowing full well that you might get blindsided and knocked unconscious, but also courage . . . and a bit of recklessness. Generally speaking, it helps to be a little crazy if you're going to play on special teams.

In that regard, and in others, my experience as a US Army infantryman proved invaluable. I don't mean to sound sanctimonious, but the fact is, when you've spent a year in Iraq and a year in Afghanistan, when you've lived without most of the creature comforts we take for granted in America, when you've been wounded in combat and witnessed the slaughter of your friends . . . the experience puts things in perspective. On the worst day of training camp, I reminded myself of what it was like at COP Keating or in Sadr City. When I sprinted wildly down the field, trying to hold my lane on kick coverage, I thought about what I'd already endured and how anything that might happen on that field would pale in comparison.

It was a bit of a balancing act, trying to appreciate everything I now had in my life without holding others to the same standard. We are all products of our unique and individual experiences, and if mine had been more dramatic than most, well, that didn't give me the right to preach. I will always be proud of my service, and as time goes by I find that I am more capable of letting go of the things I did wrong and the guilt associated with coming home when others did not.

Sometimes Coach Swinney will make reference to my experiences in front of the team, and I'm okay with that. When I first got to Clemson, though, I wasn't quite sure how to handle it. Obviously, that's something I can't control. People are going to think of me as a combat veteran first and an athlete second. But I wanted to be a football player and contribute to the Clemson Tigers. The fans could think what they wanted, but in the locker room I was determined to be just one of the boys. In that space it didn't matter where you were from or what you did before you got there. It didn't matter whether you were black, white, Hispanic, or whatever. If you could play, then you would play.

That said, there were times when I had to bite my tongue while listening to some of my teammates complain about how brutal it was to practice in the sweltering heat of a South Carolina afternoon.

Try riding in an armored Humvee through the streets of Baghdad in the middle of July! Try going a month without electricity or plumbing. Try shitting into a hole in the ground and then burning your feces.

Every once in a while I'd make a comment, but I'd try to keep it light. For example, there was the time at dinner when one of the guys complained about the food. First of all, Clemson has an amazing training table, with a wide assortment of selections, all professionally prepared. It's restaurant-quality food – and you can eat as much of it as you want! To me, it seemed like a pretty good deal. But experience shapes perception, doesn't it?

"Man, this sucks tonight," one of the guys said. "I can't eat this shit again."

I laughed.

"You know, we used to kill our own chickens in Iraq. If we were lucky, we wouldn't get sick afterward."

I scooped up a big mouthful and smiled.

"Just sayin'."

"Oh, shit . . . my bad, dude. Sorry."

That was about the extent of it. I neither expected nor wanted anyone to feel sympathy for me just because of my military service; nor did I expect my experience to in any way shape their appreciation for the relative comfort of their own lives. No one had forced me to enlist. I served because I wanted to serve. Sometimes, in certain contexts, a little good-natured ribbing was permitted. For the most part, though, I kept my feelings to myself and used my service experience as a source of both motivation and perspective.

There was a day in the middle of August that provided a number of "firsts." It was our first intrasquad scrimmage, my first reception, my first big hit, and my first injury. They all happened at roughly the same time.

I ran a short route, slanting toward the middle, caught the pass, and got absolutely swallowed by one of our linebackers. Guy was about six-foot-one, 240 pounds. It felt exactly like running into a wall. I was strong for my size and as muscular as I've ever been, but this guy did not move an inch when our bodies collided. The force of the blow reverberated through my skull. But that wasn't the worst part. He drove me into the ground with a textbook tackle. I had no way to break my fall, and I remember thinking, just before we hit the turf, *Oh, this is going to be bad.*

And it was.

As we landed I felt something strange in my shoulder, a pulling sensation, almost like my arm was being separated from my body. Then everything went numb, from my shoulder to the tips of my fingers. Not wanting to reveal the extent of my discomfort, I jumped to my feet, slapped the linebacker playfully on the back of his helmet with my good arm—"Nice stick, man"—and jogged back to the huddle.

Within a minute or two the numbness and adrenaline began to wear off and the pain set in. The next play was another pass. I distinctly recall standing at the line of scrimmage and praying that the ball would not come my way. Thankfully, it didn't. The next play was a running play, so I was nothing more than a decoy. By that point I was in excruciating pain. There was no way I could keep playing. I jogged toward the sideline and tried to eject my helmet, but the mere act of lifting my arm chin-high caused me to freeze in my tracks and double over in pain.

"Daniel, what's wrong?" one of the coaches said.

"It's my shoulder, Coach. I'm done."

He looked at me quizzically, but I kept walking straight to the bench and sat down. I felt helpless. I couldn't take off my helmet, jersey, or pads. It felt like I was wearing a hundred pounds of gear, and all the pressure was on my shoulder.

In an instant, one of the trainers was at my side.

"What's up, D-Rod?"

"I don't know. I can't even raise my arm."

He did it for me, taking my elbow gently in his hands and slowly lifting it in the air. It hurt like hell. Then he helped me take off my pads and proceeded to examine my shoulder.

"Probably separated your AC joint," he declared, after only a few seconds. "Let's get some pictures."

They don't mess around with injuries at Clemson. We have a first-rate training and medical staff, and in no time at all I was whisked away to the training room to undergo X-rays. It took only a few minutes to confirm the suspected diagnosis: a torn acromio-clavicular joint. The AC joint connects the clavicle to the shoulder blade. When I hit the ground, the joint had been damaged. Simply put, I'd suffered a separated shoulder. It was, in fact, among the most common of football injuries, and it had occurred in typical fashion: a hard tackle with arms pinned.

A separated shoulder can be a serious injury, requiring weeks, if not months, of rehabilitation, and since the joint has been weakened and loosened, there is the distinct possibility of recurrence. A separated AC joint is evaluated and graded on a scale of 1 to 6. Grades 1 through 3 are considered partial separations and usually do not require surgical intervention. Grades 4 through 6, which are less common, typically are treated surgically and result in a very long recovery period. My injury was diagnosed as a grade 2 separation. In all probability, I'd be out somewhere between one week and one month.

When the news was delivered, I felt completely deflated. I'd been working so hard and had overcome so many obstacles to reach this point, and now it was all going to come to an end. A scholarship player can afford to get hurt. The school and the program have invested in his future, and he will be given every opportunity to heal and prove himself all over again. I felt like I had no safety net. I was a diminutive twenty-four-year-old walk-on who hadn't played football in nearly seven years. There was no margin for error. I had just screwed up – big-time. A single play, a single tackle, and my career was now effectively over.

"Hey, relax," the trainer told me, no doubt sensing my anxiety. "We'll have you out there in no time."

That, of course, is the mantra of every trainer in every athletic program. These guys deal with devastating injuries and soul-crushing disappointment on a daily basis; it is their job to remain calm and upbeat, to provide a glimmer of hope and reassurance to athletes who believe that the worst has happened. In my heart, I knew that this was not the end of the world; this was not life and death. It was merely a setback. If the worst thing that happened to me while I was in college was that I didn't get to play football, well, that wasn't so bad. I felt sorry for myself for maybe a day or two, and then I remembered why I was there in the first place. I thought about Thomson and Mace and the other guys at COP Keating. I thought about my father.

I thought about all the soldiers who had been killed in Afghanistan and Iraq, or those who had come home without arms or legs, guys who struggle mightily and heroically just to get through each day. And here I was, fretting and whining about a separated shoulder?

Get a grip, Daniel!

I was briefly but profoundly disgusted with myself for indulging in even a shred of self-pity. Then I attacked my rehab with all the strength I could muster. It's not easy to spend hours in the training room getting treatment while others are in meetings. It's not easy to stand on the sideline and watch practice, especially when you haven't yet earned a spot on the team. But you can control only so many things in life, and what I have learned is that effort and attitude are variables to embrace. After the initial shock wore off, I never lost faith. There was a reason I hadn't been killed in Afghanistan. There was a reason I had found my way to Clemson. I used to think that life is a series of random events, of people and places banging into each other and making a lot of noise, that we are all just sort of floating along, hoping for the best.

Maybe that's true. Maybe not.

Maybe there is some sort of cosmic plan. And perhaps there are signposts along the way to serve as guidance. I don't know. But I had to believe that I was brought home from Afghanistan in one piece to serve some sort of purpose. I wouldn't exactly call football a noble calling, but I did think that by chasing a seemingly impossible dream and dedicating myself fully to it, I would honor the memories of my friends. I couldn't quit on that now. There was a system in place at Clemson. People got hurt all the time. Yes, my situation was more precarious than most, but I had to believe that I would get back out on the field and have another opportunity to prove myself. They wouldn't shut the door so quickly.

I worked as hard as I possibly could at rehab. I took extra treatment and pestered the trainers daily (or several times daily) about pushing up the schedule.

"When can I get out there?" I asked.

"Not today."

"Tomorrow?"

"We'll see."

A week and a half passed before I was cleared to practice. My shoulder still hurt, but my range of motion had improved dramatically. I don't envy team doctors or trainers: they are put in the difficult position of balancing the safety and well-being of a student-athlete with the needs of the team and the often unrealistic and self-destructive desires of the athlete himself. I don't know a single football player who hasn't, at one time or another, covered up an injury or lied about the extent of an injury. Our goal, at all times, is to get back on the field. Sometimes we are our own worst enemy. I probably came back too early, and maybe that's why I ended up popping my shoulder again the following season. Or maybe it would have happened anyway. At the time, though, I didn't care, and I don't have any regrets about it. I pushed and nagged the training staff to give me clearance at the earliest possible moment. I figured I had nothing to lose. If I went out and reinjured the shoulder, well, so be it. At least I would have given it my best shot. The only thing that was unacceptable was the idea of getting cut from the team without ever getting another chance to show what I could do. If I was going to go down, I wanted to go down swinging.

Bolstered by a few rolls of athletic tape and oversized, ultra-foam shoulder pads, I returned to the practice field. The pads were so big and bulky that I looked and felt ridiculous, but at least I was able to finish training camp as a player rather than a spectator. I had given it my best effort. Whether that would be sufficient, I wouldn't know until I walked into the locker room the day after camp ended and saw that Coach Swinney had posted the final team roster. There was no phone call or e-mail or text. I was just one of the guys who had been invited to training camp and who hoped to see his name on the board that day. The list was posted alphabetically, so it took me only a few seconds to find the spot where my name would appear. Or not appear. I took a deep breath. I could feel my heart pounding.

There it was:

DANIEL RODRIGUEZ

I'm not sure how long I stood there, staring at the board, making sure my name didn't magically disappear. Not long. I stuffed my hands into my pockets and walked away slowly. As soon as I got outside I pulled out my phone and called my friend Stephan.

"Dude . . . you're not going to believe this."

14

THE UNEASY JUXTAPOSITION OF who I was and what I represented came into full focus on August 19, 2012. This was Fan Appreciation Day at Clemson University. It sounds like a quaint little event, right? Well, it's actually one of the biggest days on the school's athletic calendar, and until you've been through it, there's no way to be adequately prepared. You hear about football being a big business at Clemson, and indeed the numbers are staggering: 80,000 fans a game and $40 million in annual revenue. (In the ACC, only Virginia Tech generates more football money.) A recent study by the Strom Thurmond Institute at Clemson found that each home game is worth $733,000 in net revenue for the state of South Carolina's economy, and $542,000 for the local economy.

But it's easy to forget about the people behind those numbers, as mind-boggling as they might be. As you approach the Clemson campus from almost any direction, you'll find the road dotted with giant orange tiger paw prints, like a trail of bread crumbs leading hungry fans to Memorial Stadium. As if they could possibly get lost! As on many college campuses with Division I football programs, the stadium is the largest and most striking facility. A half-dozen times each year it is filled to capacity for Clemson football games; the parking lot fills days in advance with RVs and SUVs carting folks in from all over the state for an extended session of tailgating. These are the people who make Clemson football the near religion that it has become. I sort of knew that before I even came to the school, and the coaches and returning veterans did their best to impress upon the rookies just how lucky we were to have the support of some of the best fans in college football.

"Just wait," they'd say. "You'll see."

Fan Appreciation Day is like an annual open house, during which the program and the university, as well as the players and the coaches, pay tribute to the folks who make Clemson football what it is. Not just the high-rolling booster but also the little guy who might not even get to a game in person (Clemson tickets are not easy to come by); the fan who follows the team passionately and has a closetful of orange T-shirts and sweatpants and shorts; the kids who have posters of quarterback Taj Boyd or wide receiver Sammy Watkins (both NFL-bound) on their bedroom walls. Fan Appreciation Day is exactly what it purports to be: a day for all of us to say "thank you."

I don't know what I expected, but I sure wasn't prepared for the massive turnout that late summer day, nor for the interest and affection so many fans directed my way. We were seated at tables spaced throughout the upper level of the stadium. We wore our jerseys so that we would be easily identifiable. (I had been assigned number 83.) Fans could then walk slowly around the inside of the stadium, stopping to chat with players, get autographs, pose for pictures. It's designed to be a loose, informal event, a friendly celebration between fans and the players they see on Saturdays but rarely get a chance to meet. In reality, though, it was much more than that.

I'd always loved sports and had my favorite athletes when I was growing up. But I don't think I had any idea what it meant to be a true fan until that day, when I saw thousands of fans lining up outside Memorial Stadium for a chance to shake hands with Clemson football players. Some of them had driven three or four hours to get there, only to wait patiently in line for another hour or two (or three) before gaining access to the stadium. There is no admission charge, and therefore no official attendance figure, but there must have been 10,000 people there that day. It was breathtaking . . . and humbling.

For me, it was also a little overwhelming.

I was a first-year walk-on hoping to make the travel team and get some time covering punts and kickoffs. I was simultaneously the smallest and oldest player on the roster (not usually a good combination). Why would anyone care about meeting me? On a team brimming with all-Americans and future professional football players, why would anyone want DANIEL RODRIGUEZ scrawled across a jersey or poster?

I had greatly underestimated both the loyalty and knowledge of the Clemson fan base, as well as the extent to which they supported and appreciated the efforts of the men and women who serve in the US military. Like I said, my story had been reported both in the national media and on the various websites devoted to college football in general and Clemson football in particular. But when you are inside the story, you don't realize how big it has become, or how much it means to people. Moreover, I figured that, with the noise dying down a bit by this point, no one would really care about the fact that there was a veteran on the team. I didn't consider myself special or unique; I was just a Clemson football player.

Or so I thought.

And then the fans showed up, one after another, not just asking for autographs or a picture or a handshake, but also expressing genuine appreciation for the job I had held before coming to Clemson.

"Thank you for your service," they said. Over and over and over. Occasionally they would add, "I'm sorry about your friend." And

I could see in their eyes the heartfelt emotion. More than a few had friends or relatives who had served in Afghanistan or Iraq. I could tell that some of them had been deeply affected by war. As a combat vet, it's just something you sense.

I was one of the very last players to leave the stadium on Fan Appreciation Day. It was both exhilarating and exhausting. I don't think I realized until then just how much of my life belonged to other people and the depth of the obligation that came with being a survivor. I wasn't just a Clemson football player, and I wasn't just a veteran. I was some weird amalgam, and if people found inspiration in what I was trying to do, well, who was I to discourage them?

A few days later the travel roster was posted. Once again, my name was on it. At that point it became real. That's when I knew I had earned my uniform. The fact is, football at Clemson is a serious deal. Winning games is important, and you don't win games with charity cases.

Our first game was Saturday, September 1, at the Georgia Dome in Atlanta, against defending national champion Auburn. Talk about a baptism by fire! The night before the game I called my buddy Brad Larson from my hotel room. We'd kept in touch since Afghanistan, and I just wanted him to know that I was thinking about him and the guys before I took the field. Brad had also played college football, so he would have some idea of what I felt.

"This is crazy," I told him. "What am I doing here anyway? Can you believe it?"

"Yeah," Larson said. "I knew you'd make it."

"Thanks. I don't mind saying – I'm a little nervous."

"Ah, screw it, man. You've got nothing to lose, man. You've already proved that you can do it and that you belong there."

There was a pause, and then a laugh.

"Just lie down and sacrifice your body," Larson said. "You're pretty good at that."

· · ·

We lost the coin flip, and the next thing I knew I was on the field for the opening kickoff of the 2012 season, against a team that just eight months earlier had been the best team in college football. How wild is that? Talk about getting a new lease on life! I remember feeling incredibly nervous as we jogged out onto the field and lined up. My heart raced, and my stomach did somersaults.

Just don't screw up. The whole world will see it.

And then I realized: I had nothing to lose. I'd already proven a lot of people wrong just by getting this far. I'd made good on my promise to Thomson. I had found a way to honor his memory, and the memory of all the other guys who had fallen at Keating. There was nothing left.

I played with reckless abandon that day, running balls to the wall on every kickoff and punt, throwing my body into places it probably did not belong, hitting anything that got in my way. I didn't make a single mistake, I didn't get injured. We beat Auburn, 26–19, and I was part of it.

The following week, on September 8, we played against Ball State in our home opener. This was my first opportunity to run down the hill into Memorial Stadium, into Death Valley, accompanied by the roar of 80,000 Clemson fans. This time I was more excited than nervous, in part because Ball State was a smaller, unranked program (Clemson was number twelve in the country) and the game was likely to be lopsided. I knew going in that I'd see a lot of time on special teams; if the score got out of hand, I might have an opportunity to get some snaps at wide receiver. And that's exactly the way things worked out. We scored on five of our first six possessions, jumped out to a 45–10 halftime lead, and basically cleared the bench in the second half.

Midway through the fourth quarter I made the first reception of my college career – a little four-yard pass in the right flat. It all happened so quickly that I didn't even have time to process it. But I remember feeling a sense of relief that I hadn't dropped the ball, that I had fielded cleanly the very first pass that came my way. Several seconds had gone by and I'd already returned to the huddle before I realized that the crowd was giving me a standing ovation. A few guys patted me on the back, said, "Nice job," and the game went on. To them, it was no big deal. I was a wide receiver at Clemson; I was supposed to catch the ball.

The stands were probably only about two-thirds full by the time the game ended, but the remaining fans rushed the field, as they do after every home game at Clemson. (We're one of the few programs that permit this practice.) It was fun and chaotic – an amazing emotional rush – to be out there in the middle of that sea of humanity, celebrating with fans and fellow students. Little kids surrounded me, grabbing at my legs, pushing pens and markers in front of me.

"Daniel, can I have your mouth guard?"

"Can I have your cleats?"

"Will you sign my program?"

Yes, yes, and yes.

A bunch of my friends from back home had come to the game, along with my mother and sister. When things finally calmed down a bit, they made their way out onto the field. It's funny – my mom knows almost nothing about football, or any other sport for that matter. Growing up, that was a father-son thing. My mom only occasionally came to my games, and she'd usually be the one reading a book in the stands. My senior year in high school, about halfway through the season, she came to one of our football games. I kept looking up in the crowd and noticing that she was barely paying attention. But then, after the other team scored a touchdown, I spotted her clapping politely. After the game, which we won, I asked her why she was rooting against us.

"I didn't realize you were the team in the black helmets," she said sheepishly. "Sorry."

This time, though, she knew which team to applaud: the team in the orange uniforms.

"And number eighty-three," she said with a smile. "I looked you up in the program."

"Okay, Mom. Thanks."

Even my high school friends, who are notorious and relentless ball-busters, seemed impressed. It was all a bit surreal, especially the postgame meeting in the locker room, when Coach Swinney gathered everyone together and handed out game balls and other plaudits. I was sitting there at my locker, soaking it all in, thrilled just to be a part of it – to have been on the field with guys like Sammy and Taj – when Coach Swinney changed courses.

"And let's not forget this guy." He looked at me, pointed at my locker. "Six years out of high school and he gets his first catch. Daniel!"

The locker room filled with the sweetest sound of applause. It was hard to fathom. Three years earlier I'd been in Afghanistan. Two years earlier I'd been on the verge of taking my own life. One year earlier I was a community college student who had some crazy, vague notion of playing college football.

Life is strange indeed.

For the most part I was just one of the guys, which is exactly what I had hoped to become. I worked hard in practice and in the classroom. I played in every game, mostly on special teams, although occasionally at wide receiver as well. For a first-year special teams player, I received more than my fair share of media attention; every time we went into a new town, some reporter wanted an interview about my "story," which often made me feel a little uncomfortable. But I learned to deal with it and to use it as a way of honoring servicemen and women in general, but especially my fallen brothers in Afghanistan. I never sensed any jealousy or animosity from my Clemson teammates, who were uniformly supportive and welcoming. And admittedly, there were times when my status as an older player and a military veteran had some unexpected fringe benefits.

For example, one of the Clemson football team traditions is tossing all of the freshman players into a training room cold tub. If you've never seen one of these, well, it is exactly what it sounds like: a huge tub filled with cold water and ice. After games or par-

ticularly difficult workouts, injured and aching players will sometimes immerse themselves in the tub. It's easier and more practical
than applying ice to a multitude of sore joints or muscles. While
the cold tub is undeniably effective at providing relief from swelling and inflammation, it is also excruciatingly uncomfortable. The
temperature is typically around forty degrees, so settling into the
cold tub is not unlike taking a late-winter plunge into a lake, just
after the ice has broken. It's not just cold; it's mind-numbingly
frigid. Still, it's a necessary and well-utilized piece of rehabilita-
tive equipment.

It's also a rite of passage for freshmen who otherwise would
have no use for the cold tub.

You never knew when it was going to be your turn. The returning players might grab two or three guys in a single day. Or they
might not grab anyone over the course of an entire week. By the
end of the season, though, all of the freshmen would have taken a
polar bear plunge. It's funny to watch – the whole team standing
around, clapping and chanting, ten or fifteen of the biggest older
guys wrapping up some poor freshman and carrying him to the
cold tub. The freshmen always fight, of course; that's half the fun.
And they always lose.

I kept waiting for my turn, but it never came. They just passed
me by. No one ever explained it, and I never asked. It might have
had something to do with the fact that I was not an ordinary
freshman, by virtue of age and experience. It might have been out
of respect for my service. I don't know.

Fights among teammates are fairly common in all levels of
football, especially during training camp. Guys get tired and frustrated and take it out on their teammates. It's rarely a big deal. No
injuries or lasting grudges. But it does happen. Interestingly, no
one has ever tried to pick a fight with me, regardless of how irri-
tating or annoying I might be. I got in a wrestling match with one
of the bigger guys on the team once and managed to maneuver
him into a leg bar. He started yelling, "Oh, shit! Oh, shit!" and tried

to tap out. Everyone else was laughing, making fun of him. Most of the guys know at least a little about my military background. They may not know the details, but they know I have killed people and, worse, that I have seen my friends die. For whatever reason, in certain circumstances, they keep their distance.

Occasionally, if we're joking around, wrestling, someone will say something like, "Watch out for Daniel, man. You don't want to mess with him."

Like I'm Chuck Norris or something.

I find it hysterical. In any hand-to-hand confrontation, however serious, size will usually prevail, unless you really know what you're doing. I have training, but when the other guy is six inches taller and a hundred pounds heavier? I'm almost always going to lose. Ninety percent of the guys on the Clemson football team could break me in half if so inclined. Lucky for me, they've never shown an interest.

I was fortunate that my first year at Clemson coincided with the best season the football team had enjoyed in many years. We went 11-2 overall and 7-1 in the ACC. It was the program's first eleven-win season in more than thirty years. After beating LSU by a point in the Chick-fil-A Bowl, we ended the year as the ninth-ranked team in the country, according to the coaches' poll, which, if you ask the coaches or players, is the most accurate poll. We were number eleven in the Associated Press poll and number thirteen in the BCS (Bowl Championship Series) rankings.

For me, though, the highlight of the year was Saturday, October 20, when we beat Virginia Tech, 38–17, on Military Appreciation Day. On that afternoon, as I stood at the top of Memorial Stadium, waving an American flag before leading my teammates into Death Valley, my two worlds collided. I was a football player for the Clemson Tigers — which still, even two-thirds of the way through the season, was hard for me to comprehend — and on this day I was an honorary captain. But I was also a soldier, a survivor of one of the worst battles in the Afghanistan conflict. And I was comfortable, for a change, with the duality of being both a football player and a soldier. The flood of emotion I felt on that day is hard to put into words. I thought about Thomson and Mace; I thought about my father, himself a veteran, and how this was his birthday.

It all seemed right. It seemed appropriate.

There was no guilt. Only pride.

15

T HAT FIRST SEMESTER WAS by far my most challenging at Clemson. I had developed a solid work ethic and
time management skills before I arrived on campus, but
the twin responsibilities of playing Division I football and maintaining a solid academic record as a political science major proved
much more difficult than I had anticipated.

I realize that many people – even die-hard college football
fans – are skeptical about the very notion of the "student-athlete."
Certainly there are some programs and athletes and coaches who
have helped perpetuate the stereotype of the big-time college
football player (or basketball player) as someone who couldn't
find his way to a classroom without an assist from MapQuest.
In my experience, though, college athletes are nowhere near the
apathetic students they are so often portrayed as being. The vast
majority of Division I college athletes will never earn a living in
their chosen sport. The dream dies hard for everyone, but eventually, in almost all cases, it does die. The trick is to prepare for that
day and to take advantage of the opportunities that come with
being a scholarship athlete. Most of the guys I've gotten to know

at Clemson – including those who have a legitimate shot at the NFL – are smart enough to go to class, do their work, and make sure that they emerge with a degree.

But it's not easy.

Football at Clemson, as at any other BCS program, is serious business and requires a substantial commitment in both time and energy from everyone associated with the program: coaches, players, support staff. It's not like high school ball, where you practice for a couple hours after school, play a game on Friday night, and switch to basketball when fall gives way to winter. It is a full-time commitment, seven days a week, twelve months a year. The NCAA places a weekly limit of twenty hours on a student-athlete's participation in a given sport, but this refers to official team events, such as practice, games, meetings, and weight training sessions. It does not include additional time spent by an individual who wants to make sure he understands the playbook, informal workouts, or travel time. It's no exaggeration to suggest that being a Division I college football player is a full-time job; nevertheless, you are expected to take a full load of classes (although that load is often reduced somewhat during the season) and perform well enough in the classroom to maintain eligibility. Your scholarship depends on it; more importantly, your future depends on it.

I am proud to be a Clemson football player, but I am just as proud of having become a strong student. If you polled my high school teachers and administrators, they would probably be more surprised by my academic success than my athletic success. In high school, at least I'd been a very good athlete; I'd been a dreadful student. There was no way I was going to slip back into the routine of just trying to get by.

The truth, though, is that despite working my butt off during my first semester at Clemson, I struggled to maintain a B average. Now, there's nothing wrong with a 3.0 GPA. A lot of athletes – hell, a lot of *students* – would consider that perfectly acceptable. I did not. But I realized that the slight slippage in my classroom performance was not due to lack of effort. I was working just as hard as

I ever had, but the sheer volume of material I had to digest on a political science track was more than I could manage while trying to earn playing time on the football team. I'll put it bluntly and honestly: the last thing I wanted to do after a long day of classes and a three-hour football practice was come home and read and highlight four chapters of textbook material, along with writing a paper. It was simply too much. On many nights I would doze off on my couch, with an open book on my chest.

Knowing that the work wasn't going to get any easier, and unsure of what I would do with a political science degree anyway (I wasn't interested in law school or a career in government), I changed my major to sports marketing, with a concentration in athletic leadership and parks and recreation. I found political science interesting, but I wanted something more sports-related, in part because I figured that with all the connections I was making through football, changing my major to sports marketing would give me more career opportunities after college. I could tell just a couple weeks into the second semester that I'd made the right decision. It's not so much that the workload is lighter in sports marketing, although there is less reading and fewer papers are required. It's just different. It's more a hands-on approach, working with youth sports groups and preparing projects directly related to the kind of work I might be doing. There's more flexibility in the schedule, which is certainly beneficial during the football season, when there is barely a free minute in the entire day. My grade point average went back up to 3.5 that semester, and it's remained at least at that level ever since. That means as much to me as anything else I've accomplished in my life. I know my father would be proud.

The delicate tap dance of balancing my own ambitions with the expectations of others continued in the spring. I worked out very hard, had a good spring minicamp, and prepared for my second season of ACC football. My mind-set, though, was somewhat different than it had been one year earlier, when the very notion of wearing a Clemson uniform was so far-fetched that it had seemed almost pure fantasy. Now I had a year under my belt. I knew the Clemson system, and I was comfortable as a student-athlete. I fit in well with the other guys on the team, and I understood the way things worked. My spot on the team was secure. As long as I maintained a positive attitude and avoided a career-ending injury (no small accomplishment at this level), there would be a place for me on the team. I'd have a Clemson uniform, and I'd be out there on special teams every weekend, returning and covering kickoffs and punts. Nothing wrong with that. A lot of guys dream of having just such an opportunity. I'd been one of those dreamers just one year earlier.

But as long as I was on the team I was going to work as hard as I possibly could to earn more playing time. I didn't think of myself as a novelty act, and I didn't want anyone else to think of me that way. So I asked for meetings with the coaches and media relations people during the offseason to discuss the handling of my particular situation as we moved forward. This was a tricky thing to address, because obviously I am proud of my military service and I would never want to do anything to disrespect the Army or the men with whom I served.

I explained to everyone that I didn't want to turn my back on what I was before I came to Clemson. I understood the significance of my position there, and I was not offended in any way by the attention I'd received. It was (and is) humbling. The courtesy and respect that people display toward me is overwhelming, and I continue to be moved and awed by it. And I am still learning how to deal with it on a personal level. I will never be anything but grateful to the people who appreciate our men and women in uniform. But I hoped that there was some way to steer some of the interviews toward the subject of football as well. It was with that same attitude of transparency and humility that I approached the coaches.

Before camp opened, I sat down with Coach Swinney and a couple of the position coaches and respectfully placed my cards on the table. I appreciated everything they had done for me, and I understood that we had a mutually beneficial relationship. Every time my name was announced during a Clemson football game, I received a standing ovation. It was heartwarming, and I couldn't have been more grateful.

"But I don't want to be known just as the guy who fought in Afghanistan," I said, hoping that it came out the right way. "I'm a football player. I'm a part of this program, and I want to be recognized as that."

It could have backfired spectacularly. The coaches on our staff are some of the hardest-working people I have ever known. They work ridiculous hours all season, then take about a week off before hitting the recruiting trail. They travel all over the country, not just in the Southeast, in search of the highest-caliber athletes they can find. Every year, at every position, we sign five-star recruits who could have played at any program in the country. There is an investment in these players, an obligation to get the most out of them and help them become players capable of leading Clemson to a national title. The simple truth was this: the program had invested a lot less in me (or any other walk-on) than it had in most of our recruits. Logic and human nature (and the practicality of business) dictated that most of the coaches' time and energy would be devoted to the players who had been most heavily recruited. I was not one of those players, and by telling the coaches that I expected to compete with them for playing time and to be viewed through a similar prism, I risked the possibility that they would think I was arrogant or selfish.

But they understood completely and were very gracious, although I do think they were somewhat surprised. When I first arrived at Clemson, I'd had a nagging sense that I had been given a uniform based on something other than my ability and all the hard work that I had put in. I was thankful but conflicted. I knew I was capable of succeeding without having anything handed to me, and that awareness was what drove my efforts in the offseason: to show everyone that a publicity stunt had turned into something unexpected.

"I think I deserve more playing time this year," I reiterated to Coach Morris, who coaches our receivers. "You just have to trust me."

He smiled. "I do trust you, Daniel. And you've had a great camp. But you have to remember — you're not the number-two player at your position. You're number five or six overall. It's my job to put another receiver in who I think is more inclined to have a productive season."

That hurt. I disagreed with his assessment. I also understood it. Kids who had been heavily recruited were going to get every chance to prove their value before I was put in the lineup. As always, the eye test worked against me. I could run perfect routes and catch every pass that came my way. I could win every sprint and outwork everyone in the weight room, but at the end of the day I was still five-foot-eight, 175 pounds. I didn't look nearly as impressive as someone six inches taller and fifty pounds heavier. There was nothing I could do about that.

In high school this was the sort of attitude that drove me nuts. Now, though, I have learned that some things are beyond my control. Every athlete has to learn that a coach might view him differently than he views himself. It's a matter of being patient and waiting for the right opportunity. Eventually, I figured I'd go out and make a play they didn't expect me to make, or catch a pass in traffic and hang on to the ball despite getting slammed.

I remained optimistic, especially when training camp ended and the coaches told me I was one of the most improved players on the team. I made the travel squad again; more significantly, I was placed high enough on the depth chart at wide receiver that I was no longer a member of the scout team during practice. That had been one of my roles the previous year — to run plays for the scout team against our first-team defense. Now, though, I was part of the regular rotation among receivers. I started getting compliments from our quarterbacks, Taj Boyd and his backup, Cole Stoudt. They would stick up for me, telling me to hang in there and be ready at any time.

From the very beginning of the season I played more than I had in the previous year. All of my numbers improved. I was second on the team in punt return yardage; I doubled my number of receptions. In every possible way I felt like I had become a more productive member of the team.

I even scored the first touchdown of my college career.

It happened on November 23, which, fittingly enough, was Military Appreciation Day. We were playing host to The Citadel, a private school with a proud military tradition, but one with a smaller, less ambitious football program. Clemson, meanwhile, was in the late stages of one of the best seasons in program history. We were ranked eighth in the country and had been as high as third before losing to eventual national champion Florida State. Once again I was given the privilege of carrying the flag into Memorial Stadium, and once again I couldn't help but think of Thomson and Mace and all my buddies as I stood at the top of the Stadium, waving the flag and listening to the crowd roar. There were a number of veterans in the stands that day, including some with whom I had served. I felt proud to be representing them, to be representing all of us.

This time, though, I found that I was able to transition more quickly to focusing on the game itself. Given that I was in the regular rotation of receivers and the game was likely to be one-sided, I thought I would probably see a significant amount of playing time. And that turned out to be the case. We jumped out to a 14–0 lead in the first quarter and a 42–0 lead at the half. I returned just about all of our punts that day, and I played virtually the entire second half at wide receiver. Instead of my usual ten or twelve snaps, I got somewhere between thirty and forty. And when you get more reps, well . . . you have a much better chance of finding your way into the end zone.

I'd been close before, running three consecutive sweeps near the goal line in a blowout win over Wake Forest early in the year but not quite getting in. Now we were very late in the season. I might not get many more opportunities.

Early in the fourth quarter, with Cole Stoudt having replaced Taj Boyd at quarterback after Taj threw five touchdown passes, we drove deep into Citadel territory. Twice we gave the ball to fullback Darrell Smith, but we couldn't get him into the end zone. I thought we'd give him one more shot, but on fourth down, from the Citadel two-yard line, we called a jet sweep. I lined up in the left slot. On a jet sweep, the entire play moves in one direction — in this case, to the right. It's a power play in which the quarterback, working out of a shotgun formation, has the option to run, pass, or, most likely, hand or pitch the ball to the slot receiver, who is sweeping from the left. Probably 90 percent of the time, however, the ball will be pitched. So I knew this was my play, my chance. Unless something very strange happened, I'd be getting the ball.

As Cole executed the count, I went in motion. The ball was snapped. Everything happened so quickly. Cole pivoted to his right and immediately flipped a little shovel pass into my stomach as I ran in front of him — a distance of no more than a foot. I don't think he considered any of the other options. I caught it on a full sprint, moving laterally, left to right, a few yards behind the line of scrimmage, and tucked the ball under my arm. In front of me there was a perfect block, and then another, and suddenly there was a gaping hole and a sea of green. I angled toward the end zone without even breaking stride and sprinted across the goal line un- touched.

I'll take credit for not screwing up, but I have to be honest: it was the biggest hole I have ever seen. I think I would have scored from ninety-nine yards out. That's how much room there was. But that's okay. Football is in many ways the ultimate team game. I don't care how great a quarterback you are, or how fast a tailback. If you don't have big guys up front who can move the earth and create space (while rarely receiving the credit they deserve), you won't accomplish anything.

The crowd, predictably, went absolutely nuts. Matt Porter, an- other wide receiver, was there to greet me first. And then Sam Cooper, a tight end. They both gave me hugs and patted me on the helmet. I honestly couldn't hear what they said, as the noise in the stadium was deafening. A couple seconds later Cole Stoudt met me in the end zone, smiling and yelling. I jumped into his arms, and he held me aloft. It was the fourth quarter of a blowout, but I felt like we'd just won the national championship. Coach Swinney always says that when you hit the end zone, you should respond like you've been there before. Maybe I overreacted. If so, I apologize. No offense intended. But the truth is, I hadn't ever been there before . . . and it felt great!

I kept the ball — there was no way I was giving it up. That night, for the second time in my life, I was the subject of a video that went viral. Twitter blew up, as they say, in response to the highlight reel of Clemson versus The Citadel, which focused almost exclusively on a single, meaningless play in the fourth quarter: a touchdown by an undersized, twenty-five-year-old walk-on wide receiver. There were hundreds of e-mails and phone calls. I tried to respond to every one of them.

"Thank you," I said . . . over and over.

"Thank you."

Epilogue

My situation continues to evolve, but . . . so far, so good. As I write these words it is late March of 2014. We are two and a half months removed from beating Ohio State in the Orange Bowl and a top-ten ranking in the final BCS poll. I didn't get a chance to catch any passes in that game, didn't make any tackles, but I got plenty of time on special teams and felt like I earned the ring that came with victory. I keep it in a glass case at home, flanked by my Bronze Star and Purple Heart.

If that seems an odd juxtaposition, well, it isn't to me. More than anything else, the medals are tangible reminders of the men who lost their lives in Afghanistan on October 3, 2009. Without their sacrifice, I have no medals. At best, my mother has them, awarded posthumously. Without their sacrifice, I don't have the opportunity to play football for Clemson and be part of a team that plays and wins in the Orange Bowl.

Without their sacrifice . . . I have nothing.

So, as far as I'm concerned, the medals and the ring belong together, forever linked.

I've become much more comfortable with the attention that

comes with my role. I'm in a unique situation, and I understand that. But I belong here now. I've earned my place on the field and on the Clemson team. Even some of my buddies, the guys who used to give me some good-natured crap for even thinking I could play Division I football, are amazed at the way things have turned out.

"Wow," my friend Joseph said. "Who would have thought you'd be a contributing member of the Clemson Tigers?"

I don't know where or how the journey will end. We have a few wide receivers graduating in the spring, and I hope to move even higher on the depth chart. Realistically, I should be fighting for some significant playing time next season. After that, who knows? I believe in setting goals and working hard to achieve those goals, but I think you have to be careful about trying to map out your life.

"What's your five-year plan?" someone will say to me.

My answer: "I'll tell you in five years."

It's not that I have anything against being prepared and thinking about the future. But if I've learned anything, it's that you have to be open to all possibilities, because life is full of challenges and surprises and opportunities. I have some friends and acquaintances who have very carefully structured their lives in such a way as to ensure security and avoid risk. They've gotten jobs and started trying to climb the corporate ladder; they want to buy a house, get married, raise a family. There is nothing wrong with any of that. I want some of those things too.

Someday.

But I'm not in a hurry to get there, and I have no idea what road I will take. Along the way I presume there will be detours and setbacks, disappointments and triumphs. I'll figure it out by following my gut . . . my heart. When I left that battlefield five years ago, I felt like I hadn't earned the right to go on living. But I had. It took me another year or so, a year in which depression and PTSD nearly got the best of me, but eventually I figured it out. The only responsibility I had as a survivor of Kamdesh was to live a life free of fear, a life devoted to something more than just pragmatism, a life worthy of the second chance I was given.

I'm not talking about living recklessly or dangerously. I'm talking about embracing every moment, trying to figure out what brings me joy in life and going after it.

After that worst of all years, I came to my senses and put all my energy and focus into going to college and playing Division I football. If not for what happened in Afghanistan, I don't know that I would have had the strength or the courage to do that. I woke up one morning, thought about Thomson and Mace . . . thought about my dad . . . and felt a little sickened by the way inertia and fear had taken over my life.

So what if you fail? Do what makes you happy.

It was so simple . . . and so liberating.

Nothing is guaranteed, nothing given. I've seen guys wake up one morning and leave in a body bag the next. There is no promise of tomorrow. I know that now. And because I know it, I can freely and confidently make decisions based on what I want to do with my life, rather than trying to do only what I think I should do, or what other people expect me to do.

What does that mean? Well, I'm not exactly sure. I'll have my degree in December. That will be one of the proudest days of my life, because I know how much it will mean to my family and what it would have meant to my father. Maybe I'll stick around and play another season of football while pursuing a graduate degree; maybe not. I've done some public speaking and really enjoy it. I like the idea of staying involved with sports. I've talked to some people who think I might be able to find a niche in Hollywood or somewhere in the entertainment industry.

There are no limits — only options.

I also believe in my heart that I can play in the National Football League. If I can stay healthy and continue to improve, I'll give it a shot. What's the worst that can happen? I'll go through camp and get cut. I can live with that. But I honestly believe I have a chance to make an NFL roster.

Maybe that sounds crazy. But stranger things have happened.

Five years ago, when my home was a mortar pit in Afghanistan, I dreamed every day about playing Division I college football. That seemed kind of crazy too. And now . . . here I am, decked out in orange on Saturday afternoons, sprinting into Death Valley in front of 80,000 of the wildest fans in college sports. I am an honor student and an athlete.

Believe me, anything is possible. I am living proof.